Streams of Revenue

Streams of Revenue

The Restoration Economy and the Ecosystems It Creates

Rebecca Lave and Martin Doyle

The MIT Press
Cambridge, Massachusetts
London, England

© 2020 Massachusetts Institute of Technology

All rights reserved. No part of this book may be reproduced in any form by any electronic or mechanical means (including photocopying, recording, or information storage and retrieval) without permission in writing from the publisher.

This book was set in ITC Stone Serif Std and ITC Stone Sans Std by New Best-set Typesetters Ltd. Printed and bound in the United States of America.

Library of Congress Cataloging-in-Publication Data.

Names: Lave, Rebecca, 1970- author. | Doyle, Martin, 1973- author.
Title: Streams of revenue : the restoration economy and the ecosystems it creates / Rebecca Lave and Martin Doyle.
Description: Cambridge, Massachusetts : The MIT Press, [2020] | Includes bibliographical references and index.
Identifiers: LCCN 2019047639 | ISBN 9780262539197 (paperback)
Subjects: LCSH: United States. Federal Water Pollution Control Act Amendments of 1972. | Wetland mitigation banking—United States. | Stream restoration—Economic aspects—United States. | Restoration ecology—Economic aspects—United States. | Ecosystem services—United States. | Environmental policy—Economic aspects—United States.
Classification: LCC HD1683.U5 L38 2020 | DDC 363.739/47—dc23
LC record available at https://lccn.loc.gov/2019047639

10 9 8 7 6 5 4 3 2 1

Contents

Preface vii
Acknowledgments xi

1 Introduction 1
2 Market-Based Approaches to Conservation 11
3 How Stream Restoration Was Born, and What Came of It 29
4 How Markets, and Mitigation, Came to Be Accepted Forms of Environmental Regulation 49
5 The Actors in Stream Mitigation Banking 73
6 How Mitigation Banks Work, and the Biography of a Bank 97
7 The Streams That Mitigation Banking Creates 121
8 Conclusion: Can Markets for Ecosystem Services Fix Conservation? 147

Notes 157
References 175
Index 187

Preface

One of the most influential, and perhaps surprising, developments in environmental policy in recent decades is the idea that we can protect the environment from the negative impacts of economic development by making environmental protection itself more economic. The goal is to reduce environmental harm not by preventing it, but by pricing it. Want to build a housing development on a piece of land threaded with streams? With an environmental market in place, you can do that as long as you pay to offset the damage through restoration of comparable streams elsewhere. Or, in an example that may be more familiar, want to keep emitting greenhouse gases? Fine. You just have to buy carbon credits produced by reducing emissions at another site. Starting in the early 1990s, U.S. environmental policy has supplemented command-and-control regulation (thou shalt not) with market-based approaches (thou shalt pay for your harm) in an attempt to improve conservation outcomes. There are now many environmental markets in the United States (and internationally) that are intended to improve conservation outcomes for everything from prairies and streams to woodpeckers and flowering shrubs.

Even in the United States, where capitalism has long been something close to a national religion, this shift toward market-based environmental management raised some eyebrows. There have been heated debates about economic theory, ecological value, and the details of policy. But at this point in time, environmental markets in the United States are more than two decades old and are firmly established. Haphazard, deliberately vague, and patchy policies have been smoothed out and (at least to some extent) standardized. What is not at all clear is whether these markets have actually improved environmental well-being. This book is the first sustained attempt to find out. Using stream mitigation banking (the market for rivers and streams under Section 404 of the Clean Water Act) as a case, we explain where market-based approaches came from, how they work in practice, and what they do on the ground.

Rivers and streams in the United States could use some help, as they have taken quite a pounding since European settlers arrived. They have been straightened, shortened, and put in pipes underground. They have been dammed, diverted, and cut off from their floodplains. They have been dredged, buried in sediment, and dredged again, and they have been polluted to the point of biological death. Almost anytime there was a choice between the well-being of a stream and human ease, the stream lost.

Efforts to prevent or at least undo harm to streams began in the late 1800s, but only grew legislative teeth in late 1960s and early 1970s. The Clean Water Act, in particular, was spectacularly successful in many ways. As one example, it is now possible to swim in most rivers and streams in the United States without having to take a heavy course of antibiotics afterward. The question is how to get us the rest of the way: how do we prevent further harms to rivers and streams, and even improve their ecological, chemical, and physical character and function? Can a market for streams do what command-and-control legislation has (thus far at least) failed to do?

The answer to the latter question is no, or at least not yet. The idea of allowing much-needed development to harm ecosystems as long as we restore comparable ecosystems elsewhere turns out to be quite hard to operationalize. It is very difficult to ensure equivalence between ecosystems that are harmed and those that are restored. Further, we are not yet able to reliably restore most (perhaps all) ecosystem types; natural systems are highly complex, and we are far from understanding the full scope of that complexity, much less being able to reproduce it. Finally, in addition to being complex, ecosystems are messy, dynamic, and highly interconnected; standardizing them into simple, tradeable commodities in order to create robust markets is certainly doable, but it raises unsettling questions about what, if anything, such simplified versions of ecosystems actually achieve. We thus argue that ecosystem service markets, very much including stream mitigation banking, have not delivered on the conservation goals of their advocates and should be radically reconfigured.

We have written this book with a strong emphasis on clarity and accessibility. We hope it will reach multiple audiences, from those of you studying to become environmental managers in the public, private, or nonprofit sector to those of you who already do such work. At some point in your careers, it is very likely that you will be asked to help set up an environmental market, to keep an existing one running, or to manage a project that is part of a market. This book has much of what you need to know about where these markets come from and how they work in practice. You will not find heavy theory or science in here, but suggested readings in the endnotes provide entrance points if you want to dive in. We also hope this book will be of interest to river scientists trying to figure out what is going on at their field sites, to ecological and environmental economists who have been central to conceptualizing and critiquing market-based approaches, and to advocacy groups evaluating whether or not to support pricing environmental harms.

The stakes here are high. We humans damage the world around us in many ways. Regulations are intended to limit that damage: to provide a ceiling beyond which environmental degradation should not rise. If market-based approaches cannot build and secure that ceiling, we need to change them.

Acknowledgments

This book was a long time in the making. Our first conversation about mitigation banking (in fact, our first conversation ever) took place by phone in 2006 when Rebecca was a graduate student at UC Berkeley and Martin was an assistant professor at the University of North Carolina.[1] In the thirteen years since, we submitted, resubmitted, resubmitted again, and finally won a grant from the National Science Foundation to fund this work (BCS 1213827), conducted research throughout the United States, wrote multiple articles, gave dozens of talks on environmental markets, switched institutions, and during all of that time were physically in the same room fewer than half a dozen times. Nevertheless, there has been a consistency in idea-sharing that has been unusually productive and delightful, and allowed us to sustain the project over time and space.

Throughout this process, we collaborated with Morgan Robertson, a political ecologist at the University of Wisconsin and one of the most knowledgeable people on the planet on wetland mitigation banking. Though he did not help to write this book, many of the ideas we present here are a product of more than a decade of collaboration and discussion in which he was an integral part.

The social science component of this project was entirely dependent on people's willingness to talk with us. Our human subjects protocol does not allow us to list you by name, but there is no way we could have done this work without you, and we are immensely grateful. Thank you!

We are also grateful to colleagues both inside and outside academia who helped to frame this project and hone its results. At Indiana University (where Rebecca is now), Ilana Gershon, Tom Gieryn, and Eden Medina listened to and reflected on multiple iterations of this work. At the University of North Carolina and at Duke University, Todd BenDor and Emily

Bernhardt were thought partners throughout much of the work. Frank Magilligan and Margaret Palmer have helped us wrangle this sprawling subject into coherence over the years. Although we never formally interviewed them as part of this research, Palmer Hough and Eric Somerville at the EPA provided very useful historical context on the development of mitigation banking, as did Dave Owen. Doug Thompson has been a wealth of information and understanding about the historical roots of restoration in the early twentieth century; we drew heavily on his painstaking and excellent work. David Lansing helped us come to grips with the literature on carbon credits. Most recently, as we were developing the argument in the last section of the conclusion to this book, timely critical feedback from colleagues at the University of Cambridge revealed some important holes in our thinking.

A number of graduate students helped with aspects of this research. Julia Ferguson and David Gordon were part of the initial nationwide survey of stream mitigation banking that helped us pick the states where we focused our work. Curtis Pomilia helped with transcription and Susan Powell tracked down the roots of mitigation in environmental policy. Jai Singh collected much of the geomorphic data in North Carolina and Eric Nost was involved throughout, most particularly with our research in Oregon.

At the MIT Press, Beth Clevenger provided thoughtful feedback and great enthusiasm (and if you've ever written a book, you know how precious the latter bit can be), and the manuscript review process has been simply fantastic.

Rebecca's Acknowledgments

Hooray for my colleagues in the Geography Department at Indiana University for creating such a positive and respectful work environment, and for embracing the unfamiliar in accepting monographs as legit scholarly products. Indiana University, more broadly, has been an unusually supportive institution for me. My community here in Bloomington has been a consistent source of comradery and outrageously good food: Steph, Reynard, Sarah, Tessa, Charles, Sara, Mark, Kylie, Eric, Cristian, Eden, Ilana, David, Maria, and Edgar, among many others. I am so grateful to have landed here given the deep weirdness of the academic job market. I continue to be inspired by my kickass colleagues outside IU. Particular thanks to Julie Guthman, Becky Mansfield, Kendra McSweeney and Wendy Wolford for helping me navigate the gendered absurdities of academic life, and to Phil Mirowski and Sam Randalls, who were there in the early days of this project, helping me to think better, smarter, and more deeply about the political economy of environmental science.

Sam and Nell make everything better with dumb jokes, thoughtful company, and unfailing encouragement to channel Bone Claw Mother rather than Midwestern Nice Girl.

I am profoundly grateful that unlike my previous book, this one was not steeped in untimely losses, though Ruth Gibson Snyder (1917–2016) is still much missed.

Last thing: working with Martin for nearly fifteen years, particularly the process of cowriting this book, has been an entertaining, thought-provoking, and egalitarian collaboration. I will miss working with you, my friend!

Martin's Acknowledgments

I began talking to regulators and mitigation bankers in North Carolina fifteen years ago, and over that time, their patience in educating me, willingness to take repetitive phone calls, and readiness to review all manner of my writing have been tremendous. Most notable are Adam Riggsbee, John Preyer, George Howard, George Kelly, Todd Tugwell, Steve Martin, and Dave Lekson, among many others. Mike Wicker (U.S. Fish & Wildlife Service) has played a consistent, behind-the-scenes role in steering mitigation banking toward positive results, and in encouraging academics to research the benefits and detriments of banking; streams, rivers, and wetlands in North Carolina have benefitted tremendously from his efforts. Two mitigation bankers deserve particular credit, or blame, for my interest in working on mitigation banking: Don Carr and Bud Needham. I regret that Don passed away before this book was finished; Bud and I lost a guide through the policy swamps of Washington, DC, and a great friend. The restored ecosystem at Timberlake is a fitting tribute to Don's relentless vision of how mitigation banking can leave lasting benefits for ecosystems, and particularly for birds.

Finally, working on this project has required me to read books and think thoughts that are far beyond my normal intellectual universe. I would not have done so had it not been for Rebecca's contagious intellectual enthusiasm.

1   Introduction

Martin Dairy Creek used to be a weed-lined, straight-as-an-arrow ditch, passing through pastures and farms in rural North Carolina. The channel itself was a few feet wide and a couple feet deep, and rarely carried more than an inch or two of water, situated as it was in the headwaters of the watershed. The channel had been straightened decades earlier and its banks had since begun to erode, creating mixtures of wide, raw banks along some reaches and large silty bars on the streambed in others. The constant erosion and deposition of sediment degraded the habitat and made life challenging for any fish or aquatic insects that tried to make a home in this typical rural American waterway.

Then in 2017, bulldozers arrived. Martin Dairy Creek's banks were stripped bare of vegetation to make room for a platoon of big yellow machines that set to work remeandering the creek. The channel was reformed to be shallower and slightly wider, with near-*perfectly* regular meander bends. Small, adolescent trees were planted in carefully spaced sequences and patterns along the creek's banks, each the same height and age. A series of nearly identical riffles were constructed, each with well-sorted, well-placed gravel and cobble. A mostly innocuous, occasionally rambunctious rural creek had been transformed into an elegant, symmetrical work of engineering. Like a road or a bridge, this creek was now very clearly designed and constructed (figure 1.1).

On the opposite side of the planet, in Australia, sits the terrestrial equivalent of this carefully rationalized aquatic system. This particular landscape had previously been a mixture of forest and farmland. Now, however, there are rows upon rows of trees, mainly eucalyptus, but also large uniform expanses of pine trees. Each tree is the same age, having all been planted

Figure 1.1
Aerial image of Martin Dairy Creek, North Carolina. The stream flows from top to bottom, with the portion upstream of the farm road being unrestored—and perfectly straight—while the downstream portion is restored into almost perfectly symmetrical sine wave meander bends.

simultaneously. Each tree is equidistant from its neighbors. This forest did not accumulate over time by natural process, or by piecemeal, uncoordinated decisions of various landowners; like the stream in North Carolina, this Australian forest was planned, designed, and constructed.[1]

There is something not quite natural about these ecosystems and their clean, symmetrical forms. There is no confusing the perfectly proportioned stream with its unruly, unmodified kin, nor the linear rows of trees with an old growth forest (though not all carbon forests are so obviously designed, there are no rules that encourage more natural planting plans). In each case, these ecosystems have been made visually coherent and biophysically distinct from their surroundings. They have pieces that are comparable to other systems—trees, riffles, meander bends—and individually make sense, but are startlingly artificial when combined. They are now strange ecosystems to behold.

Reconfiguring ecosystems to suit human desires is not new. What is newer is that each of these systems was modified under the banner of ecological restoration; they were "restored." Humans intervened in an ecosystem they considered degraded in an attempt to return it to health. And what is really new, only a few decades old, is the rationale for restoring these disparate systems: "the market." Like a rapidly growing number of ecosystems around the world, they were restored to create a novel type of commodity. The buyers of these odd ecosystems, however, were not interested in owning a wiggly creek or a linear forest; in most cases these individuals or organizations never set eyes on the ecosystems they purchased. The buyers of these ecosystems only did so because they were required to participate in a particular environmental market, making them participants in a broader, nascent restoration economy.

Buying and selling ecosystems through environmental markets has been the subject of volumes of research. Such markets have drawn advocates and critics, engaged in debate ranging from appropriate treatment of economic minutiae to whether markets and the burgeoning restoration economy can save us from the impending catastrophe of climate change.

But the debates have largely sidestepped the question of just what kind of landscapes these new markets might produce. Behind every environmental market transaction there is an ecosystem: an actual place whose biophysical conditions are changed when capital changes hands. These ecosystems are the manifestations of environmental markets. These ecosystems—with all their potential for artificiality and contrived nature—bear the fingerprints of the market's invisible hand; they are the manifestation of the restoration economy.

Selling Nature in Order to Save It

The environmental movement has long worked to protect nature from the most destructive impulses of capitalism. Whether by setting aside protected areas like national parks to be preserved from human disturbance, moderating the use of timber or fisheries to produce sustainable yields, or restoring ecosystems to undo anthropogenic harm, the goal of environmental conservation often has been to force the invisible hand of the market to squeeze the natural world a little less tightly. Now, market forces—channeling capitalism, or bending it at least—are increasingly seen as the best, perhaps only way to save nature.

The idea that traditional forms of environmental regulation are insufficient, and that we should sell nature in order to save it, began gaining traction in the 1980s. It is now firmly, if surprisingly, established in environmental policy circles, promoted by presidential administrations as otherwise distinct as those of Obama and Trump. The notable early successes of the Clean Water Act in improving water quality in places like Cleveland, or of the Endangered Species Act in bringing iconic species such as bald eagles back from the brink of extinction are often dismissed as costly and inefficient. In their place, a broad range of market-based policy approaches have been proposed, from cap and trade to eco-labeling to impact investing. These quite different policy frameworks share a core claim that would have been anathema to most environmentalists even twenty years ago (and still is to many): the path forward is not to protect nature from capitalism, but to tie the two together as tightly as possible. The approaches of major environmental organizations are harbingers of this change: the World Wildlife Fund and The Nature Conservancy (TNC) have major programs now on corporate engagement, environmental markets, and impact investing, with TNC going so far as starting its own investment banking operation—NatureVest.

This is a momentous shift in thinking about the environment, and it has been hotly debated in the United States and internationally. Rather than refight those battles, this book is centered on a more pragmatic pair of questions:

> What does it take to put market-based approaches into practice? And what are the tangible consequences for ecosystems of doing so?

To answer these questions, we focus on one of the oldest and most robust environmental markets: stream mitigation banking under the Clean Water Act. While seemingly mundane, or even innocuous, stream mitigation banking is often held up as an exemplar for how markets can be created, adapted, and scaled in terms of economic and ecological impact.

Markets for Ecosystem Services

Ecosystem services is a catchall term for the things nature provides society free of charge, such as the crop pollination provided by bees, or wetlands' utility as giant natural water filters. Many environmental markets focus on putting a monetary value on those services, and then creating the conditions that make it possible to sell them. The many varieties of what are referred to as *markets for ecosystem services* (MES) share a common set of claims: (1) growing human needs for housing, food, transportation, employment, and so on, make at least some amount of ongoing environmental damage inevitable, and given that we cannot stop development; (2) the best approach is to stop trying to prevent negative environmental impacts and instead require compensation for them. Imagine, for instance, a proposed factory that would provide much-needed new jobs, but would have the environmental consequence of paving over a wetland if allowed to be built on the proposed site. Instead of insisting that the factory owner find another site, or cease the project altogether, an MES approach would require the owner to quantify the ecosystem services lost through wetland impacts (known as *debits*), and then to buy an equivalent or greater amount of the same ecosystem services (known as *credits*) produced by restoring an equivalent degraded wetland elsewhere. Effectively, MES are commodity markets, although the commodity for sale is not a crop or production input, such as grain or timber, but is instead the service provided by a particular ecosystem.

We describe such markets in detail in chapter 2, but for now the key thing to note is that while calculating debits and offsetting them through the purchase of credits sounds straightforward, it is remarkably complex in practice. Making a standardized, saleable commodity out of complex, messy, above all *interconnected* ecosystems and their services turns out to be substantially harder than making a commodity out of trees or wheat. For example, how can we be sure that the particularities of the wetland to be restored are equivalent to the unique characteristics of the wetland that would be lost at the proposed factory site? And how do we cope with the myriad uncertainties of whether we can even restore wetlands in general, let alone restore the functions lost from this particular wetland in this particular place?

These are thorny questions. Each market grapples with them in different ways, from the simplified approaches used to trade endangered species habitat to the almost unwieldly complexity of carbon credits (both discussed in more detail in the next chapter). What is perhaps most notable—given the common portrayal of MES as a leap forward in achieving environmental goals—is how little we know about how these projects are put together in practice and what their outcomes actually are. Most pointedly, what kinds of ecosystems do MES produce? To answer that question, this book presents a detailed empirical study of the intertwined physical and social processes at work in a specific ecosystem service market from conception to construction to implementation, moving from ideas of what an ecosystem should be to what actually exists in the ground when a market-based, restored ecosystem is constructed.

Stream Mitigation Banking

The specific market that we examine is for stream ecosystems, the industry, practice, and political economy of which are subsumed under the phrase *stream mitigation banking*. The 1972 Clean Water Act (CWA) was intended to protect the chemical, biological, and physical integrity of the "waters of the United States." A particular part of the CWA—Section 404—requires that anyone physically impacting a water of the United States, including streams, must get permission from the federal government to do so: they must receive a 404 permit. While Congress likely assumed that the regulatory agencies implementing the CWA—the U.S. Army Corps of Engineers (Corps of Engineers) and the Environmental Protection Agency (EPA)—

would deny many permits to prevent harm to these ecosystems, the vast majority of permits have been granted, as the agencies have yielded to the political costs of limiting development, be it new homes, factories, or roads.

Rather than deny permits altogether to protect the nation's freshwater ecosystems, the agencies arrived at a workaround known as the *mitigation sequence*: avoid impacts, reduce impacts, and only then compensate for any unavoidable impacts. In practice, however, it turned out to be far more politically palatable to let developers offset their project's impacts on a stream by restoring a comparable stream elsewhere than to ask them to rework the project to avoid or reduce its impacts altogether. While developers initially did the restoration themselves, a new approach arose in the late 1990s—stream mitigation banking. Under this system, an entrepreneur would speculatively restore an ecosystem and generate a "bank" of stream credits. These credits could then be sold to developers to fulfill the permit requirements set by the regulators—the Corps of Engineers and the EPA. In theory, as more mitigation banks emerged in an area, developers would have multiple bankers competing for their business. This competition could thus create market-like conditions for stream restoration credits.[2]

Over a two-decade period—from 1998 to 2018—the regulations and practice of stream mitigation banking evolved from a series of isolated, bespoke, one-off curiosities to a well-regulated industry and the beginnings of a "restoration economy." The first stream mitigation bank was approved in 1998 in North Carolina. A wide variety of developers subsequently went to the stream market—from shopping mall developers to state highway departments to public utilities and airports—and as a result more than one thousand stream mitigation banks were in operation in forty states as of 2018.[3]

Overview of the Book

Social scientists have studied (and often critiqued) the underlying rationales of market-based environmental management; for their part, biophysical scientists have studied (and, likewise, often critiqued) the underlying assumptions of ecological restoration, most typically by examining the failures of particular projects. That has left unexamined everything in between. What does it take to go from the idea of MES to actual functioning markets? Just as important, what are the specific environmental consequences of the markets once created? What is actually constructed on the landscape as the end result of an ecosystem service market, and what decisions had to be made along the way in order for it to be built that way? Tracing the path of a particular market allows us to understand the interrelations of policies, science, concepts, personal relationships, engineering, and standards of practice that underlie any environmental regulatory market.

This book is about that path, from start to finish. By tracing the process of creating an ecosystem service market from conceptual beginnings to physical manifestations, we can begin to understand its fingerprint on the landscape. We trace the roots of stream mitigation banking, the challenges of balancing ecological and economic concerns, and the physical consequences of how we have done so to date. The history and evolution of stream mitigation banking are particular, but not unusual; all environmental markets will have a similar genesis, evolution, and implementation, contorting science, policy, and politics to create a market and the commodities for sale within it. Although market-based environmental approaches, including stream mitigation banking, are thus far relatively minor in global economic terms, their potential impacts are deeply consequential: environmental policy shapes the landscapes around us and determines the long-term prospects of vulnerable species, ecosystems, and human communities. As markets have become a preferred regulatory instrument for environmental policy, their actual operation and effect, rather than theoretical underpinnings, becomes critical to society.

The chapters in this book are loosely grouped into three sections. The first (chapters 2, 3, and 4) considers what a market for ecosystem services is and does, and how one was created for streams. The second (chapters 5 and 6) draws on our fifteen years of social and physical fieldwork across several states, but primarily in North Carolina, to explain the various parties involved in making stream mitigation banking function, and how they go about accomplishing this. The final section (chapters 7 and 8) describes what we know about the actual environmental consequences of stream mitigation banking, particularly whether the market that was created delivers on ecological promises and expectations.

More specifically, chapter 2 provides an overview of MES in theory and practice, focusing on the challenges that all ecosystem service markets face in addressing what we consider to be the two key negotiated elements of any such market: reconciling equivalence and uncertainty. How do MES policy-makers balance the conflicting goals of economic and ecological functionality? How does that vary across different kinds of ecosystem markets, whether carbon markets or habitat for endangered woodpeckers? Chapter 3 introduces readers to the history of stream restoration, and the relevant science and engineering necessary for any ecosystem service market intended to work in streams. The 150-year-old practice of stream restoration has shifted over time from attempting to improve habitat within streams to creating entirely new stream channels. Why did people begin intervening to improve stream ecosystems, and how have those improvement goals changed? Chapter 4 plunges into the history of market-based approaches to environmental management, from the work of John Dales in the 1950s to the incorporation of such approaches into federal policy. How did the idea of selling nature in order to save it gain such momentum, and how was it converted from idea to policy and practice?

Chapter 5 introduces the cast of characters in the stream mitigation banking community, from the federal agency staff members who set up and regulate the mitigation banking market to investors who provide the funding to initiate a bank. How do dynamics among these players influence mitigation policy and practice, and shape how they address concerns about uncertainty and equivalence? Chapter 6 walks through mitigation banking in practice, highlighting the surprising complexity of this seemingly simple trade of debits and credits. Focusing on the history of a particular North Carolina stream mitigation bank, we ask how do bankers, regulators, and the other key actors keep a functional market for stream credits running?

Chapter 7 investigates the physical consequences of how mitigation actors, policies, and practices in North Carolina resolve the tensions between the economic and ecological goals of stream mitigation. Through a detailed set of geomorphic (i.e., physical) surveys of streams in North Carolina, including those restored under the auspices of mitigation banks, we quantify the actual physical imprint of this ecosystem service market on the fluvial landscape (the hydroscape), and thus begin to understand its peculiar biophysical consequences. Finally, in chapter 8 we return to our initial questions about the environmental implications not only of stream mitigation banking, but of MES more broadly. We argue that markets for ecosystem services have not delivered on the conservation goals of their advocates, and thus need to be radically reconfigured either to strengthen equivalence between destroyed and restored ecosystems, producing narrow but more certain ecological improvements, or to embrace the chaos and dynamism of natural ecosystems, producing far less certain, but potentially much better ecological results.

We turn now to chapter 2, and an overview of the goals and challenges of markets for ecosystem services.

2 Market-Based Approaches to Conservation

The overarching rationale for market-based approaches to environmental conservation is that they are more efficient for society than non-market-based approaches. Instead of blocking development projects to prevent environmental harm, market-based conservation approaches allow that harm so long as it is offset by environmental restoration elsewhere. The goal is to prevent net environmental losses, and perhaps even create environmental gains. The common language for describing this is that *debits* (environmental harms) are compensated for via the purchase of *credits* (environmental improvements).

This sounds straightforward, and clearly has some appeal to both market and conservation advocates: there are now markets for ecosystem services on every continent except Antarctica, designed to address a wide range of issues from species habitat preservation to water quality improvement to atmospheric carbon sequestration. Despite their geographical and environmental variety, these markets face a common set of issues that each must address if they are to successfully conserve the environment via economic incentives.

This chapter first lays out what, exactly, a market for ecosystem service is. Next it explores the fundamental challenges MES face along with the common tactics used to address them. We then illustrate how these core challenges are addressed in practice via the examples of forest carbon credits and conservation banking.

Common Features and Shared Issues

What do we imagine when we think of a market? Put simply, two (or more) participants voluntarily exchange a good or service for money, whether buying a loaf of bread or paying for a haircut. The voluntary part is key: a person may choose to purchase a particular loaf of bread or they may choose not to; similarly, the baker is under no obligation to sell the product of their labor. Further, as we imagine a market, we often assume there will be multiple products that might meet a purchaser's needs, and that they will choose among those products based on their own preferences or priorities. Price is one obvious criterion, but a purchaser's choices may also be influenced by the quality of the goods or services, their particular characteristics, or the interchangeability of the products or services offered for sale.

Markets for ecosystem services, by contrast, typically belong to another category of market—a regulatory market—in which participants enter the market out of government compulsion, not out of choice. In the words of one EPA staff member we interviewed: "At the end of the day, we can *say* the people are gonna do voluntary restoration, but I'm gonna hold that one of the biggest drivers in any of the ecosystems services markets is that people do it because of regulation and they have to."[1]

In regulatory markets, purchasers may not actually want to purchase the product or service they are buying. It is simply a means to an end: meeting regulatory requirements. There is therefore no reason other than price for a purchaser in a regulatory market to choose one product or service over another as long as the product meets regulatory requirements.

An example of a more familiar regulatory market is vehicle emissions inspections. In order to relicense a vehicle each year, many states require that the vehicle must pass an emissions inspection. Importantly, the requirements of the inspection are mandated by the state, and every certified inspection is, by design, identical and interchangeable. Because of government standardization and regulatory compulsion, there is no market competition based on quality; all competition is on price or possibly convenience of the inspection stations. Further, the purchaser has no incentive to seek out a higher quality inspection because they are not entering the market voluntarily. In fact, purchasers are not in the market for an inspection at all; what they seek from the transaction is the sticker confirming regulatory compliance of their vehicle's emissions level. This distinction between voluntary and regulatory markets is important because most markets for ecosystem services are regulatory markets: buyers enter the market to purchase compliance, not ecosystem services (table 2.1).

Table 2.1
Key differences between voluntary and regulatory markets

Free market	Regulatory market
Voluntary purchase: buy something because you want to	Mandatory purchase: buy something because you are required to by regulators
Variety of goods/services for sale, at a range of prices	Very limited range of goods/services for sale, determined by regulators; variation primarily by price
Competition, and thus innovation	Competition only on price; very limited innovation

Regulators (i.e., government staff) play an outsized role in regulatory markets in comparison to their role in a voluntary market. Regulators determine most of the central characteristics of an ecosystem service market, including what the commodity for sale is, such as tons of carbon, acres of species habitat, or emissions certification for vehicles. Regulators also determine what specific requirements must be met in order to create those commodities. Finally, regulators create the demand for these commodities: they determine what types of impacts (debits) require the offsetting purchase of the commodity (credits), and they monitor whether the appropriate commodity has been purchased given the impacting activity. In many ways, the government role in regulatory markets distorts them to the point that they are not particularly market-like at all.

Nevertheless, MES are advocated as a market-like approach for regulatory agencies to achieve conservation goals. And MES do carry some characteristics of markets. While the regulated community must participate in the market, the people or organizations who produce credits for sale enter the market voluntarily and typically as entrepreneurs. Also, there are price differentials—sometimes large, sometimes quite small—between credit providers, and people purchasing credits to offset environmental harms can choose from whom they purchase their credits. As such, there can be competition between providers and price-based selection by purchasers. Finally, competition on price between credit providers occasionally drives innovation, another characteristic of markets.[2]

The key consideration is that markets for ecosystem services must perform a balancing act between the needs of the market and the realities of regulatory compliance. Critics and thoughtful proponents have put forward a fairly consistent set of concerns about whether or not ecosystem service markets actually deliver their intended environmental benefits or their presumed market-like advantages. These include concerns about:

- Whether or not regulators have the capacity to monitor and enforce standards of practice;
- How to ensure that the credits produced survive in perpetuity (referred to as *durability*) rather than being themselves negated by future development activities, such as species habitat being bulldozed for a future housing project or a carbon-sequestering forest being consumed in a fire;
- How to ensure social equity, given that ecosystem services removed in one place are rarely replaced by resources in the immediate geographic vicinity;
- Whether the benefits at the compensation site would have been created anyway under existing requirements, typically referred to as *additionality*; and
- The importance of the time lag between when ecosystem services are destroyed by development and when they are restored to produce credits, particularly in markets intended to address biodiversity loss.[3]

Some of these issues are considered by MES advocates to be straightforward to address. For instance, the durability of habitat compensation can be ensured through conservation easements.[4] Even issues that are difficult to resolve are not viewed by MES advocates as dealbreakers, but rather as subjects for policy adaptation or as opportunities for another market innovation. For example, while it may be difficult to protect forests used to sequester carbon from forest fires, the durability of the sequestration credits sold can be addressed via required insurance contracts if a fire does result in the loss of the offsetting forest.

There are two central concerns with MES, however, that both critics and supporters acknowledge have the potential to undermine their rationale entirely: establishing equivalence, and addressing uncertainty.

The first central concern facing any ecosystem service market is *equivalence*—whether the benefits produced or gained at a compensation site are equivalent to the benefits lost at the developed site (typically referred to as the *impact site*). Without equivalence, the rationale for a market-based compensation/offset approach to environmental management crumbles.

Strict equivalence obviously is impossible: the ecosystem at any given site is too complex and contingent, too particularly a product of its unique eco-social history, to be completely or exactly replicated elsewhere. Such ecological purity, however, disallows the entire project of MES. Thus, some accommodation is needed. Instead, supporters argue for something more generalizable: rather than exact replacement of damaged ecosystems, the goal of an ecosystem service market should be net enhancement of equivalent ecological structure and function, or of a discrete set of ecosystem services.[5] Assessing even this somewhat relaxed form of comparability between debits (the damage at the impact site) and credits (the improvements conducted at the mitigation site) requires paring away the ecological specificity of particular sites, an act of simplification that is itself not a simple task. Many critics argue that it cannot be done, while supporters argue that it is difficult but doable.[6]

Uncertainty is a second central concern for any ecosystem service market. If we cannot be reasonably sure that the actions we take to produce credits actually create the ecological benefits we seek, the entire project of MES is moot. More simply, MES require restoring something: uncertainty is whether that restored ecosystem results in the ecological benefits intended. This uncertainty has both physical/ecological and social/political aspects. In both cases, it centers on our ability to control short- and long-term environmental outcomes. On the physical front, uncertainty can revolve around the very notion of ecosystem restoration generally: are we able to successfully restore ecosystems at all? Can we obtain our desired outcomes and preserve them over the long term? On the social front, uncertainty revolves around whether regulatory frameworks will change with shifts in political power, and also whether human actions on site or nearby will affect the efficacy or durability of restoration at a particular site. There is widespread agreement that any credible ecosystem service market must provide satisfactory responses to these concerns, demonstrating our ability to control environmental outcomes to produce the results we seek.[7] It is worth noting, however, that even strong advocates of MES agree that while many ecosystems can be reliably restored, there are some that are so difficult to restore or recreate that impacts to them cannot be offset, and thus should not be allowed.[8]

Addressing Equivalence
Different MES attempt to address equivalence and uncertainty in different ways, depending on their geographic, regulatory, and environmental

context. Typically, questions of equivalence are addressed through the metrics by which the commodity for sale is defined, while questions of uncertainty are addressed through the regulatory framework that sets the rules for that market.

The overarching purpose of an ecosystem service market is to create a socioeconomic system in which ecosystem damage can be offset. But because no ecosystem can be exactly replicated, the goal of MES is to incentivize (and require) the conservation of *some aspects* of the impacted ecosystem. Markets for carbon, for instance, do not require conservation of underground coal to compensate for emissions of carbon from coal-fired power plants; rather, they require conservation of atmospheric carbon, thus enabling a newly planted forest to compensate for extracted and burned coal. Markets for stream temperature do not require installation of water-chilling services; rather, they require conservation of thermal loading (i.e., solar input) to streams, thus enabling planted riparian vegetation along headwater streams to compensate for increased warm water inputs from an industrial facility.

In short, equivalence requires a dramatic reconceptualization and abstraction of ecosystems into only those narrow, limited aspects that society deems relevant to conserve at that time. These limited aspects can be functions (e.g., biogeochemical processes such as carbon sequestration or nitrogen retention), structures (wetlands, streams, species habitat), or communities (specific species, or groups of species). *Without this abstraction from complex ecosystem to function, structure, or community, MES are impossible.* If equivalence were taken literally, the only way to offset the impacts of digging up and burning coal would be to create coal and replace it underground; by abstracting out only one aspect of coal—its contribution to atmospheric carbon—a market for carbon becomes possible because there are numerous potential ways to produce offsets for sale (not to mention numerous emitters of CO_2 who would need to purchase offsets for their emissions). The key thing to note is that the more abstractly equivalence is defined, the thicker and more robust the potential market because of the numerous possible ways to produce the equivalent characteristic, and the numerous potential purchasers of that surrogate characteristic.

This abstraction of ecosystem aspects (function, structure, community) to create equivalence requires distilling entire ecosystems into a small set of metrics that are measurable and translatable between sites. This is the central pivot of equivalence: the metrics used in MES must be able to capture both debits and credits and so capture key attributes of sites that are damaged and those that are conserved. MES require that we be able to assess whether there is equivalence between ecological loss and ecological gain, and they require metrics that quantify these losses and gains. Metrics thus convert ecological complexity into a simplified set of characteristics that can be measured, regulated, and sold. The ecological specificity of the impact and conservation sites must be radically reduced to an ecologically coherent core indicator or set of indicators. This simplified metric or indicator, when placed in a regulatory market context, becomes the measurable commodity to be bought and sold. In the parlance of MES, this becomes the *credit* for sale.[9]

In any ecosystem service market, simplicity is crucial for enabling comparison of the equivalence of ecosystem debits and credits, but it is not sufficient to ensure a smoothly functioning market. To function well, markets require commodities that are not just simple, but also stable and predictable for market participants. Those producing credits must know that if they go through the effort and cost of production (i.e., restoring a site), there will be a market for those credits—demand—in the future (see chapter 5). Those who are purchasing credits will be more willing to do so if the regulations requiring the purchase are durable, thus providing legitimacy to the incurred costs. Because this is a regulatory market (with credits defined by a regulator), if regulators frequently change how equivalence, and thus credits, are defined, that creates significant regulatory uncertainty for credit producers. Vice versa, credit purchasers need to be sure that when they purchase a credit, it will extinguish their regulatory liability; if there is any uncertainty about this, then there will be far less willingness to use this type of market mechanism for regulatory compliance. Thus, both credit producers and purchasers require that the ways in which equivalence between credits and debits are defined remain stable, or they will be very reluctant to enter the market.

Creating these simple, stable commodities out of complex, dynamic ecosystems, and thus ensuring equivalence between debits and credits, is a far more difficult task than it may initially appear. Ecosystems are characteristically dynamic; they are in constant flux over the time scale of days (e.g., ecosystem production by day; respiration by night), seasons (e.g., floods in spring and droughts in summer; organismal hibernation), and even decades and centuries (e.g., organismal recruitment; migration; forest succession). While some of these changes are predictable, others are not: invasive species or natural disasters such as forest fires or hurricanes have profound impacts on most aspects of the ecosystems regulated via MES. Quite simply, *ecosystems are characterized by a lack of the very same simplicity, stability, and predictability on which functional markets depend.*

Reducing the particularities of an ecosystem to establish equivalence and define a simple, stable commodity for sale requires grappling with ecosystem dynamics in two ways. From the perspective of a regulator, the system restored must be sufficiently stable or controllable so that what is assessed represents what will exist over some period of time; it must not simply be a snapshot of a condition that may soon degrade. Thus, it must be possible to control the measured characteristics of a system, the system itself must be invariant, or the metrics used by the regulator must be able to integrate over time to capture some average condition that accounts for natural instability but draws attention to degradation or failure of conservation.

For instance, if the equivalent ecosystem service is nitrogen retention in riparian vegetation, then measuring (directly) nitrogen reaching the stream can vary tremendously on whether that measurement occurs during late-winter runoff (when flow and nitrogen loading are high and plant growth minimal) or during late-summer (when flow and nitrogen loading are small and plant growth high). Alternatively, the metric could focus on characteristics of riparian vegetation, which are far less variable; while the number of plants per square meter is an imperfect surrogate for the actual function of interest, density of riparian vegetation provides a more stable metric of nitrogen retention for regulators and for market participants. Thus, riparian vegetation could be used as a proxy for equivalent nitrogen retention in large part because it is temporally stable and is an integrative measure over time.

In sum, equivalency in MES is addressed through highly simplified metrics. These metrics distill complex ecosystems into what is perceived to be their most critical functions or attributes. The metrics must also be relatively stable in the face of natural fluctuations or social dynamics, or both; that is, the particular function or characteristic that metrics quantify must be static, or at least controllable, over the lifetime of a conservation project in order to meet market needs.

Compensating for Uncertainty

Markets for ecosystem services, and ecosystem restoration more generally, are inherently uncertain (as discussed in chapter 3) because of the wide variety of functions underlying ecosystems and the peculiarities of people and markets. To be blunt, *it is unclear whether many types of ecosystem restoration actually reverse the ecological damages they are intended to undo.* In an attempt to address these eco-social uncertainties, MES require standards of practice, typically in the form of regulatory frameworks developed by public agencies or authorities. In some cases, the participants in an ecosystem service market—those who will produce the credits for sale, or those who will be required to purchase the credits, or both—are consulted in setting the basic rules for these regulatory markets; in most cases, however, public agency staff develop regulatory frameworks for MES on their own, although iteratively based on experiences. Because MES are regulatory markets, regulatory frameworks effectively set the rules to address fundamental concerns and questions, most notably:

- Who is required to purchase credits and under what circumstances (e.g., must impacts by public agencies be offset, or only those by private industry)?
- What counts as a compensation site, what standards must be followed, and what specific aspects of a compensation site generate credits (e.g., what physical or biological characteristics must exist at a site for it to count as a compensation site)?
- What are the temporal characteristics of the market (e.g., how soon can credits be sold? Are credits needed prior to impacts)?
- What are the spatial/geographic characteristics of the market (e.g., how far away from an impact can an offset site be located)?

Regulatory frameworks can address and potentially alleviate many sources of uncertainty for credit providers, purchasers, and regulators, but these frameworks must do so in a way that does not stifle the potential market. This forces trade-offs between different kinds of uncertainty. For example, in order to address regulatory uncertainty about whether or not an endangered animal will be able to survive the loss of its habitat, most MES intend that new, conserved habitat should already be present before any credits can be sold. However, this requires credit providers to invest a great deal of money to build a conservation project long before any generated credits can be sold, creating tremendous financial uncertainty for credit providers. In this type of regulatory approach, a credit provider has to wait a long time before realizing even the potential to generate a return on their investment, along with experiencing uncertainty about how many credits the project will generate and whether there will be buyers for those credits in the future. To balance these competing sources of uncertainty (i.e., to balance regulators' need to ensure endangered species have access to high-quality habitat with credit providers' unwillingness to participate in a regulatory market without some reasonable expectation of profit), the regulatory frameworks for MES often allow credits to be sold by producers before the credit site has been fully completed and assessed. That is, credits can be sold that do not yet exist.[10] This is a mechanism developed by regulators to strike a balance between the uncertainty of credit providers and the uncertainty associated with the needs of a species or ecosystem, a constant tension and balancing act for any ecosystem service market.

There is also high uncertainty about the long-term prospects of conserved ecosystems. Will a project continue to provide ecological benefits over years or decades, or will it either degrade over time or be destroyed for a new development project? Can we control the site itself and the impacts of outside forces upon it sufficiently well to obtain the environmental outcomes we seek? MES typically require a monitoring period after conservation project completion to demonstrate some ecological effectiveness over time. But again, the regulator must balance the needs of market uncertainty with those of ecological uncertainty. The regulator could minimize ecological uncertainty by requiring monitoring and demonstrable benefits for many years, or even decades, allowing only very slow, gradual release of credits over time. This would place tremendous uncertainty on the credit provider, however, as they would be forced to internalize uncertainty over how their conserved project performs over time, recognizing that they cannot control broader environmental conditions that inevitably drive site performance (e.g., droughts, fires, invasive species). Alternatively, if the regulator allows the credit provider to have immediate financial returns in very short periods of time, there is significant uncertainty for the ecological trajectory of the site.

A trade-off to balance the uncertainty of long-term disposition with the needs of the market has been to combine several years of monitoring with conservation easements: regulators typically mandate that compensation sites be monitored for several years (e.g., five to seven years for streams and wetlands) and then maintained in perpetuity (often via conservation easements managed by state agencies or private land trusts) to ensure that the ecological benefits created via MES will not be lost to subsequent development.[11] This assumes that even if we cannot control what happens at the site and the benefits of the conservation activities themselves prove transient, the land will not be developed, providing at least a minimal level of conservation and reduction of ecological uncertainty for the future.

A particularly problematic source of uncertainty is whether many kinds of ecosystem conservation can be accomplished successfully. In some cases, ecosystem conservation and restoration are relatively novel in terms of type or scale, and thus best thought of as emerging science and technology.[12] In other cases (such as stream restoration; see chapter 3), ongoing science and long-term monitoring raise questions about the efficacy of what were thought to be well-established practices.[13] Most scientists and regulators accept the fact that restored ecosystems will have biological communities and functions that are poorer (or at least different) from their undisturbed counterparts, or that restored ecosystems take a period of time to gain functions comparable to undisturbed systems. That is, the basic efficacy of ecosystem conservation, which undergirds market-based approaches, is highly uncertain.

In order to address this most basic source of uncertainty while still allowing MES to proceed, regulators use *trading ratios*, by which a particular number of debits can only be offset by a higher number of credits. Importantly, trading ratios are intricately linked with metrics that address equivalency issues in myriad ways, as we will explain. Trading ratios work in very much the same way that *factors of safety* do in engineering. For example, when designing a bridge, there are sources of uncertainty when calculating the size of a pier or the stiffness of a beam. Engineers conduct rigorous analyses to specify such dimensions, but then increase the final value by some percentage to offset the risks associated with uncertainty in scientific precision or accuracy present in the many analyses leading to that final value. If the analyses suggest that a bridge pier should be 1.5 meters in diameter, the engineer may use a safety factor of 2, and recommend a pier 3 meters in diameter. Factors of safety are used to quickly mitigate the effects of the many inevitable sources of uncertainty in any design project that cannot be fully accounted for or controlled. Similarly, if regulators feel the science underlying a particular type of stream restoration—say, restoration of cold-water small streams for an endangered frog species—is fairly certain, then a small trading ratio can be used, perhaps 1.5:1 (i.e., 1.5 units of restoration are needed to offset 1 unit of impact). If instead regulators are uncertain about the scientific basis of this kind of restoration, then a larger trading ratio may be used in an attempt to compensate for the uncertain outcome (e.g., 5:1). As scientific understanding and experience increase the likelihood of success (and uncertainty decreases), the trading ratio can become less lopsided.

Regulators also use trading ratios to address issues of equivalence: larger trading ratios can be used to compensate for a lack of equivalence between impact site and compensation site. In the case of wetland markets, if a conservation site is to be used to compensate for an already degraded impact site, then a trading ratio of only 1.5:1 or 2:1 might be used. But if that same conservation site were to be used to compensate for impacts at a nearly pristine site, then a trading ratio of 6:1 might apply. Similarly, geographic proximity of a conservation site to an impact site typically is considered ecologically beneficial because it increases the similarity between the functions and communities lost and those gained via conservation. Thus, regulators apply lower trading ratios for nearby compensation sites, and higher ratios for more distant sites. A similar approach can be used to address temporal disparities, or even differences in types of systems; for example, a certain type of ecosystem impact is offset by compensation of a different type altogether, and the greater the difference in types, the greater the trading ratio applied.

There are multiple reasons to use trading ratios, but a fundamental one is that trading ratios enable the continued use of simplified metrics to represent complex ecosystems. While the sources of uncertainty are real, they are also quite subtle and complex. Distinguishing the ecosystem variations of impact and compensation sites between locations or types or timing at the level necessary to ensure that a trade results in equal amounts of functional loss and gain (equivalence) would push the bounds of science while also requiring significant data collection, analysis, and expertise to be deployed for each individual transaction. Such effort would undermine one of the chief rationales of market-based approaches—improving the efficiency of complying with environmental regulation—by creating untenable delays and increasing the costs of each transaction. Each impact would need to be studied in detail before deciding how many credits would need to be purchased on the market; meanwhile, each restoration site would likewise need to be studied in exceptionally high detail. These delays and associated costs would preclude any market from developing at all. By subsuming all of these sources of uncertainty into trading ratios, regulators are able to continue using the same metrics of site assessment for both impact and compensation sites. Regulators can also respond to scientists' calls for higher precision, or to environmental advocates' concerns that markets result in the loss of net ecosystem function, by hedging with higher trading ratios. Thus regulators can say that regardless of the effectiveness of restoration, the end result is a net gain in permanently conserved land (through the requirement of easements coupled with >1:1 trading ratios). Moreover, this approach of using higher and higher trading ratios also increases the flow of credits through increasing demand from impactors, thus bolstering the overall market side of MES. Quite simply, trading ratios amplify and accelerate both sides of the balancing act that regulators must negotiate: increasing a trading ratio decreases the ecological risk that the restored ecosystem will not offset damages, while simultaneously increasing the demand for more credits (i.e., increasing the thickness of the market). Trading ratios offer regulators and market participants a ready cure for many of the underlying uncertainties in MES. Yet using trading ratios obscures the fact that they do not address the root causes of uncertainty; rather, all of the uncertainty of ecosystem restoration is subsumed under the umbrella of trading ratios.

Trading ratios have received considerable attention in the literature about MES. In studies of the economics of trading ratios, it is presumed that their creation and application is unproblematic.[14] Yet there is substantial debate as to whether ratios are an adequate avenue for addressing this fundamental uncertainty.[15] Studies that carefully consider the uncertainty of restoration efficacy find that to ensure equivalency would require trading ratios many times higher than those typically used.[16] This raises questions about what, exactly, trading ratios are addressing. After all, if attempts at restoration are fundamentally inadequate, simply expanding their scope and scale through greater numbers of restored ecosystems—a result of higher trading ratios—seems unlikely to produce desired conservation results. Thus, there is not yet consensus as to whether uncertainty can be successfully addressed via regulatory frameworks.

Credit Definitions and Regulatory Frameworks in Practice

Perhaps the easiest way to understand how MES address these complex issues of equivalence and uncertainty is to see how two quite different ecosystem service markets—forest carbon credits and species conservation banking—address them in practice via credit definitions (metrics) and regulatory frameworks.

Example 1: Forest Carbon Credits

The Clean Development Mechanism (CDM) is a market-based regulatory framework for addressing atmospheric carbon and associated climate change laid out in the Kyoto Protocol. Under the CDM, developed countries required to offset their greenhouse gas emissions can purchase offsets from developing countries. In this MES, the commodity for sale is the Certified Emission Reduction unit, which can be produced by a range of possible activities (e.g., replacing coal-fired power sources with solar arrays or capturing fugitive emissions of powerful greenhouse gases), all of which are exactingly specified in the CDM. Particularly in comparison to the complexities of defining equivalence between ecosystems, defining equivalence between tons of CO_2 emitted or reduced is relatively straightforward: a unit of CO_2 is neither internally complex nor in any way specific to the eco-social context that produced it. The source of complexity and uncertainty lies in which types of projects are allowed to produce those relatively simple credits.

Initially, the CDM specified that Certified Emission Reduction units could be produced by reducing carbon emissions, but not by absorbing (i.e., sequestering) greenhouse gases after they had been emitted, such as via reforestation. Put differently, credits could be produced by reducing *sources* of emissions, but not by producing *sinks*. This type of constraint on the market is possible because it is a regulatory market not a voluntary one, so that the commodity for sale (i.e., credit) is created by government fiat rather than by voluntary participation and creation.

Advocates for including reforestation projects in the CDM as an allowable mechanism of producing Certified Emission Reduction units argued that terrestrial carbon sinks could play a crucial role in greenhouse gas reductions by absorbing excess emissions until developed countries could feasibly reduce them, creating a "wooden bridge" into a clean energy future. Critics were skeptical about the impermanence of these credits: there was a very real possibility that Certified Emission Reduction units sold for carbon sink projects could vanish abruptly due to natural or human disturbances (e.g., forest fires), destabilizing the CDM market and efforts to combat climate change.[17] Dutschke and Angelsen, for example, identified five major issues that could lead to early re-release of carbon including risks from natural disturbances, from climate change, and from direct human reversal of reforestation via logging, burning, or neglect.[18] Critics thus were concerned about the durability and stability of credits over time in the face of profound broader uncertainty.

After extensive debate, the CDM was expanded to include sink projects in 2003 via the Afforestation and Reforestation protocol.[19] The uncertainty about whether reforestation projects would be able to sequester carbon reliably even over relatively short timespans became a central topic of debate, and the way in which reforestation was eventually accepted into the CDM reflects this: unlike conservation projects intended to persist in perpetuity, credits from reforestation come with set expiration dates. Rather than trying to achieve permanence, these credits are predicated on impermanence. In the case of temporary Certified Emissions Reduction units, for example, the credits expire every five years; even long-term Certified Emissions Reduction units have a maximum lifespan of forty years. Once credits expire, their initial purchasers must find other sources of Certified Emission Reduction units to offset their impacts.

The development of the CDM has been heavily influenced by the concerns of the scientific community, as demonstrated by the complex and carefully specified metrics and guidelines for producing carbon sequestration credits. While concerns for market viability are clearly present, imperatives for stability and simplicity seem to have taken a backseat to attempts to address the plausible uncertainty about physical and social risks.

It is perhaps unsurprising, then, that the CDM market is not functioning as well as its advocates had hoped, with credit prices at a mere fraction of their original values.[20] Carefully addressing issues of uncertainty and equivalence came at a steep cost: the credits for sale were widely perceived as too complicated and unstable and thus not worth the investment, and the carbon market has been anemic at best.

Example 2: Species Conservation Banking
While the U.S. Endangered Species Act (ESA) is often portrayed as the ultimate inflexible regulatory hammer, the ESA in fact allows impacts to habitat

of federally listed species (e.g., threatened or endangered) to occur as long as they are offset by habitat conservation elsewhere.[21] These offsetting projects are often called *conservation banks*, and are comparable to mitigation banks used for offsetting dredge/fill impacts to aquatic ecosystems (introduced in the previous chapter). The rationale for conservation banking at the federal level stems from the ESA's prohibition of *take* (i.e., harm, harassment, or killing) of individuals from endangered species or destruction of their habitat. Conservation banks allow take to occur as long as there are offsetting conservation measures elsewhere, providing the equivalent ecosystem service of habitat for the species in question.

Like most other MES, there are no voluntary participants in the conservation banking market. Rather, credits are purchased from conservation banks because of regulatory compulsion, typically by land or oil/gas developers, and increasingly by large land-intensive alternative energy projects such as wind and solar production facilities. Regulatory agencies determine what characteristics must be present for a conserved ecosystem to count as a conservation bank for a particular species, and thus to produce habitat credits for sale.

The first conservation bank was established in the United States in 1995 in California. As late as 2002, conservation banks could only be found in California, and even as of 2015, more than three-quarters of the 137 federally approved conservation banks were in that state.[22] As of 2013, 73 percent of conservation banks were private, for-profit ventures. These banks vary in size by three orders of magnitude, from eight acres to just over four thousand acres, and have been established to compensate for impacts to a wide range of protected species, from tortoises to foxes to bats.[23]

Compared with the highly detailed international regulatory framework for forest carbon credits, the regulatory framework for conservation banking is quite limited and case specific. There was no federal guidance for conservation banking at all until 2003, and even that is far less detailed than the regulatory framework for Certified Emission Reduction units. Also, unlike forest carbon credits, conservation banking depends primarily on preservation of existing high-quality habitat rather than restoration or creation;[24] according to one study, 94 percent of conservation banks through 2005 were primarily preservation projects.[25] Thus, uncertainty in this ecosystem service market is addressed because the habitat protected is already of very high quality, so the risks of unsuccessful restoration are greatly reduced, and via trading ratios determined by comparing the quality of the habitat at the credit site to that at the impact site.

How equivalence—and thus the actual conservation credits for sale—is determined is specific to each bank and the species preserved there.[26] Early in the history of conservation banking, credit determination methodologies were often quite complex, based on careful, nuanced attention to the ecological needs of specific species. For example, in 1998, credit calculations for vernal pool banks in Central California paid careful attention to equivalence, taking into consideration the size of the proposed bank, the rarity of the type or types of vernal pools included, the relative rarity of the endangered species at the site, the condition of the habitat, and its long-term feasibility based on surrounding land uses. The result of this ecologically specific definition of equivalence between impact and credit sites was a complex set of calculations dependent on careful ecological surveying combined with a healthy dose of best professional judgment. This state of affairs seems not to have lasted long; by 2008 vernal pool credits were calculated on the far simpler basis of acreage, as are 91 percent of conservation banks nationwide.[27]

Another illustrative example of conservation banking is the market for the federally listed red cockaded woodpecker. Breeding pairs of woodpeckers are the lynchpin of species survival, and would be a suitable metric in terms of scientific and ecological rationales. However, the birds themselves are difficult and resource intensive to monitor. Moreover, their viability and breeding are subject to myriad external factors beyond the possible influence or control of credit providers, constraining the durability of any credit (based on breeding pairs) that might be created. Rather than establish a market based on breeding pairs, regulators instead established credits for this species based only on acres of suitable habitat. Yet even this relatively simple metric has proven difficult to sustain and regulate: while there is supposed to be careful long-term monitoring to ensure that high-quality habitat is maintained, such monitoring has been "haphazard and limited, and it is not at all clear whether these banks are supplying the habitat for which they were established."[28]

In conservation banking for ESA compliance, concerns about stability, ease of measurement, and durability have superseded attempts to address complexity, unpredictability, and equivalence. The market for conservation credits appears to be doing very well even if we cannot determine whether the target species are in fact being conserved.[29] *But these experiences demonstrate the tightrope ecosystem measures and metrics must walk: precise enough to represent the ecosystem while nebulous enough to allow a market to operate.* This is the balancing act that all MES must confront.

Conclusion

Markets for ecosystem services share a set of issues that must be addressed, regardless of whether their focus is carbon sequestration or woodpecker habitat. First, any ecosystem service market must determine how it will define *equivalence* between the impact and compensation sites and manage the trade-offs between ecological complexity and economic stability. Second, any ecosystem service market must find ways to address the many physical and social forms of *uncertainty* about whether credit producers can actually deliver gains equivalent to the losses we expect them to offset. Therefore, regardless of the impact they are intended to address, MES face a series of trade-offs between ecological and economic concerns, balancing the requirements of robust markets and ecosystems.

We turn now to the history of the regulatory market at the heart of this book: stream mitigation banking. How and why did humans begin intervening to improve the ecological health of rivers and streams? How have those interventions evolved over time? And how did they set the stage for creating an ecosystem service market for streams in the 1990s?

3 How Stream Restoration Was Born, and What Came of It

Streams and rivers play an outsized environmental role. In a purely geographic sense, they are relatively rare; only a small portion of any landscape is a flowing aquatic system. But these fluvial systems have very broad impacts. They are crucial not only for aquatic organisms, but also for many terrestrial organisms that need water to survive. Further, rivers and streams are central to physical and chemical processes across watersheds because of their role as integrators: everything flows or is washed downhill, converging into them.

Both physical and chemical properties have been essential features of the economic and political landscape in the United States, and thus have been subjected to tremendous anthropogenic impacts. European settlers used rivers as their primary arteries of transportation, harvesting timber from hillsides and routing it along rivers downstream to ports. To quicken the downstream journey of their timber and to provide easier passage for their rafts, canoes, flatboats, and steamboats, settlers removed gravel bars, snags, logjams, and boulders and straightened river channels, rapidly clearing out almost every navigable waterway throughout the Northeast and upper Midwest. Dam building came next to provide power for the mills that converted raw timber and grain into lumber and flour, which were easier to ship and brought higher prices. Most colonial villages from New England to Georgia were built around a grist mill, and the eighteenth- and nineteenth-century industrialization of America depended on waterpower from mill dams peppering nearly every river, stream, and tributary.[1]

When the federal government entered the picture through its water resource management agencies, particularly the Corps of Engineers and the Bureau of Reclamation, the scale of river change increased dramatically.

Along the lower Mississippi River, the Corps of Engineers straightened the channel to speed floods and riverboat traffic: the length of this massive river was reduced by 150 miles in the first half of the twentieth century. Other agencies were just as busy straightening and dredging rivers; one nationwide estimate put total stream and river modification at 200,000 miles, or about 6 percent of the total length of stream miles in the United States.[2] This does not even account for the dams built nationwide: by the close of the twentieth century there were as many as 85,000 dams greater than ten feet tall, and perhaps as many as two million dams overall if you included all the other smaller structures that blocked streams, sloughs, and tributaries across the nation.[3] These structures radically changed the character of the rivers and streams on which they were located, both upstream and downstream.

There were equally profound changes to the water that flowed in those rivers. America was long an agricultural society and still is in many regions, such as the Midwest. Food production has come at the expense of rivers and streams. The explosion of forest clearing and row crop agriculture triggered vast soil erosion and the muddying of tributaries; the most common pollutant in twenty-first-century streams and rivers is sediment. As America industrialized, rivers were befouled by the decaying cattle carcasses from meat processors adjacent to the waterways in Chicago, the oil refining wastes of heavy industry that lined the Cuyahoga River of Cleveland, and the burgeoning petrochemical empire along the Mississippi River near Saint Louis. Even where these industrial pollutants were not spewing into waterways, the exploding population's municipal waste flowed directly into rivers for decades. Today, the runoff of fertilizers from farms and suburban lawns flows untreated into America's streams and rivers.

Rivers were, and are, the gutters of society. And just as individuals and groups oppose this environmental damage today, scientists, engineers, and fishermen in earlier times sought out ways and opportunities to undo the damage being done to rivers.

Early Forms of Stream Restoration

Environmental restoration is based on the idea that we can undo the environmental damage we have caused.[4] This compelling vision of humans as beneficial members of ecosystems has made restoration an increasingly central part of the global environmental movement since the mid-1970s. Restoration has far deeper roots, however, stretching back at least to the late 1800s in the United States.⁵ Some of the earliest efforts to restore aquatic ecosystems took place in the backwoods of the Catskill Mountains of upstate New York in the 1870s under the auspices of fly fishermen in search of trout. Rivers in the Catskills were isolated from much of the industrialization occurring elsewhere, so they were not befouled by chemical waste or urban sewage. They were physically degraded, however: the local timber industry not only had removed trees, but also had manipulated the streams and rivers to get the timber out by straightening and clearing their channels.

This physical degradation, along with the loss of riparian (i.e., river-bordering) vegetation, caught the attention of fishermen worried by declining trout populations, who then wrote about trout stream degradation in popular magazines such as *Forest and Stream*. John Spencer Van Cleef was particularly prolific in both his fishing and his writing about how the physical form of rivers affected trout. He had a clear view of what was degrading trout streams: "I have become satisfied that the destruction of the trees bordering on these streams and the changed condition of the banks produced thereby, has resulted in the destruction of the natural harbors or hiding places of the trout." The importance of Van Cleef's explanation was that it made clear that this habitat destruction was reversible: "I believe it possible to restore most of our streams . . . especially when they are under the control of clubs or associations who can make the effort."⁶

Van Cleef and a few other trout fishermen had intuitively combined several important ideas that would shape stream restoration for the next century and a half. They linked the physical condition of a river with the presence or absence of trout, and in so doing viewed the bed of a river, the vegetation along its banks, and how water flowed along the channel as malleable. If humans could restore these characteristics of a stream to a semblance of their natural condition, early restoration practitioners assumed, the ecosystem—particularly the trout—should follow. This was one of the earliest rationales for stream restoration, and it has been given a rather flippant slogan drawn from the 1980s movie *Field of Dreams*: build it and they will come.

Over the next decade, private fishing clubs were organized in the Catskills and other areas outside large eastern cities. Beyond acquiring and preserving land, the clubs focused their attention on restoring trout streams. In the 1870s, Van Cleef developed methods for manipulating the features of streams to increase trout habitat, the implementation of which became a hobby for club members between their fishing outings. They used the materials available in the Catskills—logs and boulders—and placed them in particular configurations and locations with the hope of attracting trout to their stream reaches again. They built miniature dams—weirs—across channels to create pools upstream and fast-flowing riffles downstream. They brought in larger rocks to build *vanes* in the river—partially submerged barriers to flow, like hydraulic speedbumps. They tried different shapes and combinations of structures in an effort to make things just right for trout. While their efforts were novel, they were largely ineffective, in part from a simple limitation of scale: a few hundred feet of restored stream makes very little difference in a watershed of a hundred square miles.

The increase in scale required to make stream restoration at least theoretically effective was made possible when emerging research from a group of fisheries scientists at the University of Michigan was combined with the very activist role of the federal government during the Great Depression. In the early 1930s, University of Michigan researchers began a concerted focus on improving habitat conditions for trout to restore the fishes' ability to naturally reproduce. Some of the earliest formalized, scientifically based guidelines for restoring streams were developed from their work, encapsulated in a nondescript pamphlet titled *Methods for the Improvement of Michigan Trout Streams*.[7] It eventually became a cornerstone document of habitat improvement for stream restoration through much of the mid-twentieth century.[8]

The specific restoration techniques the scientists from the Michigan School advocated were quite similar to what had been done by the hobbyists in the Catskills a half century earlier. Working within the existing stream channel, they constructed small dams and weirs, and placed boulders and logs in particular shapes and spacings in attempts to create more varied hydraulic habitat within the confines of the existing river channel. Importantly, the sinuosity (i.e., the layout, or course of the river) and banks were treated as fixed aspects, while the in-channel aspects of the river were considered malleable targets of intervention. Over the second quarter of the twentieth century, river scientists at the University of Michigan published dozens of articles in prominent journals. These studies formed the basis

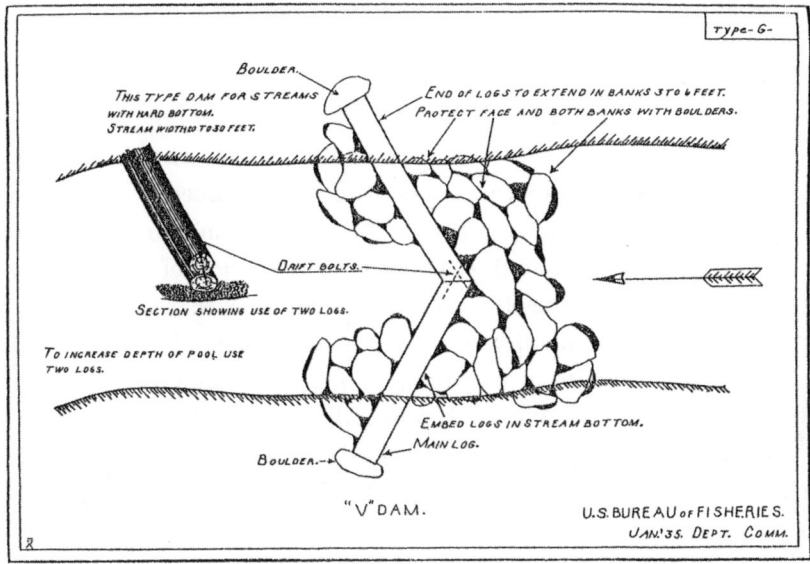

Figure 3.1
Example of channel restoration "V" dam design from 1935. *Source:* Design from Type G, U.S. Bureau of Fisheries 1935, 17.

from which longer-term evaluations and guidelines were developed, and as students matriculated from Michigan and populated government agency positions elsewhere, their ideas about the utility of trout stream restoration as a management technique diffused nationally as well.[9]

An accident of timing allowed the work of these scientists to jump scale from the limited interventions of Catskill fishing clubs to wide distribution across the nation. Government work programs were a key feature of the early years of the Great Depression, and the people in those programs needed something to do. Small stream restoration was ideal for one of the primary New Deal work programs, the Civilian Conservation Corps (CCC), because it required very few technical skills, was done in rural areas of the United States where unemployment was high, and relied on locally available materials such as logs and boulders.[10] No one knew whether the tactics from the University of Michigan would work, but the ecological risks paled in comparison to the potential economic and political benefits. During the early 1930s—the initial peak of the Great Depression—around thirty-one thousand structures were constructed on over four hundred mountain streams for the purpose of restoring habitat for trout. By 1936 the CCC had altered almost five thousand miles of streams.[11]

The efforts to restore streams, especially by employing instream hydraulic structures, continued on through the mid-twentieth century, with methods largely identical to those the CCC and Michigan scientists used during the 1930s. Restoration work was done, and well documented, in Michigan, South Dakota, Montana, Tennessee, New Mexico, and throughout the upper Midwest,[12] and it had three key features. First, most of the work was in-channel restoration: the physical dimensions and shape of the river were left intact. Second, restoration was based on the assumption that desired ecological benefits, such as bigger trout populations, would follow from physical improvements. And third, even at the time there was no clear evidence that these techniques actually worked. Based on a thorough analysis of data collected at the restoration projects, there is no evidence that they had any positive ecological effects at all.[13]

Reconfiguring Channels

All of the efforts of the Catskill fishermen, the Michigan scientists, and the CCC workers were concentrated down in the stream; they worked within the existing streambanks and streambed, and built structures to modify how water flowed within the *existing* channel. And yet many of the problems they wanted to address stemmed from physical alterations of the channel through straightening or the construction of dams and levees. Restorationists could see clearly that something was physically wrong with the shape (or *morphology*) of these rivers and streams, but they were unsure how to fix it because there was no way to identify what an appropriate, healthy morphology for any given reach would be. Looking at historical photos or maps to see what had been there before was almost always irrelevant: changes in land use throughout a watershed inevitably affect the amount of water and sediment a river or stream needs to carry. What restorationists needed was a way to determine what the shape of a given reach of stream channel should look like now in order to successfully transport the water and sediment it currently received. In the 1980s, there were significant leaps in restoration science, engineering, and audacity that together finally made this possible, transforming reconfiguration of stream channels from a dream into a common practice.

The leap in science was the result of a paradigm change in fluvial geomorphology—the study of river form and processes. Up through the middle of the twentieth century, geomorphology was a primarily descriptive discipline. Geomorphologists were narrators of process, describing how landscapes evolved. Geomorphology texts and journal publications were dense with photographs and a few maps, in combination with long explanations of the formation of particular types of landscape in different regions of the world.

And then came the quants. Starting in the 1950s, a group of geomorphologists began quantifying landforms rather than describing them. Articles and texts from geomorphologists had fewer and fewer pictures, and more and more graphs and tables of data. Instead of summary statements, equations summarized concepts. Fluvial geomorphologists laid out the processes that formed rivers in equations of force and motion, and distilled the shapes of rivers themselves down to a surprisingly tidy set of quantifiable relations, referred to as *hydraulic geometry equations*.[14] Studies in the United States and abroad demonstrated that once coefficients and exponents were adjusted for the particular conditions in a given watershed, hydraulic geometry equations could be used to describe almost any river or stream within it. This gave river morphology a sense of rule-like behavior, and even a sense of predictability.

Hydraulic geometry equations link the morphology of a river directly to the amount of water it carries or the size of watershed that it drains. Key features of a river—such as width and depth—are functions (dependent variables) of an independent variable such as discharge or Drainage Area, and are expressed as a set of equations:

Width = $a(DA)^b$

Depth = $c(DA)^f$

The power of this new way of thinking was that it converted rivers into a series of equations, and thus made stream morphology calculable. Over the next half century, river scientists fleshed out these numeric relations and patterns with increasing subtlety and precision. Hydraulic geometry equations went from generalizations to predictions that river engineers could deploy to design flood outlets or move a river under a new bridge overpass.[15]

For stream restoration practitioners, the hydraulic geometry equations were nothing short of revolutionary. In theory, once discharge was

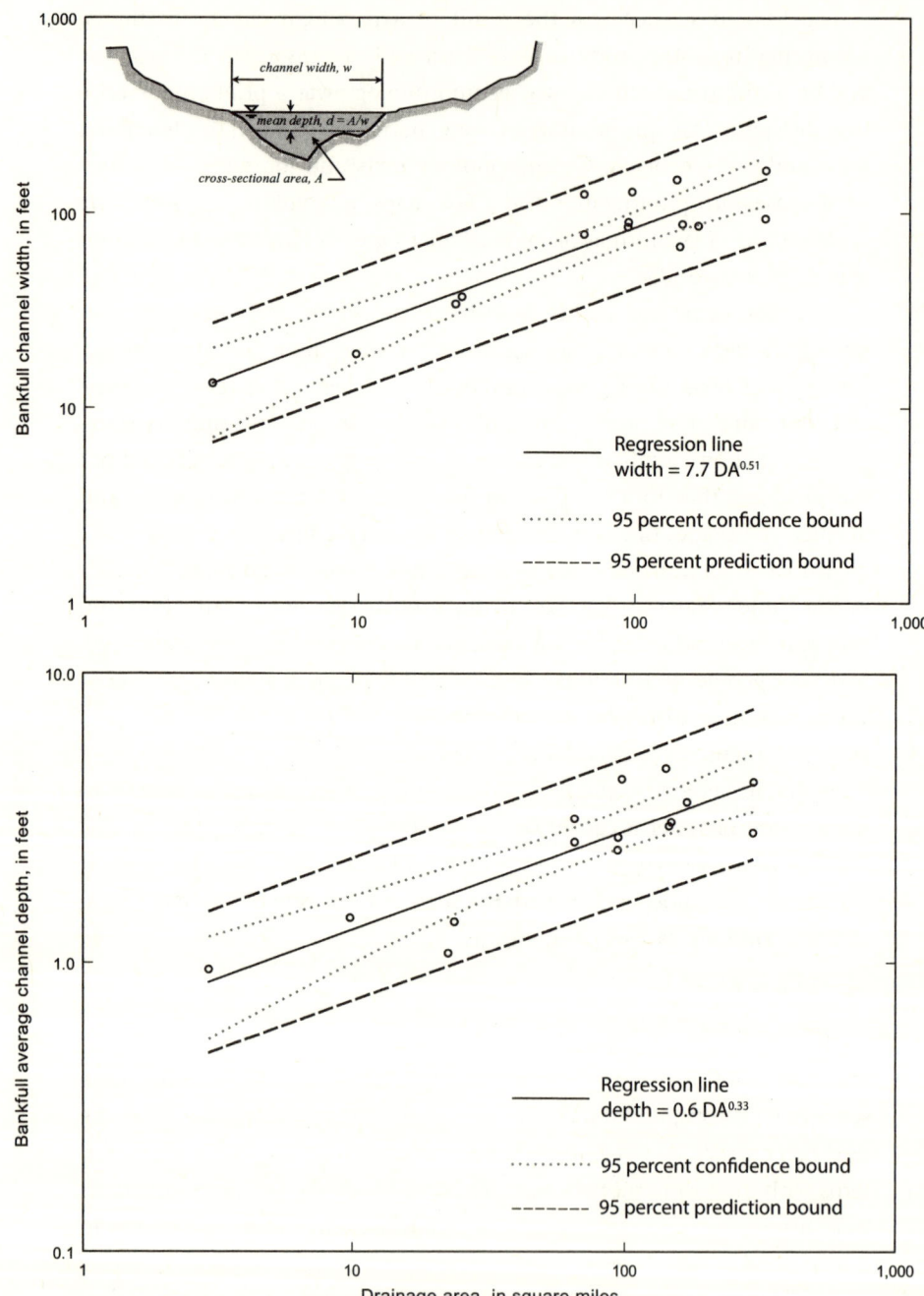

quantified or drainage area measured on a map, any river or stream whose form had been altered by human actions could be redesigned to fit its current conditions. Starting in the early 1980s, groups and individuals in different parts of the United States used these equations to restore streams through full channel reconstruction rather than just manipulating instream conditions.

This departure really was startling. There were no direct precedents for the channel reconfiguration work these restorationists were doing, and the potential for catastrophic failure was all too real. As described by one of the pioneers of channel reconstruction, Greg Koonce, "When we started Inter-Fluve [a consulting firm focused on stream restoration], we just started building pools and riffles into existing streams with a backhoe." But then they moved toward changing the entire river, which for them was a very big step (figure 3.3). Koonce recalled: "The first re-meander we did was totally scary."[16]

Koonce and other early practitioners of channel reconfiguration had the hydraulic geometry equations, but not much in the way of guidance for how to make them work in practice. They had to employ a trial-and-error approach to see what worked and what didn't. As consultant Jim MacBroom explained, when he started trying to figure out how to rework channel morphology, "there really wasn't what we think of as design guides or manuals on how to design a channel for something other than a rigid boundary, prismatic type of geometry."[17] Consultants like Koonce and MacBroom were pioneers, trying out different approaches for locations and conditions all over the United States: Greg Koonce worked in Oregon and Montana; Jeff Haltiner worked in California and the Pacific Northwest; Jim MacBroom and Robbin Sotir worked throughout New England and the Southeast, respectively. Other early practitioners were part of the vanguard

---

Figure 3.2
Example of hydraulic geometry relationships for width and depth as a function of drainage area. Each data point represents a specific measurement location along a river, and the trend lines are found through regression techniques. Note that the axes are logarithmic, so the variation is significant, and the regression relationships are power functions. *Source:* This particular figure and set of relationships was derived from a subset of data in Dudley 2004, although there are many publications and studies that develop nearly identical figures and relationships.

Figure 3.3
Example of channel design and construction at Joe's Creek, Oregon, by Inter-Fluve, Inc. A completely new channel was designed into existing sediment (top panel), requiring estimation of stable channel width, depth, and alignment. Note inclusion of woody debris in final constructed channel (bottom panel). Photos: Greg Koonce.

of federal agencies focused on restoration: Dave Rosgen (an employee of the U.S. Forest Service during this period) worked in Idaho, Montana, and Colorado, and Doug Shields (Corps of Engineers and U.S. Department of Agriculture) in Mississippi. There were a surprisingly limited number of academics who were part of this initial vanguard of geomorphologists actually implementing stream restoration designs, including Jim Gore (University of Wyoming) and Matt Kondolf (University of California); the academic research community more broadly would not engage stream restoration practice for another decade.[18]

Initially, these early channel reconfiguration practitioners worked largely in isolation in part because they were located in different regions of the country, and in part because the auspices under which they worked were wildly different. For example, consultant Greg Koonce began his work restoring streams on private land, bankrolled by wealthy landowners or land developers putting in hobby ranches. He based his early work on developing designs for streams that would improve trout fishing, going so far as to advertise in fishing magazines that targeted this clientele (figure 3.4). Doug Shields, in contrast, worked initially for the Corps of Engineers and then the U.S. Department of Agriculture's Agricultural Research Service. He was effectively doing extension work for farmers in the Deep South, trying to develop lower-cost practices to stabilize rapidly eroding streams. Dave Rosgen, a U.S. Forest Service employee at the time, was trying to minimize damage to streams from logging. Each of these restorationists only gradually became aware that they had company in their startling departures from past restoration practice.

But from this early starting point, interest in stream restoration really took off, and demand for designs outstripped the supply of people who had actually done reconfiguration projects. The uniqueness of these individuals' experiences and the growing demand for stream restoration design meant that their knowledge was valuable, and was one of the only sources of stream restoration know-how. Many in this early cohort developed short courses to teach others how to do stream restoration. A majority of stream restorationists in the United States who came along after this cohort, even decades later, got their initial education through these short courses. This includes many twenty-first-century stream restoration designers, but also many federal and state agency employees who have gone on to regulate stream restoration efforts. Indeed, in the absence of formal academic

Figure 3.4
Page of advertisements in *Rod & Reel Magazine*, 1988. Note advertisement for stream restoration designs.

certifications in stream restoration, short courses played an outsized role in the intellectual establishment of the restoration economy.

Among this early group of stream reconfiguration practitioners, by far the most influential was Dave Rosgen, a former U.S. Forest Service employee turned consultant. A protégé of Luna Leopold (who had developed the hydraulic geometry equations in the 1950s), Rosgen quickly became the most nationally recognized figure in the stream restoration movement, including being profiled in *National Geographic*. His well-known approach to restoration—Natural Channel Design—became the most practiced method of stream restoration design in the United States.[19] Although Rosgen completed many restoration projects, his primary influence on stream restoration as a discipline and industry came through his role as an instructor. Rosgen's series of short courses continues to be a primary source of stream restoration education in the United States; by one estimate, as of 2012, approximately two-thirds of stream restoration practitioners and regulators in this country had taken at least one of his Natural Channel Design short courses.[20]

In addition to short courses, several influential textbooks and handbooks were published between 1996 and 1998, including Rosgen's *Applied Geomorphology*, Brookes and Shields's *River Channel Restoration*, the Federal Interagency Stream Restoration Working Group handbook,[21] and Ann Riley's *Restoring Streams in Cities*. Some of these books reached very wide audiences. However, Rosgen's book was the one considered synonymous with "how to do restoration." The U.S. Forest Service, for example, purchased copies of Rosgen's book for every hydrologist at the agency.[22]

Because of their large role in restoration, it is important to understand what was covered in these books and short courses, and what was not. Perhaps surprisingly, given the common image of restoration as intended to produce clean water and happy fish, the courses and texts focused almost exclusively on geomorphology. The texts were riddled with equations and specific best practices for anything related to the physical form and function of a stream or river, but offered little more than generalities for anything related to water chemistry or ecology. The instructors for the short courses and the authors of the texts listed earlier were similarly almost exclusively geomorphologists and hydraulic engineers. Improvements to water chemistry and ecology were called out as goals, but the assumption was that reconfiguring channel morphology was what was needed to reach those goals. Many of the short courses, including Rosgen's, did not address how to understand (much less improve) nutrient pollution, or even the basics of aquatic ecology.[23]

Just as important, Rosgen's 1996 textbook, which supplanted most of the other geomorphic texts for restoration practitioners, and his short courses emphasized channel stability above all else (further discussion to follow). While some early channel reconfiguration practitioners emphasized bioengineering approaches, with deformable materials such as vegetation shaping a reconfigured channel that could move or change over time, the more common approach deployed in the field and taught in short courses made liberal use of logs and boulders in the same way that hydraulic engineers used concrete and riprap: to make sure a redesigned channel stayed where it had been put.

Thus, this fairly rapid development of stream restoration had some clear points of kinship with Van Cleef's nineteenth-century efforts, and the Michigan School's work in the early twentieth century. The scope of intervention may have shifted dramatically, but the restorationists' reliance on natural yet nondeformable materials, and their assumption that getting the physical form of the channel right was both necessary and sufficient for the recovery of ecological communities and processes, were all too familiar; many of the types of stream intervention (when not completely remeandering a stream) were eerily familiar recreations of the approaches and techniques used seventy-five years earlier (figure 3.5).

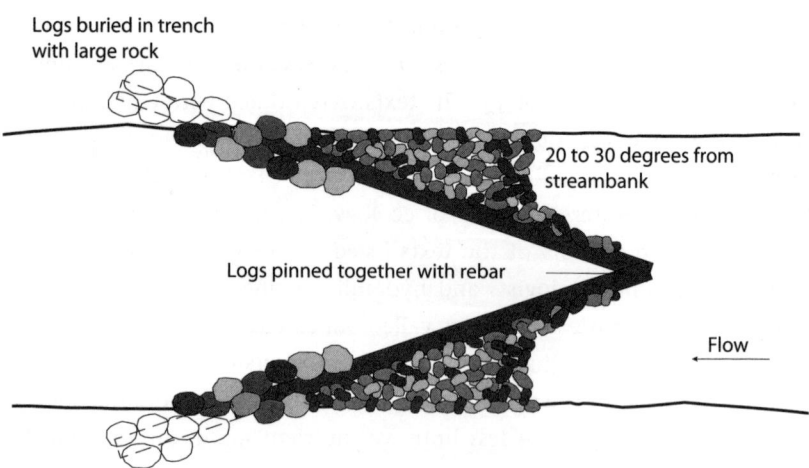

Figure 3.5
Example of early twenty-first-century channel restoration design structures used by the Pennsylvania Fish and Boat Commission; note similarity with 1930s-era design (see figure 3.1). *Source:* This figure is an adaptation of the Log Cross Vane design in Lutz 2007.

Stabilizing Unstable Hydroscapes

During the mid- and late 1990s, channel reconfiguration projects became increasingly common geographically and numerically as the restoration economy developed; hundreds of projects were built each year, hundreds of millions of dollars were spent, and a community of practitioners became established. Stream restoration no longer was limited to isolated patches around where early leaders happened to be located: it proliferated and expanded into most regions of the United States. Restoration also expanded out of rural or isolated places and into cities and suburbs through the work of urban stream restoration pioneers such as Ann Riley in the San Francisco Bay Area.

Via the short courses described earlier, the stream restoration community drew in people with training in fisheries biology, geology, geography, forestry, landscape architecture, and engineering, among other fields. Yet despite this diversity in backgrounds, the majority of practitioners employed a basic approach to stream restoration drawn from Rosgen's Natural Channel Design short courses. That approach was to develop hydraulic geometry equations for a region and then use those equations to design restored streams based on the assumptions that a) restored streams will be stable, and b) that stability will bring improvement in water quality and ecology (the "build it and they will come" approach pioneered more than a century earlier by Van Cleef and his colleagues).

The development of the restoration economy in any given region typically went something like this. First, a critical mass of restoration practitioners and the agency staff who were funding or reviewing their projects (or both) attended Rosgen's short courses. Thus inspired, they worked together to survey *reference reaches*: relatively untouched reaches of streams that, importantly, were believed to be physically stable. The goal of surveying reference reaches was to develop the backbone of technical tools for Natural Channel Design-based stream restoration: *regional curves*. Regional curves are the hydraulic geometry equations particular to a given physiographic region from which new channel designs could be derived. Finally, these regional curves would be adopted as the basis for appropriate design parameters for stable channels.

Why the emphasis on stability? After all, dynamism is one of the defining characteristics of rivers and streams. Healthy, functional streams move over time both across the landscape via meandering along with constant reworking of sediment through erosion and deposition. Why has stream restoration focused so heavily on stability? The answer to that question is complicated, and requires some backtracking into the different ways stability is interpreted in scientific and practical contexts.

The form of any given reach of a stream is determined by its balance of inputs and outputs of water and sediment; if the amount of water or sediment shifts, the shape of the river will adjust to those changes. If there is a long-term balance in this water and sediment budget, then the river is considered to be in equilibrium. Importantly, a river in equilibrium can and does move. The migration of rivers shapes the basic topography of landscapes, such as flat valleys or *oxbow lakes* (former channels now cut off from the river), and many aspects of river ecosystems are in fact dependent on this natural shifting of rivers.[24]

But other kinds of channel movement can be symptoms of negative human impacts rather than of natural dynamism. Rivers and streams can adjust dramatically in response to changes in upstream or downstream conditions. For example, when the land use in the surrounding watershed changes, water and sediment loads are often significantly affected. Deforestation increases both the amount of water and the sediment load entering rivers and streams when trees and their soil-binding roots are removed, causing fluvial systems to change their shape until they return to equilibrium with the new conditions in their watershed. Urbanization causes similarly profound changes: converting land surfaces from forests (or agriculture) to paved and guttered hillslopes dramatically increases the amount of water in a river while decreasing the amount of sediment. Rivers typically respond to urbanization by eroding their bed and banks—becoming deeper and wider. They might also change their sinuosity by becoming straighter.

The key thing to note is that rivers and streams can take years or even decades to adjust to changing watershed conditions and reach a new equilibrium. Complicating this, urbanization and other land-use changes are rarely one-time, single-place events. Development typically occurs in different parts of a watershed over time; first road and sewer building, then neighborhoods in one area, and then a shopping mall elsewhere, for instance. If a river is adjusting to chronically changing conditions, it will be constantly out of equilibrium. But if watershed conditions remain static for a period of time (i.e., if changes associated with urbanization cease for years, or even decades), the river channel should come into equilibrium with these new conditions on its own.

The question, then, is how to tell the difference between the natural dynamism of a healthy stream channel versus problematic, chronic instability. One of the key ways in which the hydraulic geometry equations came to be used in stream restoration was to determine which kind of channel movement was in operation in a particular reach, a use far different from any the equations' developers ever intended. In restorationists' hands, hydraulic geometry equations were used to compare the form of a channel to what would be expected given the regional curves; if there was a mismatch, then that site was presumed to be unstable and thus in need of restoration, regardless of whether the channel had the capacity to adjust to its new conditions on its own.

Eventually, indicators of stream channel instability became synonymous with poor stream restoration design in the Natural Channel Design community (which was itself synonymous with stream restoration across much of the United States). Given that the hydraulic geometry equations allowed a practitioner to design a stream that should be stable, instability meant that the designer got something wrong. And one of the key indicators that was used in assessing instability (and equilibrium) was river bank erosion. *Thus, if a restored stream had any type of bank erosion, even erosion caused by a stream restoring its equilibrium with its changed watershed, then that project was considered a failure.* Stability came to mean being fixed, and not adjusting at all.

There is some controversy over whether Rosgen intended his students to interpret his calls for stability so literally.[25] Regardless, it's quite clear that they have. As Kris Vyverberg, a state agency staff member, ruefully noted, "Rosgen folks are talking about *stability* stability. . . . I can't speak to Dave's perspective on stability, but as . . . [Natural Channel Design] is applied in the field, people seem to believe stability means the channel won't move."[26] This contradiction between the goals of restoration practitioners and the most accepted principles of river science caused conflicts between the restoration science and practice communities that persist to this day, and have shaped the development of stream mitigation banking, as we describe later.[27]

Restoring Streams without Fish

The fixation on stream channel stability was in part the result of another broad trend in stream restoration generally: through the 1990s and on into the twenty-first century, stream restoration was fully in the realm of the physical sciences and engineering, with little engagement from biological or chemical science. As mentioned earlier, hydrologists, geomorphologists, and civil engineers were the primary personnel developing the techniques, standards, and methodologies; they were the ones teaching the short courses, writing the books and handbooks, and doing the actual design work. Indeed, whereas the earliest days of stream restoration in the Catskills and Michigan were led by efforts at restoring trout, the burgeoning late-twentieth-century restoration economy focused on restoring stable channels. There was some justification for this in that much scientific work had demonstrated that ecosystems were negatively impacted by unstable stream morphology. However, the underlying focus on geomorphic controls of stability permeated the practice, and eventually came to dominate. This was not to say that geomorphologists overtly asserted that stable, meandering channels were both necessary and sufficient; they generally only left it at necessary. But they did not argue that it was insufficient.

Over the first decade of the twenty-first century, ecologists began more heavily engaging in stream restoration and their work showed that channel reconfiguration may (sometimes) be necessary, but that it was nowhere near sufficient. Systematic studies showed that restoration efforts were not producing positive impacts, whether for biotic communities or water quality. This was perhaps best summarized in an analysis of seventy-eight restoration projects, which concluded: "Most projects were successful in enhancing physical habitat heterogeneity [i.e., physical conditions]; however only two showed statistically significant increases in biodiversity rendering them more similar to reference reaches or sites."[28] That is, of seventy-eight different projects, only two worked to at least some degree. This was an almost identical endpoint reached by the work proliferated (and monitored) by the University of Michigan program in the 1930s, along with subsequent programs: there was little to no evidence that restoration projects produced the *ecological* improvements they were intended to provide.[29]

How Stream Restoration Was Born, and What Came of It

Restoration in the Late Twentieth Century

By the mid-2010s, the U.S. stream restoration economy had three overarching characteristics. The first was the presumption that restored streams should be stable; the approach most used to achieve stability was Natural Channel Design and the application of hydraulic geometry equations. The second characteristic was the increasing realization that restoration attempts were not generating ecological or water quality benefits to degraded streams. And third was the increasing distrust between practitioners of streams restoration (whether in the design or regulatory communities) and the scientists who studied streams because of their heated disagreements over Natural Channel Design.

But by then geomorphology-based stream restoration was central to the restoration economy and firmly incorporated into environmental policy and regulation whose outcomes were at best uncertain. And one key driver of that economy was the rise in markets for the ecosystem services from streams under the U.S. Clean Water Act.

4   How Markets, and Mitigation, Came to Be Accepted Forms of Environmental Regulation

> USED TROUT STREAM FOR SALE.
>   MUST BE SEEN TO BE APPRECIATED. . . .
>   "We're selling it by the foot length. You can buy as little as you want or you can buy all we've got left. . . . We're selling the waterfalls separately of course, and the trees and birds, flowers, grass and ferns we're also selling extra. The insects we're giving away free with a minimum purchase of ten feet of stream."
>   "How much are you selling the stream for?" I asked.
>   "Six dollars and fifty-cents a foot," he said. "That's for the first hundred feet. After that it's five dollars a foot."
>   "How much are the birds?" I asked.
>   "Thirty-five cents apiece," he said. "But of course they're used. We can't guarantee anything."
>   "How wide is the stream?" I asked. "You said you were selling it by the length, didn't you?"
>   "Yes," he said. "We're selling it by the length. Its width runs between five and eleven feet. You don't have to pay anything extra for width."
>   —Richard Brautigan, *Trout Fishing in America*[1]

As late as the early 1980s, market-based approaches to environmental management were little more than a twinkle in economists' eyes. Yet today there are national and international cap-and-trade markets for carbon dioxide and other pollutants, conservation and water quality credits are for sale in many developed countries, and the idea of payment for ecosystem services is common in international environmental policy circles; even the Ecological Society of America became an advocate for market-based techniques for saving the environment. How did putting a price tag on nature come to be viewed as a good way to save it? How has that viewpoint shaped and reshaped environmental regulation and management over the last thirty years? And how did it come to be such a major driver of stream restoration practice in the United States that the surrealist dream of 1960s counterculture icon Richard Brautigan in the epigraph sounds eerily close to actual practice?

The Concept of Environmental Markets in Society

A good place to start to understand how markets entered environmental management is along the Great Lakes in the middle of the twentieth century. On the banks of Lake Michigan, there was a group of outspoken scholars at the University of Chicago—Milton Friedman most notably—who were doing their best to reshape the world economy. The Chicago School was characterized by strong beliefs in markets, private property, and minimum government intervention and other elements of what are typically referred to as *neoliberal* approaches. Their solution to almost all the ills of society was predictably nongovernmental: health care should be privatized; electrical utilities should be deregulated; students should be able to choose schools based on vouchers.

To their east, along the shore of notably polluted Lake Ontario, the economist John Dales was of a similar bent but a bit more pragmatic about environmental management. Rather than theorize about the global economy, he devised a market-based approach to the pollution in Lake Ontario through a thought experiment. Dales did not assume the pure market solution: that a voluntary market of willing buyers of reduced pollution would emerge, finding a market-driven price point at which some polluters would be willing to cease polluting. Rather, he assumed that a government-created mandate would be needed to create a scarcity of clean Great Lakes water. Dales then reasoned that this proposed regulatory market must have something to trade—a commodity—and that the government should create it: the right to emit pollutants into the lake. Polluters, such as factories or sewage treatment plants, would be issued pollution permits that they could either use themselves to continue polluting at their current rate, or sell to other polluters. If they reduced their pollution sufficiently, they would have extra permits they could then sell; if they needed to increase their pollution, then they would have to purchase permits from someone else. Government agencies interested in improving water quality could reduce the number of permits for a given ecosystem over time, thus constraining total pollution by increasing the scarcity of the permits. The value of remaining permits would increase, thus increasing the economic incentive to reduce pollution.

This was all a thought experiment initially, part of the rise of neoliberal approaches after World War II.[2] By the late 1970s, however, Dales's ideas (along with those of other economists in universities and think tanks) began to spread into the U.S. federal government. Explicit promotion of market-based alternatives to command-and-control regulation began, in fact, with President Jimmy Carter.[3] Carter's Executive Order 12044 promoted regulatory reform in order "to achieve legislative goals effectively and efficiently . . . , [without imposing] unnecessary burdens on the economy."[4] Carter's Regulatory Council, for example, was charged with developing a list of innovative techniques and recommendations to "find ways to achieve their goals with reduced burden on the private sector . . . [while also promoting] innovation, putting private ingenuity to work, [and] finding better long-term solutions to regulatory problems."[5] The Regulatory Council's Project on Alternative Regulatory Approaches promoted eight primary strategies, most of which have clear ties to the kinds of neoliberal approaches Dales and the Chicago School economists promoted. As described in a 1980 report, the list of alternative approaches began with:

- Marketable Rights: Distributing a limited number of rights to scarce resources that private parties can then buy, sell, or trade as market needs dictate. This can remove the government from difficult, contentious, and lengthy decisions about who can "best" use the limited resources.
- Economic Incentives: Using fees or subsidies (rather than government-enforced standards) to encourage private sector achievement of regulatory goals. This approach removes the government from having to eliminate or directly restrict unwanted activity, but creates an incentive for the private sector to limit the activity itself.[6]

The remaining approaches included "Performance Standards" to increase flexibility by replacing regulations that spell out particular paths to compliance (i.e., command-and-control); "Compliance Reform" to supplement government enforcement with "market-oriented mechanisms including third-party compliance monitoring . . . and supervised self-certification"; "Enhanced Competition"; "Information Disclosure" to "replace centralized government decisions with informed freedom of choice among many users," and "Voluntary Standards." Yet while this and other Carter administration initiatives talked the neoliberal talk, very little neoliberal walking seems to have occurred at the time. The ideas and scaffolding were put in place, but little action taken.

President Ronald Reagan picked up where Carter left off, making regulatory reform (which he unsubtly restyled as "regulatory relief") one of the "four pillars" of his initial platform and encouraging the federal regulatory agencies to embrace neoliberal practices. Immediately after he took office, Reagan took the notable step of requiring agencies to demonstrate that the economic benefits of any major proposed regulation exceeded its costs.[7] He established a high-powered group—the Taskforce on Regulatory Relief—chaired by Vice President Bush, to operationalize the cost/benefit analysis of federal regulation. By his second term, however, Reagan had backed away from this agenda and no longer emphasized regulatory reform.[8]

In the late 1980s, President G. H. W. Bush continued what Presidents Carter and Reagan had set in motion, but increasingly put the ideas into actual practice. He replaced the Task Force on Regulatory Relief with the White House Council on Competitiveness in 1989, putting Vice President Dan Quayle in charge. In 1991, Bush gave the Council additional powers to directly revise regulation when mere review did not have the transformative impact he had hoped.[9]

Bush's implementation of the Clean Air Act Amendments (signed in 1990), which included an emissions trading system to reduce acid rain, was a crucial turning point in the acceptance and growth of environmental markets. In an approach clearly indebted to John Dales, the amendments reduced the total emissions allowed over time and allowed permits for emissions to be traded, thus creating an incentive for industry to reduce emissions overall and market-like conditions to do so. The resulting trading program was widely viewed as a success as emissions fell by almost 60 percent over the next twenty-five years while the costs of the reductions were less than anticipated (which was attributed to the trading approach). The acid rain reduction-trading program is widely viewed as the policy experiment that put environmental markets on the map, though it took some time for market-based approaches to spread.[10]

The Clinton administration (1993–2001) brought a new political party into the White House, but like his predecessors he used an early Executive Order to establish a regulatory review council, the National Performance

Review, led by his Vice President Al Gore.[11] Clinton tasked the National Performance Review with increasing flexibility, reducing regulatory burden, and reducing costs of compliance, thus striking notes almost identical to those of the Carter and Reagan administrations. The National Performance Review released a number of reports promoting neoliberal, market-based reforms, including the 1995 *Reinventing Environmental Regulation*, which argued that "[m]arket incentives should be used to achieve environmental goals whenever appropriate," and stated that while command-and-control regulation may remain a policy option:

> We must expand available policy tools to include new and innovative ways to achieve greater levels of environmental protection at a lower cost. For example, we have learned that setting "performance standards" and allowing the regulated community to find the best way to meet them can get results cheaper and quicker—and cleaner—than mandating design standards or specific technologies. We can promote both lower-cost environmental protection and innovation in pollution control and prevention technology. Using performance standards along with economic incentives encourages innovation. The lowest-cost and most effective strategies earn a greater return in the marketplace.[12]

Thus by the mid-1990s, there had been a few key, high-profile developments in market-based approaches to environmental management, most notably the Clean Air Act Amendments. However, such approaches were neither widespread nor widely accepted as instruments for environmental management generally. In addition, even the Clean Air Act Amendments involved trading in environmental pollution permits only; market participants' activities had not changed, but they now had a neoliberal twist that enabled alternative approaches to them. Yet simultaneously, a different rationale for environmental markets was emerging in academia. Environmental economists and ecologists became enamored, respectively, with the economic value of nature, and valuing nature through the concept of ecosystem services. When combined, these two initiatives proved far more effective at directing environmental management toward full-throated market acceptance.

The Ecosystem Services Paradigm

The concept of ecosystem services was fleshed out within academia during the same time period as the regulatory reform efforts previously described (roughly the late 1970s through the mid-1990s), and "ascended boldly into environmental policy discussions"[13] as the basis of market-based environmental approaches starting in the late 1990s. The ecosystem services paradigm was not conceived with intent of putting nature up for sale, however. Instead, it originated in the late 1960s and 1970s as "an eye-opening metaphor intended to awaken society to think more deeply about the importance of nature and its destruction"; the capitalistic, monetized language of ecosystem services was seen by its instigators as distasteful but necessary.[14]

The origin of the ecosystem services concept typically is traced back to work by the brothers Howard and Eugene Odum, among others,[15] and a shift in the discipline of ecology toward studying function alongside the structure and communities of ecosystems. Rather than delving into great detail about the composition or behavior of individual species within a stream or a forest, ecologists began considering ecosystems as a type of black box and focusing on their inputs and outputs. Ecosystem ecology became characterized by quantifying the fluxes of energy, materials, and nutrients. Whereas a community ecologist studying streams might focus on the number of different species, an ecosystem ecologist would now include a nitrogen budget, perhaps demonstrating how one type of stream resulted in less nitrogen leaving the watershed than another type of stream (i.e., nutrient retention). Forest ecology similarly began to focus increasingly on the rates of carbon loss or capture, articulated as masses of carbon rather than board feet of timber or the particular species within that forest.

With this intellectual pivot came an ability to frame ecosystems as providing particular functions from which humans benefitted, eventually captured in the phrase *ecosystem services* (ES). For example, a wetland is an ecosystem with particular characteristics of soil, water, and species communities. Because of these characteristics, wetlands have a particular set of functions (e.g., carbon sequestration, flood attenuation) that are often desirable to humans. Thus, wetlands provide ES at a higher rate than some other types of ecosystems, namely, a drained wetland replaced by an agricultural field or a parking lot. Early ES advocates argued that by destroying or degrading natural ecosystems, society was also losing a significant amount of "free" ES. Taking this further, other ecologists noted that society pays the monetary cost for many of these lost services—for example, by paying for new water treatment plants to replace natural filtration lost when wetlands are destroyed. Amid this pivot in the discipline of ecology, environmental scientists more broadly began using capitalistic metaphors to raise environmental awareness. By speaking the lingua franca of late twentieth-century life—monetary value—early ES proponents hoped to galvanize those to whom the language of environmentalism seemed to be unintelligible, or unimportant.

During this same period, ecological economics arose as a hybrid field of ecology and economics. Under the auspices of scholars such as Robert Costanza and Herman Daly, ecological economics fully embraced monetization of ecological functions, and introduced and advocated the approach of *ecosystem valuation* as an important way to bridge capital and nature. By quantifying the functions that a particular ecosystem provides, and then estimating the economic value of providing those functions through non-natural approaches (e.g., using a reservoir instead of wetlands to retain floods), ecological economists argued that they could quantify the economic value of all manner of ecosystems, and thus, the value of ecosystem services more generally.

In 1997, ES made the leap into environmental policy ubiquity after two germinal pieces were published. The first was an ecological economics paper in *Nature*, led by Robert Costanza, which inventoried and put a price tag on the ES performed naturally across the globe.[16] This paper had a big take-home message: the "free" services provided by natural ecosystems had a value of $33 trillion, an economic scale on par with global GDP. The second key text was ecologist Gretchen Daily's edited volume *Nature's Services*, published in 1997, which provided an approachable, readable treatment of the ES concept.[17] As Dempsey and Robertson note: "Together these publications carried the banner for a movement within policy and economics that has reached the highest levels of global environmental governance and development policy."[18]

These texts sparked the development of a wave of assessment techniques to enable valuation of the broad range of ecosystem services. The drive to save nature by incorporating it into capitalism was on, structured around work put forth not just by economists but also by leading environmental scientists. By the time the Millennium Ecosystem Assessment was released in 2005 under the auspices of the United Nations, ES had become a central, structuring framework of international environmental policy. Ecosystems were not just important—they were valuable.

Although valuation and commodification (putting a price tag on nature vs. actually selling it in a market) in theory are separable, in practice, valuation provides a necessary and absolutely critical first step, paving the way for transforming ecosystems into commodities.[19] The long-term marriage of ecosystem services with the language of capitalism made it a very smooth fit with the types of neoliberal, market-based regulatory reform under discussion in the Carter, Reagan, Bush, and Clinton administrations, as already described. Originally conceived as a tool to galvanize environmental awareness, ES morphed instead into a central tool in both justifying and implementing market-based environmental management efforts, including compensatory mitigation under the Clean Water Act.

The Evolution of Compensatory Mitigation

These initially unrelated efforts by ecologists, economists, and regulatory reformers merged to provide the scaffolding for environmental markets that shifted from trading pollution to trading ecosystems, or at least their functions and services. Compensatory mitigation under the Clean Water Act emerged as one of the prime applications and tests.

The concept of compensatory mitigation, often shortened to *mitigation*, was first applied to the environment in the 1958 Fish and Wildlife Coordination Act (FWCA). Water resources development projects of this era created staggering environmental impacts largely at the hands of federal agencies (e.g., Corps of Engineers, Bureau of Reclamation). The FWCA was an early federal, interagency attempt to reduce the environmental impacts of federal agencies' projects, but it lacked regulatory teeth: U.S. Fish & Wildlife Service (USFWS) and state wildlife agency staff's primary leverage for environmental protection was language in the FWCA that called on them to "describe the damage to wildlife attributable to the project and the measures proposed for mitigating or compensating for these damages."[20] Mitigation became a central tactic for salvaging *something* in the frequent cases where USFWS staff could not prevent damage to water resources, which were considerable: in the mid-twentieth century, the Corps of Engineers alone was responsible for channelizing over eleven thousand miles of rivers, and the Soil Conservation Service was responsible for more than twenty-one thousand miles, not to mention the channelization by nonfederal actors such as state and local agencies and private landowners.[21]

From this starting point, the mitigation policy landscape went through significant changes in the 1970s. The passage of the National Environmental Protection Act (NEPA) in 1970 put more muscle behind water resources mitigation by insisting that potential impacts be disclosed, yet gave no guidance on the extent of mitigation that entailed, or even how to define it in the first place. More consequential for rivers and streams was the inclusion of Section 404 of the 1972 Federal Water Pollution Control Act (later renamed the Clean Water Act [CWA]). Section 404 regulates dredging and filling of waters of the United States, which include streams, rivers, lakes, and wetlands, bringing them under the jurisdiction of the CWA. Impacting waters of the United States whether by draining, filling, or physical manipulation (e.g., diverting or channelizing) required a formal permit—from the Corps of Engineers, which, along with the EPA, was given joint authority for administering the CWA.

Immediately following passage of the CWA, the Corps of Engineers and the EPA remained hesitant to accept the political costs of preventing damage to aquatic ecosystems altogether, and instead latched onto mitigation as a mechanism through which permits for degrading ecosystems could be granted while requiring applicants to offset the environmental damage.[22] Mitigation grew into a central component of CWA regulation and implementation. While permits to damage aquatic ecosystems were granted readily, these permits were conditioned with mitigation requirements. The Corps of Engineers and the EPA eventually formalized regulatory guidance for mitigation that consists of three stages to be performed in order, commonly referred to as the *mitigation sequence*. These three stages are *avoidance* of impacts to the extent possible, *minimization* of any impacts deemed unavoidable, and *compensation* for unavoidable impacts via ecological restoration.

This evolution of the concept and practice of mitigation was occurring at the same time as the evolution of the types of ecosystems to be regulated. The CWA had regulatory authority over waters of the United States through the federal government's role in interstate commerce; however, the CWA did not define waters of the United States for regulatory purposes.[23] Instead, the definition of waters of the United States, and thus the regulatory scope of the CWA, was set via a series of court cases. Through the courts, waters of the United States included *traditionally navigable waters* such as rivers and lakes on which commercial traffic could move; then wetlands directly adjacent to navigable waterways; and eventually wetlands that had hydrologic connectivity to navigable waterways. With each expansion of the definition (or interpretation) of waters of the United States the types and numbers of wetlands under jurisdiction changed. When the definition of jurisdictional waters expanded (e.g., through inclusion of wetlands adjacent to navigable waters), a growing number of impacts (via the expanding definition of which aquatic systems were covered by the CWA) required mitigation as part of their permit requirements. That is, as the geographic scope of the CWA expanded (or contracted) via court case interpretations, the scope of compensatory mitigation shifted as well.[24]

Rivers and large streams were certainly considered waters of the United States, yet wetlands were the almost singular focus of early mitigation policy and activity through the late 1990s. Mitigation then was often referred to as wetlands mitigation and this still occurs sometimes. This focus on wetlands seems to have been the unintended result of a single project: the USFWS National Wetlands Inventory Project (NWI), begun in 1975.[25] Thanks to the painstaking work of staff scientists (in an era before GIS and other computerized methods for tracking land-cover change existed), it was clear by the mid-1980s that more than 54 percent of U.S. wetlands had been drained or filled to make way for agriculture or development; this averaged to a loss of sixty acres of wetland per hour since the 1780s. The staggering extent of loss spurred action by a diverse set of constituencies, from coastal environmentalists to Midwestern duck hunters. Their combined pressure led to a series of federal government actions,[26] culminating in adopting a *no net loss* of wetlands goal championed in 1988 by then-candidate and eventual President George H. W. Bush. This goal was critical for two reasons. First, including the word "net" presumed compensatory mitigation; "no loss" would have required protection, but "no net loss" presumed that impacts would be allowed as long as there was subsequent compensation. Second, the policy itself focused on wetlands, and thus a continued focus on aquatic conservation via wetlands mitigation.

It is difficult to overstate the importance of wetlands in CWA enforcement, particularly mitigation. As the EPA and the Corps of Engineers noted in their 1990 MOA (Memorandum of Agreement) on mitigation:

> In focusing the goal on no overall net loss to wetlands only, EPA and Army have explicitly recognized the special significance of the nation's wetlands resources. This special recognition of wetlands resources does not in any way diminish the value of other waters of the United States, which are often of high value. All

waters of the United States, such as streams, rivers, lakes, etc., will be accorded the full measure of protection under the Guidelines, including the requirements for appropriate and practicable mitigation.[27]

The single-minded focus on wetlands throughout the 1980s and 1990s had serious consequences for fluvial systems. Because wetlands were the focus of regulatory attention, there was a growth of wetland mitigation, yet not of mitigation of other aquatic systems, particularly streams. In fact, for much of the 1980s and 1990s, impacts to streams could be mitigated via restoration of wetlands; this practice is referred to as *out-of-kind mitigation*.

The pivot towards *in-kind mitigation* for streams (offsetting impacts to streams with restoration of other streams) finally arrived in the late 1990s in North Carolina, a state that was one of the earliest and most enthusiastic adopters of the modern wave of channel reconfiguration-based stream restoration.[28] According to former regulators with the state of North Carolina and the Wilmington District of the Corps of Engineers, the turning point was the proposed development of the Hanes Mall in High Point, North Carolina, which involved putting thousands of feet of streams into culverts, and thus effectively turning them into underground pipes. The 1998 permit for that project was the first time—as far as any of the dozens of people we interviewed for this project were aware—that impacts to streams were measured in length rather than area.

This was a key conceptual pivot: up to this point, credits and debits for mitigation purposes had been measured solely in area. This made a great deal of sense for inventorying impacts to wetlands, but was glaringly inappropriate for streams, particularly small streams. By assessing impacts in linear feet, agencies conceptualized streams as distinct from wetlands for mitigation purposes, thus moving mitigation practice (if not policy) toward more stream-inclusive approaches.[29] That same year, the first restoration project explicitly intended to provide compensatory mitigation for stream impacts—the Johns River Bank—was proposed to the Wilmington Corps District.[30] With this starting point in North Carolina, in-kind compensatory mitigation for streams spread rapidly in the Wilmington District, through the South Atlantic Division of the Corps of Engineers, into states and Corps districts along the Mississippi River, and from there into other early adopter states.

The last, but critical piece for the wetland-to-stream pivot came in 2006 with the Supreme Court's decision in the *Rapanos v. United States* case.

Through this case, and the Court's decision, the Corps of Engineers and the EPA were required to more definitively and deliberately address the nexus between navigable and non-navigable waters of the United States (and thus which aquatic resources should be under the regulatory jurisdiction of Section 404). This nexus largely was provided by small streams and tributaries—particularly very small headwater streams.[31] In the same way that expanding CWA jurisdiction to wetlands in the early 1990s had bolstered wetland mitigation, the *Rapanos* decision had the unintended consequence of inserting streams, rivers, and their tributaries more fully into the system of compensatory mitigation.

Compensatory Mitigation in Practice: The Evolution of Banking

Amid all of this evolution of policy and regulatory/legal interpretation, and the pivot in attention from wetlands to streams, there was a commensurate evolution of the financial mechanisms through which compensatory mitigation was conducted. To understand what compensatory mitigation looks like in practice, and how this changed over time, imagine a land developer (public or private) who purchases a 500-acre tract on which are scattered 60 acres of wetlands and 2 miles of stream and tributaries large enough to be considered waters of the United States. The developer—typically referred to as the *permittee*—wishes to build a certain footprint of buildings, roads, and parking lots, and associated infrastructure such as bridges and culverts. Using the envisioned footprint would require draining and filling some of the wetlands and either culverting or reconfiguring many of the streams to shift the flow of water around on the site. Because the types of streams and wetlands that exist on the site are considered waters of the United States, they are regulated by the Clean Water Act (and referred to *as jurisdictional waters*). Thus, the developer must receive a permit from the Corps of Engineers to culvert or move the streams and to drain and fill the wetlands. The Corps of Engineers will condition the permit subject to the mitigation sequence: avoid, minimize, compensate.

To enforce *avoidance*, the Corps of Engineers would require the developer to adjust the design to avoid the stream and wetland impacts altogether. Where practical and feasible, this would require changing the actual footprint of the buildings, road layout, parking lot, and other built features to avoid the aquatic resources on site, and would likely raise the costs of the project at a minimum, or at least affect its economic feasibility. Impacts to aquatic resources that could not be avoided could be *minimized*; again, this would require changing the design and thus the economic feasibility of the proposed project, but it would allow some reduced level of impact. Any remaining impacts that could not be avoided or minimized would be considered unavoidable. The Corps of Engineers would require the developer to *compensate* for those impacts deemed unavoidable via preservation or restoration of comparable streams and wetlands elsewhere, creating a type of offset program.

Figure 4.1 lays out a hypothetical example of this mitigation sequence. A developer proposes a parking lot that would ideally be located in the middle of a particular property parcel, but the size and location of the project would necessitate straightening, ditching, and putting into culverts or pipes 750 feet of stream. The regulator (Corps of Engineers) would first require the developer, as part of the permit, to avoid impacting the stream altogether. Under this scenario, the developer—now referred to as the permittee—could do so, but only by changing the location and size of the proposed project. Alternatively, the permittee could minimize the impacts by retaining the size of the project, but altering its location. The final alternative would be for the permittee to retain the initial size and location of the project, but to compensate for any unavoidable impacts by restoring existing degraded streams on the property. In this case, the permittee would restore some of the stream as well as a portion of a tributary located on the property.

For the Corps of Engineers and the EPA it is often more politically palatable to ask developers and public works agencies to compensate for damages than to redesign proposed projects. In addition, for these regulatory agencies, compensatory mitigation is far easier, and even seductive, because it avoids or circumvents tough permit decisions that might end up preventing a proposed development project. Regulators can impose strict, potentially expensive requirements (via trading ratios; see chapter 2) rather than by fully exploring and requiring avoidance and minimization, which are more demanding for the permittee.[32]

Who actually is responsible for doing the compensatory mitigation has evolved over time. In the 1980s and well into the 1990s, permittees did the mitigation work themselves, an approach known as *permittee responsible mitigation* (PRM) (see figure 4.2). As shown in the hypothetical example of

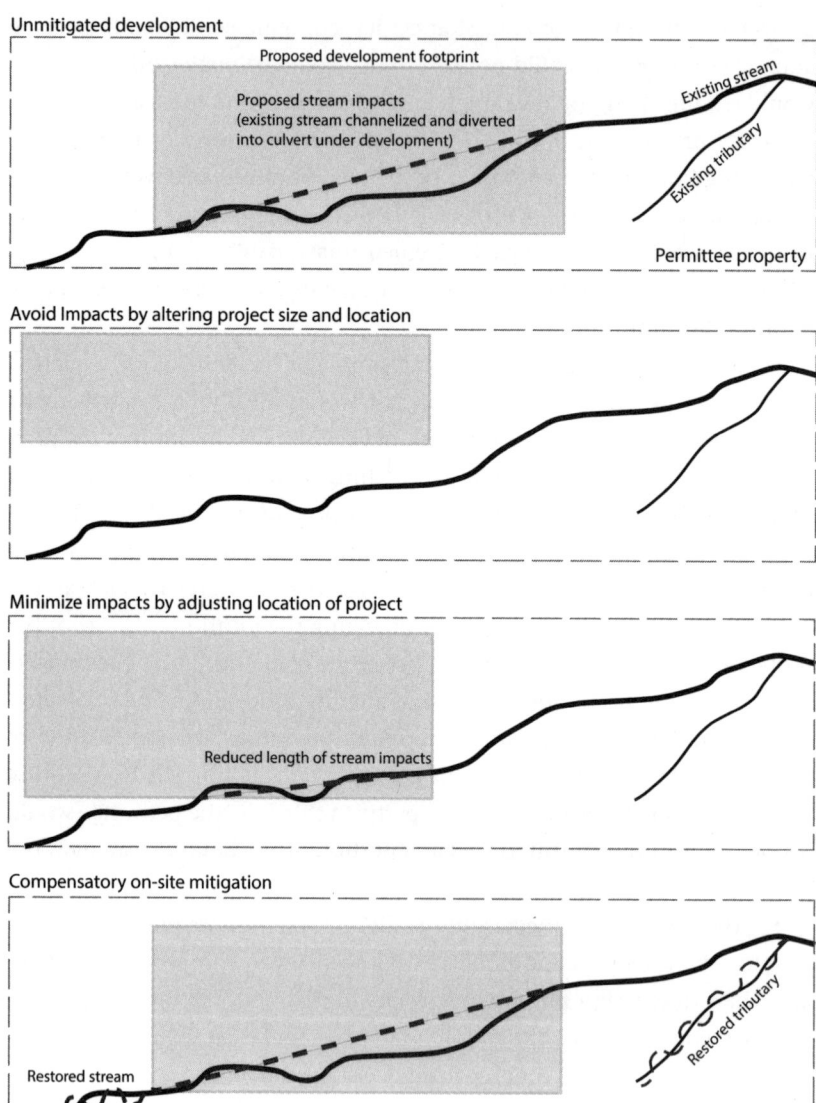

Figure 4.1
The mitigation sequence. The last step would be an example of *permittee responsible mitigation*.

Markets as Environmental Regulation

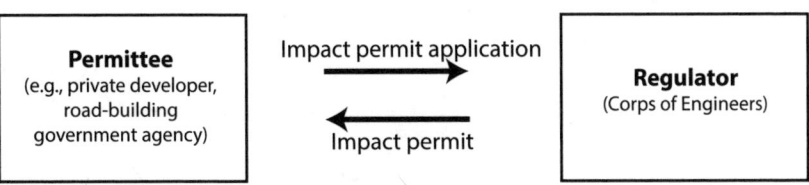

Figure 4.2
General design of permittee responsible mitigation. Note that the permit is submitted and granted via the Corps of Engineers. For decisions related to compensatory mitigation, the Corps is advised by an *Interagency Review Team* (IRT); the permittee will typically interact with the IRT throughout the mitigation process, with the final mitigation bank approval and permit being granted by the Corps.

figure 4.1, this would mean that the developer/permittee would do the restoration work (or be responsible for that work being done). In other words, the restoration of the stream and tributary shown in the bottom panel would be work completed by (or under the auspices of) the permittee. This approach made logistical sense; permittees were often landowners and had access to necessary earth-moving equipment (e.g., bulldozers), and could thus internalize the costs of compensatory mitigation as part of land development. This approach also made a lot of scientific sense because the compensation would likely occur at the same time as the impacts, and would be on the same property; maintaining this temporal and geographic proximity was considered highly relevant and important in such offset programs.

However, cracks began to appear in this mechanism of compensatory mitigation as both regulators and scientists increasingly questioned the ecological value of the permittee responsible mitigation (PRM) projects. Perhaps most notably, a review committee set up by the National Academy of Science's National Research Council to thoroughly review compensatory mitigation to date concluded: "The goal of no net loss of wetlands is not being met for wetland functions by the mitigation program, despite progress in the last 20 years."[33] Some of this blame was placed squarely on the reliance on PRM as the mechanism of mitigation: real estate developers were not necessarily skilled in ecological restoration, and their restoration efforts bore little fruit in practice despite their advantages in theory. In addition, PRM led to restoration projects that were just large enough to offset the impacts for the permittee. These smaller restoration projects are generally less ecologically effective, and are also much more difficult for regulators to monitor.

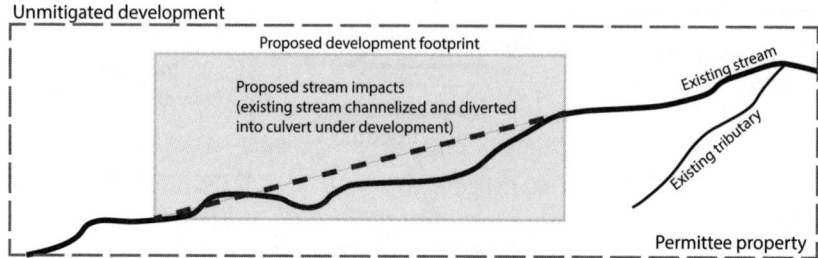

Figure 4.3
Hypothetical example of compensatory mitigation through an off-site mitigation bank.

The alternative to on-site PRM was the use of *mitigation banks*: off-site restoration projects that create an excess of compensatory mitigation that could then be used to compensate for impact projects in need of mitigation (a similar off-site mitigation mechanism is an *In Lieu Fee* [ILF] program).[34] The key distinction of mitigation banking is that the permittee is no longer responsible for the restoration work itself. Instead, a third party—a *mitigation banker*—undertakes the work of creating mitigation credits, and then markets those credits to permittees. As a hypothetical example in figure 4.3, a permittee develops a project that will generate 750 stream debits. Rather than creating restoration projects and thus mitigation credits on their own, using their own property, the permittee instead purchases the credits from a mitigation banker. This banker has developed a restoration project that created 2,000 mitigation credits; once 750 of these credits are sold, the banker retains 1,250 credits that can be sold to other permittees.

The roots of mitigation banking date back to the early 1980s as the U.S. Fish & Wildlife Service (USFWS) sought to enforce the 1958 Fish and

Markets as Environmental Regulation

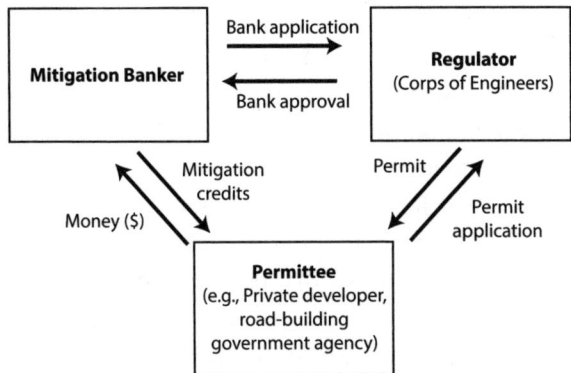

Figure 4.4
General design of compensatory mitigation banking. Note that the mitigation bank application is submitted and granted via the Corps of Engineers, but the Corps is advised by an Interagency Review Team comprised of representatives from federal and state environmental agencies; the mitigation banker will typically interact with the IRT throughout the process, with the final decision and permit being granted by the Corps.

Wildlife Control Act (described previously). In an attempt to make wildlife protection requirements more palatable, the USFWS and a few state agencies began to experiment with mitigation banks, thirteen of which were up and running by the early 1980s.[35] Importantly, the initial form of mitigation banking that the USFWS developed was not market-based, but was modeled on savings accounts (figure 4.4). In the words of one early study:

> Mitigation banking has been likened to maintaining a bank account. A developer implements measures to create, improve, or preserve fish and wildlife habitat prior to an anticipated need for mitigation for project impacts. The benefits of these measures are quantified as mitigation credits for the developer and placed in a mitigation bank account from which withdrawals can be made. When the developer proposes a project which will result in unavoidable losses of fish and wildlife resources, the losses are quantified as debits using the same method that was used to determine bank credits. A withdrawal equal to that amount is deducted from the bank balance. The debiting process can be repeated as long as mitigation credits are available in the bank.[36]

Such early mitigation banks were both noncommercial (the credits produced by the bank were not for sale) and not-for-profit. Twelve of the thirteen initial banks were developed by ports and state Departments of

Transportation for their own future permitting convenience. Effectively, they were comparable to PRM projects, but instead of each impact project having its own directly associated compensatory mitigation project, a single, larger restoration project was developed for a particular agency's permitting needs. The avoidance of all things commercial in these early mitigation banks was deliberate; in the U.S. Fish & Wildlife Service's 1988 report on mitigation banking, for example, there are multiple mentions of the need to avoid the appearance that permits were being bought or sold, and the single mention of markets was in relation to land costs, not the value of the bank for compensatory mitigation itself.[37]

However, this noncommercial, non-entrepreneurial model was short-lived. The first commercial sale from a wetland mitigation bank occurred in 1986 as an afterthought at a bank intended primarily for in-house use for the only private sector bank owner at the time, a major oil company. But that single transaction set the model for entrepreneurial compensatory mitigation banking: entrepreneurs develop a preservation or restoration project speculatively, and then sell the credits within the available market of permit-seeking developers. The first truly entrepreneurial wetland mitigation bank was built in Florida in early 1994.[38] From there, the mitigation banking industry flourished as part of the rapidly growing restoration economy in the 1990s and through the turn of the twentieth century. The mitigation industry developed most rapidly in the Southeastern and upper Midwestern United States, likely for two reasons. First, both of these regions are wet and flat, thus creating the simple physiographic conditions necessary for wetlands and numerous streams. Second, both regions—but particularly the Southeast—were experiencing extremely rapid population growth along with associated land development and road building, all of which contributed to increased demand for permits. In this region, increasing demand for credits (to ensure that road building and other public agency infrastructure projects were not delayed for lack of wetland permits) led to the creation of many private entrepreneurial mitigation banks, as well as state-administered programs and agencies whose mission was providing compensatory mitigation. These agency-administered programs often took on the form of In Lieu Fee programs, which either functioned as mitigation banks themselves or as a broker between state agency permittees and mitigation banks to ensure regulatory compliance of state agencies.[39]

Mitigation banking emerged as a practice and an industry on a largely ad-hoc basis, with the initial mitigation banks developed through individual negotiations between developers and regulatory agency personnel. The first decade of commercial mitigation banking was regulated via a disparate set of individual agreements, guidance letters, and documents specific to a particular geographic region rather than through formal, federally approved guidance documents. The scattershot nature of this initial regulation was partly the result of the fact that the Corps of Engineers, like all federal government agencies, is operated in a fairly decentralized manner. It is divided into thirty-eight districts, each of which has a high degree of autonomy (figure 4.5). Because local agency staff negotiate individual impact permits and mitigation projects, mitigation practices were developed locally, often by individual staff on a case-by-case basis.[40] These individual practices initially consolidated at the district level into local-level policies, often in the form of "guidance" documents that applied only to that geographic area,

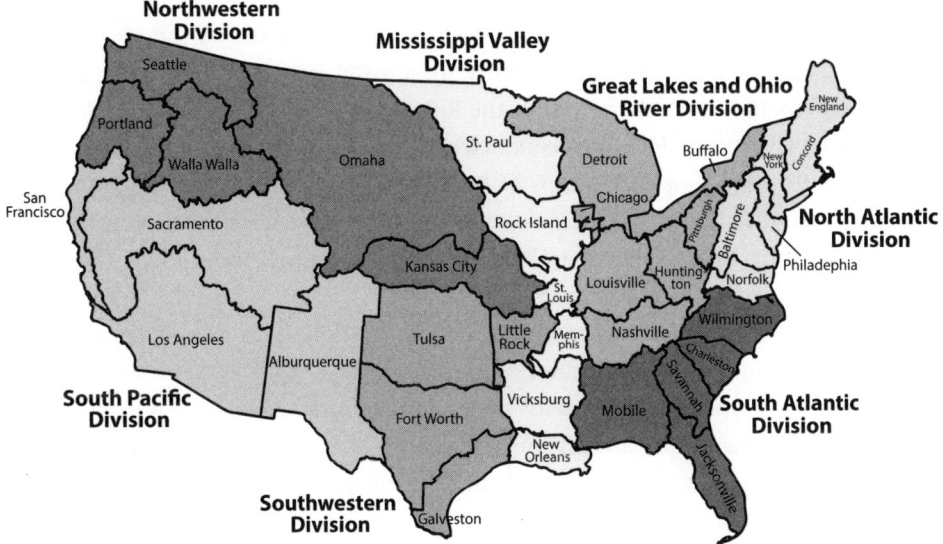

Figure 4.5
Corps of Engineers Districts and Divisions. The Corps headquarters sets national-scale policy and practices; divisions (e.g., South Atlantic Division) will typically seek some consistency across districts within their division, but most project-level decision-making is made by the District Engineer, who is located at the district level (e.g., Wilmington District).

or even a particular subregion of that area. This geographically-diffused regulatory approach led to mitigation policy variability from one region to the next in things such as trading ratios, yet also to consistency: states and Corps districts consistently relied on channel stability as a central metric of restoration success, and for the most part they still do.[41] With different approaches and standards in each district, it was difficult for mitigation banking companies to expand across districts, since doing so required adjusting to a new set of rules. Likewise, developers faced a diverging permitting landscape dependent on which state or district of the Corps of Engineers they were building in. This led to concerns that practices in some districts and states were not sufficiently rigorous compared to others.

The evolution of mitigation, particularly stream mitigation, reached a regulatory zenith in 2008, when the Corps of Engineers and the EPA released their first rule by which compensatory mitigation would be regulated nationwide: the 2008 Mitigation Rule.[42] This rule codified mitigation nationally for the first time. In many ways, the 2008 Mitigation Rule left unchanged the practices that had developed and evolved over the preceding decade; there was still a sequence from avoidance to minimization to compensation, for instance. Also, the Rule left significant deference to the district level: most decisions remained at the discretion of the District Engineers (the heads of each Corps of Engineers district). However, the 2008 Mitigation Rule did set some more defined trajectories for mitigation by establishing clear practices and preferences among the hodgepodge that had emerged in the preceding years.

Most relevant for streams, the 2008 Mitigation Rule moved toward requiring in-kind compensatory mitigation. This shift was important because it formalized demand for stream mitigation nationally. As it turned out, there were more stream impacts than had been appreciated during the era of out-of-kind mitigation, and thus the market demand for stream mitigation rose substantially.

Taken together, the *Rapanos* decision and the subsequent regulatory clarification efforts it triggered put considerable attention on stream mitigation. And when combined with the 2008 Mitigation Rule, stream mitigation banking garnered considerable attention from the regulatory community and the private sector, including bankers, designers, and investors. The conditions were set for stream mitigation banking to expand rapidly, and expand it did.

Conclusion: Operationalizing MES: Where Stream Mitigation Landed in the Twenty-First Century

From 1960 to 2010, ideas of neoliberal environmental management and ecosystem services gradually converged and were converted into actual policies and practices. Among them was mitigation banking under the CWA, which is now one of the oldest and most robust markets for ecosystem services in the world. As of this writing, there are hundreds of stream mitigation banks compensating for Section 404 impacts nationwide. Across the United States, new development projects that negatively affect the physical form of a stream, whether it be a new highway cutting across the landscape or a proposed housing complex with a stream where the parking lot could be, are involuntarily enrolled in a market where the commodity for sale is regulatory compliance in the form of stream credits. These credits are produced by entrepreneurial mitigation bankers who are regulated by agencies, but incentivized by profits. The price of stream credits has steadily increased over time: in the Southeast, for example, credits were $125/linear foot in the late 1990s, $220/linear foot as of 2002, and $300/linear foot in 2006. As of 2018, stream credits were selling in the range of $500/linear foot. While mitigation banking may not be as pure a market as Milton Friedman might have liked, it is certainly a more neoliberal form of environmental regulation than were the Corps of Engineers' efforts to restrict stream impacts altogether, or to do mitigation projects themselves. Most important, mitigation banking is actually in operation, a functioning regulatory market rather than a thought experiment in the pages of academic journals or think tank reports.

Mitigation banking is also one of the most visible and cited ways of operationalizing an ecosystem service market approach to conservation. Just as Friedman had an ideal for how markets would work, advocates of ecosystem services had an ideal that the many functions of ecosystems would generate their inherent value. But in the same way that mitigation banking became (for a while) synonymous with wetlands banking, the way stream ecosystem services are managed via banking is in some sense an accident of timing; the market that exists today is contingent on the conditions when it started. When stream mitigation banking began in the late 1990s in North Carolina, the restoration community was dominated by geomorphologists and focused primarily on channel form (see chapter 3). The timing and location of the genesis of the market for streams is clearly reflected in the *design* of the stream mitigation market itself: in much of the United States, 150 feet of impact to a stream is compensated for by the purchase of credits produced by restoring a stream of the same physical form (according to Rosgen's classification system; see chapter 3).

Further, the focus in the late 1990s by the stream restoration community—prior to the existence of stream mitigation banking—was not simply on channel form, but on channel *stability*. There were alternative approaches developed,[43] but the core restoration community was focused almost exclusively on channel stability. And nailing dynamic systems like rivers in place takes serious interventions.

This preference for serious intervention was reflected in the way that stream credits were initially defined in most parts of the United States. As regulators developed their guidance documents and came to agreements with mitigation bankers for early projects, they privileged highly interventionist approaches over less invasive ones. If regulators had applied a strict ecosystem services lens to stream restoration, they would likely have led the market toward preserving high-quality streams, or perhaps minimally intrusive enhancements, which might produce more functional ecosystem results. Instead, regulators developed approaches with a strong preference for physically rebuilding the hydroscape, and doing so in a way that locked it in place through highly stabilized channels. Regulators did this through trading ratios: to maximize the potential credits they could receive from stream restoration at a particular site, mitigation bankers had to reconfigure and completely rebuild the channel.[44]

This focus on channel form, and especially on channel stability, grew out of the particular amalgam of restoration science and policy in the late 1990s, in the particular place where stream markets first took root, which assumed that ecological and biological functions would follow once a stable channel form was in place. The result is that although the CWA is explicitly intended to protect the biological, chemical, and physical integrity of waters of the United States, the market for ecosystem services that eventually emerged for streams was built around an exchange of credits defined primarily via physical measurements that require intensive intervention in fluvial systems.[45] *This narrow version of equivalence between impact and restoration sites may ensure a robust market, but it raises unsettling questions about what, if anything, compensatory mitigation for streams actually achieves.* In the chapters that follow we examine these tensions in more depth, first through an exploration of the different actors involved in stream mitigation banking (chapter 5) and the different forms of uncertainty and equivalence that shape their actions, and then through the biography of a specific mitigation bank (chapter 6) to see how the archetypal concerns laid out in chapter 5 play out in practice.

5 The Actors in Stream Mitigation Banking

The market for streams in the United States includes a wide cast of characters, but across the many states where stream mitigation banking occurs, it centers on three primary actors: *permittees*, who trigger the whole process by proposing to damage a river or stream; *regulators*, who require the permittee to provide compensatory mitigation, and approve mitigation banks; and *mitigation bankers*, who produce stream credits (figure 5.1). Key secondary groups are *landowners*, without whose cooperation there could be no stream mitigation banks; *designers*, who set up what actually happens to streams in mitigation banks; *investors*, who provide the funds that enable mitigation bankers' work; and *scientists*, whose input is primarily indirect, through critiques of mitigation banking practice (figure 5.1). Each of these groups has different goals for mitigation banking, and different levels of concern with whether or not their work produces equivalence between streams impacted by development and those restored to offset those impacts. Each is also attempting to manage very different sets of uncertainties.

The structure and practice of mitigation banking generally (at the national scale) and locally (within a particular Corps district) are the result of the negotiations between these groups. And these national and local negotiations have increasingly profound impacts on fluvial systems in the United States as mitigation banking spreads.

Primary Actors: Their Roles and Goals

Permittees

> No one ever bought a mitigation credit without a gun to their head.[1]

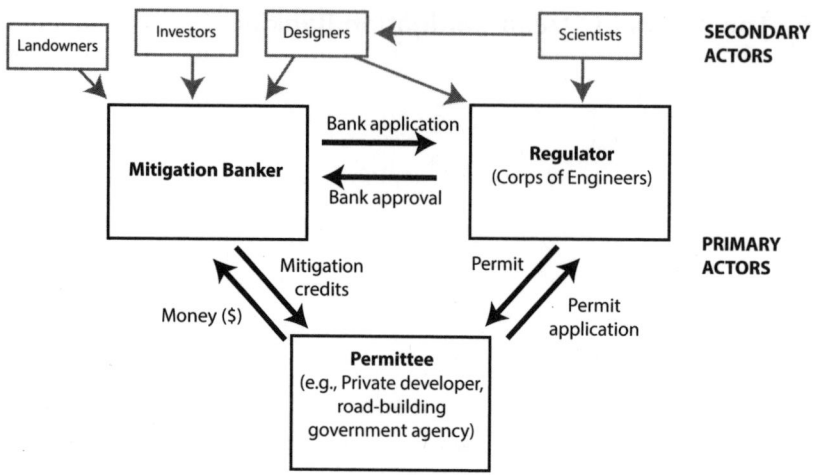

Figure 5.1
The primary and secondary actors in compensatory mitigation banking. Primary actors are the mitigation banker, regulator, and permittee. The secondary actors are landowners, investors, designers, and scientists.

Permittees catalyze the mitigation process by proposing a project, be it widening a road or building a new housing development, which would negatively affect a river or stream in a way that triggers Section 404 review, such as by straightening or moving its channels. Once a project is proposed, a regulator will review it and visit the potential impact site to evaluate its aquatic features. Based on information permittees are required to collect, regulators will determine the quantity of streams on the impact site. They will also characterize the quality of those streams (e.g., whether they are of high existing value or already degraded), and their flow permanence (e.g., perennial, ephemeral, or intermittent).[2] Regulators and permittees thus negotiate not only the official determination of the physical condition of existing streams on the impact site, but also whether or not they require mitigation, and if so, how much. All of this is decided without the benefit of biological or chemical sampling in almost all cases. Instead, the overall quality of the aquatic resources is evaluated visually on the basis of geomorphology and fairly obvious ecological measures, such as the presence or absence of large woody debris, which are readily estimated. Based on this site visit and the permittee's proposed development plans, the regulator will assign a quantity of compensatory mitigation deemed to be equivalent to the unavoidable loss from the proposed project. Permit applicants must provide that compensation—in quantity and type—or they will not be granted a permit to damage streams at the impact site.

A crucial point, then, is that permittees are not in the market for restored streams: they are in the market for a permit that will allow their project to damage a stream (see chapter 2). It does not matter to them whether the stream credits they purchase are produced via preservation of an existing high-quality stream, enhancement of a somewhat damaged stream, or total reconstruction of a poor-quality stream. Nor does it matter to them whether the ecological quality of the credits they purchase is higher or lower than other available credits. *From the permittee's point of view, credits are binary: they fulfill their permit obligation or they do not.* Thus, unlike almost any other commodity a permittee purchases, quality differences among mitigation credits (be they for streams, wetlands, or habitat) are irrelevant. And as some observers note, given the prevalence of a single restoration approach, Natural Channel Design, in many states there may not be that much difference between the quality of different credits in the first place; restoration practitioners have a strong tendency to design the same stream (see chapter 3). In the words of one restoration educator:

> Consultants are somewhat interchangeable because you get the same design approaches throughout the state. . . . There is an informal network of designers. They all seem to know each other fairly well. Many companies hired from other companies and public agencies, so at any given time there are a number of consultants who have worked for other companies and agencies.[3]

Instead of quality, permittees typically prioritize certainty of obtaining their Section 404 permits to avoid regulatory uncertainty. While the economics literature suggests that lower cost and increased efficiency will be the primary reasons why permittees choose to purchase mitigation credits rather than doing the restoration themselves,[4] data from mitigation banking suggests instead that certainty about their ability to satisfy their Section 404 permit obligations can be a bigger factor for permittees than cost per se.[5] As one of our interviewees noted:

> Most permittees don't care what the cost is. They'll write a check for just about any amount, just to shed the responsibility of mitigation. And that, I hear that from almost everybody: developers, Departments of Transportation, railroads. . . . I'm sure there's some threshold at which they'd start caring, but . . . [no one] seemed to bat an eye at writing a $100,000 check to shake a mitigation responsibility.[6]

Regulators

> We don't have time to stop our regulatory permit program and say, "Ok everybody, we're just going to stop issuing permits nationwide until we figure out what's the best possible thing we can do when it comes to stream restoration." It just does not work that way. And so, when we're dealing with an evolving science—which this is in my mind—you know, you try to incorporate lessons learned. And I think in [my state] we've done a pretty good job of that. There's some things we used to do that we wouldn't do today. . . . [C]ould we do better? Maybe, yeah.[7]

Permittees may catalyze the mitigation process, but across the United States it is the regulators, particularly staff in the regulatory offices of the Corps of Engineers, who control it. For mitigation banks, the negotiation is formally between the mitigation banker and an Interagency Review Team, which is comprised of relevant regulatory representatives (e.g., USFWS, EPA, and the state department of environmental protection). The Corps of Engineers is the lead agency on any IRT (because the Corps implements the CWA and issues permits), but other agencies will be relevant to the project and express opinions and advice on its specifics. Nevertheless, in the end, the permitting decisions fall on the Corps of Engineers, and thus, we refer to the Corps and regulators interchangeably.

Regulators strongly shape both supply and demand in mitigation banking, requiring permittees to purchase credits to discharge their permit obligations, as well as setting and enforcing the standards mitigation bankers must follow to produce those credits for sale. Regulators work at the state and national level through guidance documents and industry-wide criteria that affect all mitigation bankers, and at the level of individual projects via specific criteria included in the legal documents guiding those projects (see chapter 6).

Because stream mitigation banking occurs under the auspices of the Clean Water Act, the primary goal of the regulator is the goal of the CWA: to restore and maintain the chemical, physical, and biological integrity of the nation's waters. But regulators are also required to serve those whose actions trigger the CWA: the *regulated public* (permittees). Thus, regulators cannot demand the highest ecological quality to reduce uncertainty, or define credits in carefully specified ways to increase equivalence. If the regulators' position were that simple, the Corps of Engineers would likely be enforcing the CWA through preventing harm rather than pricing it via compensatory mitigation. Instead, regulators have to walk a delicate line, balancing ecological and economic concerns, as well as demands on their own time and resources.

Thus on a day-to-day basis, the regulator works with the permittee to assess the presence or absence of aquatic resources (i.e., streams, wetlands) on a proposed impact site; the type, quantity, and quality of those resources; and the required type and quantity of compensatory mitigation required to offset the proposed impacts. The regulator also ensures that the permittee actually purchases the required credits, and that those credits are equivalent in the eyes of the Corps of Engineers to the damage from the proposed project.

On the credit production side, the regulator works with the mitigation banker to review and negotiate the specifics of the proposed Mitigation Banking Instrument (MBI; the legal document that sets the conditions for a mitigation bank, addressed in chapter 6) for any new bank to address potential sources of uncertainty, and to ensure equivalence between the stream credits produced and the impacts they are intended to address. This process can take months or even years depending on the complexity of the proposed project. Once the bank is approved and constructed, the Interagency Review Team reviews the "as-built" surveys to ensure that what was built matches what was proposed in the MBI, and evaluates the monitoring data provided via the mitigation banker to determine whether the bank is meeting the agreed-upon *success criteria*, the legally binding performance standards a mitigation bank must meet to receive their credits (intended to address uncertainty and equivalence, among other issues).

It is important to remember that the functions laid out in the previous paragraph are fairly new for all of the public agencies involved, including the Corps of Engineers' regulatory staff. Because of the initial focus of CWA implementation on wetlands (see chapter 3) there has been limited expertise in stream restoration generally, and even less expertise in stream mitigation banking within regulatory agencies. For example, of fifteen Corps staffers across the United States we interviewed, only two had educational backgrounds relevant to the predominantly physical focus of stream restoration (in civil engineering in both cases); the vast majority had degrees in fields such as fisheries biology, aquatic ecology, or botany. As one regulator put it, "Obviously, it's not the [Army] Corps of Biologists, but most of the people in Regulatory are biologists."[8] Along with limited directly relevant formal education, many regulators also had limited opportunity for on-the-job training: while a few Corps districts have almost two decades of experience with stream mitigation, most districts have surprisingly little.

This lack of formal educational background, training, and experience in fluvial systems is compounded by the fact that managing and regulating stream mitigation is an additional role for Corps of Engineers staff, expanding their already extensive responsibilities to regulate stream and wetland impacts. Thus, almost to a person, regulators report that that they feel stretched thin, with limited capacity and resources to fulfill this new regulatory function. One Corps staffer from the southern Midwest spoke for many of his colleagues when he said, three years after the publication of the 2008 Mitigation Rule:

> The hardest thing's finding time to work on it. . . . I'm the chief of the division and I'm sitting in PDTs workin' on stream method! But, I mean it's what you gotta do. We would have revised it [the district stream mitigation banking policy] before now. I mean the [Mitigation] Rule came out in 2008! But it's just putting it into a place where you can work on it when everybody has multiple jobs they're trying to do.[9]

Mitigation Bankers

> It's a market. There's money to be made . . . via mitigation banking.[10]

The role of a mitigation banker sounds very simple: provide stream credits. Doing so requires a wide range of efforts, however (as described in more detail in chapter 6). Stereotypically, mitigation bankers' primary motivation is making a profit. In practice, however, most mitigation bankers chose this particular career path from among a vast array of entrepreneurial options because they care about the environment. Thus while making money is clearly a priority, bankers typically are not driven solely by economic concerns.

Bankers begin by assessing the likely credit demand in a particular area (the geographic *service area*) and thus the potential market into which they would eventually be able to sell the credits generated from a project.[11] Along with assessing credit demand from current and potential future permittees, bankers must also assess the competition (i.e., other mitigation banks either existing or potential/proposed), which will impact credit value or potential to sell credits. As the founder of a design and mitigation banking firm that works in several Southeastern states explained to us, there are a number of important sources of uncertainty in calculating potential demand for stream credits:

> When you model a mitigation bank, you have to guestimate what the credit prices are gonna be for like 7 to 10 years. You gotta guestimate what the market's gonna be like for the next seven years. You gotta guestimate what competition's gonna be. That's the other thing. . . . You could start a bank and it could be the best bank in the world, it could be in a great basin, with you know, a *ton* of demand for credits. And you could get a year into doing your mitigation plan and all of a sudden five other public notices [for new rival mitigation banks] could come out. And all of a sudden you realize, "Oh my god. The supply vs demand in this basin is 3:1. What the *hell*."[12]

Once bankers believe there is sufficient demand, they conceptualize and propose a project. Because the product they are producing—the stream credit—is a function of regulation, regulatory uncertainty is a make or break issue for them. Bankers typically have significant command of the nuances of relevant regulations at the federal level (e.g., CWA, 2008 Mitigation Rule), as well as the specifics of local regulations. They must also find and acquire property rights to a potential bank site. Mitigation banking firms typically have personnel who scour real estate databases to find degraded streams. In regions with a great deal of development activity and thus a high demand for stream credits, appropriate sites for stream mitigation may be mostly exhausted, creating competition between bankers for the particularly good remaining sites and another crucial source of uncertainty.

Once an appropriate site has been secured, the banker has to develop a proposed Mitigation Banking Instrument. This typically requires hiring a stream restoration design firm to develop a specific restoration and construction plan. The MBI is then negotiated and eventually (the banker hopes) approved by the regulator. Because the MBI is effectively the contract that lays out the economic potential of the project (e.g., what must be done and how many credits it will potentially generate), a cynical view would suggest that the goal of the banker in this process is to maximize credit potential while minimizing effort (e.g., costly obligations) within the MBI by starting high and then negotiating downward with the regulators as little as possible, adapting the document along the way until the parties reach something both can agree on.

However, it is important to note that all of the time and effort leading up to the approval of the Mitigation Banking Instrument is speculative from the banker's perspective: no revenue is generated for the banker until the document is approved. And there are significant costs that go into any MBI including mitigation bankers' time, attorney costs (as this is a legal document), and design costs. Thus, the more time and effort that is put into negotiating the MBI, the more up-front capital must be spent by the banker. This gives the banker a powerful incentive to submit a proposed MBI that is as likely as possible to receive quick regulatory approval rather than starting with an aggressive negotiating position and then spending months (or even years) incrementally revising the document until it gains approval. The banker benefits by having a highly efficient process, as does the regulator. The more known and "standard" the proposed project approach is, the more the uncertainty is reduced for the regulator. Further, standard approaches and practices already incorporate and address regulators' concerns about the equivalence of impacts and restoration. Finally, the more standard the project, the more efficient the process is for both banker and regulator overall. Thus an innovative approach, even one that might actually increase equivalence, may be avoided by both bankers and regulators in favor of an established approach.

Only once the MBI is negotiated can the banker get the actual project built. At different points during that process, depending on the *credit release schedule* negotiated in the MBI, the bankers will have blocks of credit to sell. At that point, they need to find buyers, another source of uncertainty for bankers. This can range from an individual developer needing only a few credits to a highway department needing to mitigate a large road-building project running across multiple regions. The key point is that selling stream credits is not as simple as selling a sofa on Craigslist: stream credits are a very specialized commodity in a heavily regulated market for which there are relatively few buyers.

Finally, it is important to realize that this entire process depends on mitigation bankers' ability to assemble the capital to fund their work, which is yet another source of uncertainty for them. With financing secured, they must manage outlays and potential incoming revenue from credit sales in a way that allows them to compensate investors and to generate profits. The costs of mitigation banks can range from tens of thousands to tens of millions of dollars, and thus the sources of capital can vary dramatically (as described in the Investors section to follow).

Each mitigation banking firm develops a particular philosophy and approach to their industry, which is reflected in the actual projects they develop. Some mitigation bankers respond to the many sources of uncertainty in mitigation banking conservatively: they choose to serve the market that exists, developing projects that are in close agreement with locally accepted practices in terms of size, location, approaches, and concepts. For example, they may only develop mitigation banks that are just large enough to meet immediate credit demand, thus reducing financing costs and the uncertainty of long-term credit demand. Other mitigation bankers become "market makers": they develop novel types of projects in terms of location (new geographic service areas), scale (i.e., very large banks), or approach. For example, Restoration Systems in North Carolina pioneered the use of dam removal for stream mitigation banking, along with large-scale coastal restoration projects in Louisiana to mitigate levee-building projects by the Corps of Engineers. These types of novel mitigation banks require longer and more uncertain negotiations with regulators, and are thus more expensive and riskier. But they have less competition compared to standard approaches and practices, and thus the potential for higher rates of return.

Secondary Actors: Roles and Goals

Designers

> There is a lot of consistency. . . . I won't say rubber stamp, but many of the designs are very similar in their approach now anyway.[13]

Like any building or road, stream restoration projects must be designed. As described in chapter 3, stream restoration design firms originated in the 1980s, often serving private landowners or grant-funded projects. In a few cases, stream designers adapted their business model to become mitigation providers themselves, taking on the tasks described in the previous section. More commonly, a mitigation banker has a project concept, project site, and budget already in hand and then selects a designer. The banker and designer sign a contract laying out the deliverables the designer must provide. The designer then works with the banker to develop a concept for the restoration site, an actual design (subject to local standards of practice, if they exist), and construction specifications (e.g., design sheets, cost specifications, construction schedules). These are the types of documents and specific input that regulators consider as part of the MBI package (see chapter 6 for more detail). Once those documents are approved as part of the MBI negotiated between the mitigation banker and the regulators, the designer will develop implementation plans and, if also contracted for such work, oversee the actual construction of the project. The heart of the designer's role is ensuring equivalence between the stream credits produced through the restoration project they design and the impacts that need to be to offset.

Like mitigation bankers, designers' motivations initially appear to be completely economic: to meet the goals of their client—the mitigation banker—so that they get paid for their work and potentially hired again for other projects in the future. But again the picture here is more complex. Designers could have chosen to specialize in many different areas of engineering or construction; those who have chosen to focus on stream restoration almost to a person do so because they have a deep interest in streams and rivers. Further, they are bound by professional standards: like the designer of a bridge or a highway, their goal is not only to satisfy their client's needs, but also to develop the most appropriate design for the particular setting based on then-existing professional standards of practice.[14]

An indication of this adherence to standards is that stream restoration designers typically do not alter their approach based on the client. If they were primarily focused on profit generation, they would use one approach for streams designed for mitigation banks and another for grant-based work, where profit is not a goal. Instead, designers insist, and data on constructed projects confirm, that they use the same design approach, with the same goal of restoring stream health, regardless of whether they are working for mitigation bankers, private clients, or government grants (see chapter 7).[15] As one designer put it, "No, there are no real differences in the design process [between mitigation and grant-funded restoration projects]. . . . You take the same stuff into consideration as far as stream mechanics."[16] Or as three designers at another firm said, when we asked whether there was a difference in the designs they prepared for grant-funded vs. mitigation projects:

D1: No

D2: Not really . . .

D3: You're still trying to get to the end product, the same end product.[17]

Even if designers tried to change their approach to squeeze more credits out of a particular site (often referred to as *credit chasing*), this departure from standard practice would raise red flags for regulators. *In effect, the designer's client is not simply the mitigation banker but also the regulator, without whose approval the project cannot proceed.* The design cannot simply optimize ecological characteristics of the eventual stream, nor can it only optimize market returns for the banker; it must also optimize (or at least be efficient) its ability to pass regulatory review.

Over time, designers have come to use an approach that is the same for bankers as it would be for a grant- or NGO-funded project; broadly accepted standards of practice are forceful in what is acceptable as a stream design. Indeed, this reflects the additional role that designers have played: that of educator. Throughout many regions of the United States, stream designers were early entrants to the field of stream restoration, certainly well in advance of regulators and long before the rise of stream mitigation banking (see chapter 3). As regulators and new entrants became interested in, and compelled to understand stream restoration, a few prominent stream designers (e.g., Dave Rosgen, Inter-Fluve, and Will Harman) began developing short courses on stream restoration design (see chapter 3). Along with staff from consulting firms and agency personnel interested in moving into stream restoration, regulators were common attendants at such courses. Designers thus educated the rest of the stream restoration community, becoming the developers and purveyors of best practices. Regulators eventually drew on such courses in developing the standards of practice to be used in their jurisdiction (e.g., district or state), which then play a crucial role in negotiating Mitigation Banking Instruments. Thus, stream designers have leverage with bankers because designers are the ones with expertise on whether a particular design is appropriate or is overly influenced by profit seeking. In sum, because of their early role in stream restoration and mitigation, designers are, in many ways, the arbiters of how compensatory mitigation affects restored streams.

Scientists

> There has been a lot of work done . . . in North Carolina and the Southeast on physical components of restoration, the channel morphology and width/depth ratio and sediment transport and all that sort of stuff. . . . [But] how do you know

a project is in fact successful . . . ? By looking at the benthos, by looking at the aquatic insects. So I spent a great deal of time selecting projects and sampling the benthos and trying to develop success criteria . . . [that have] not been accepted by any of the regulatory agencies.[18]

Many of the people involved in stream mitigation banking are trained as scientists or engineers, and would describe themselves as scientists.[19] We define the role of scientist more narrowly here: people who work for organizations whose role is the provision of data and interpretation only, and whose work is not drawn on for any specific mitigation transaction or negotiation. Thus, scientists as discussed here are those employed in academic or government research lab settings. Their focus is on studying streams, almost always without consideration of regulatory or market priorities.[20] When they do pay attention to mitigation banking, scientists tend to be critics, as they are hyperaware of the pit of uncertainty over which stream restoration hangs, as well as the enormous challenges of claiming, much less creating, equivalence between physically distant aquatic ecosystems.

One central role of scientists in mitigation banking has been in shaping the thinking of regulators about what stream restoration is. The development of stream restoration from the discipline of geomorphology, and the lack of engagement through the early to mid-2000s by the academic ecological community (see chapter 3), meant that the regulatory community was primarily interacting with geomorphologists and hydraulic engineers. Negotiations about what would "count" as stream restoration thus centered primarily on channel form and on equilibrium, a key concept advocated in early geomorphic work on stream restoration.[21] As the engineering and geomorphic scientific community engaged in stream restoration, early designers were largely drawn from this community. And this emphasis on the science of stability translated to designers emphasizing stability as criteria for successful stream restoration (see chapter 3). Thus, in the early development of stream mitigation, regulators were confronted by scientists emphasizing stability, and designers who could not only provide stable channel designs, but were also educating regulators on the benefits of such designs.[22]

While scientists have had some influence on regulators, they have been far less effective in their role as potential educators; that role has been seconded almost entirely to stream designers (as noted earlier).[23] That said, when existing frameworks of restoration have become unworkable, scientists have been called upon as purveyors of expertise and education. For example, when a mitigation bank proposed to use dam removal as a mechanism for generating stream restoration credits, regulators were unable to draw on stream designers because most of them had little experience with such projects. Instead, regulators called in scientists to assist with thinking through how this new type of restoration might be grafted into the existing framework of mitigation banking. Similarly, when more mitigation banks were being proposed in the extraordinarily flat eastern region of North Carolina—the outer Coastal Plain—it became clear that existing policies (i.e., guidance documents) were less relevant in this unusual physiographic region, where fluvial systems were very unlike streams in the rest of the state (as well as areas where much of stream restoration practice was developed, e.g. the inter-Mountain west, Pacific Northwest, and California). Scientists were one of the groups that regulators called on to help develop new guidance:

> In the work that XX and I did in the coastal plain, we met multiple times with . . . the Wilmington Corps District . . . [and] helped them devise some new language for the restoration of headwater streams. Because up to that point they had been applying definitions that were based on Piedmont and mountain systems where you needed a clearly visible valley, which doesn't make any sense in a coastal plain. So we did get involved in how to delineate a stream in that kind of setting. . . . And it was really interesting sitting down at a conference beside the lead Army Corps decision maker who in the first meetings had been saying, "Oh well, these are the rules, we can't change them." And then a year and half later sitting down beside him at a stream restoration conference and somebody was talking about a curvy channel on the coastal plain, and he was saying, "That's just silly, that's not how streams look out there." So we were able to actually . . . change minds (*laughs*). And that was a positive development.[24]

Another role of scientists has been to critique the practices and results of stream restoration, whether grant-funded or for mitigation banking.[25] The predominance of a particular approach to restoration design—Natural Channel Design—drew the ire of many stream scientists, and led to long-term animosity between scientists and designers (i.e., practitioners). However, this was largely limited to the community of physical stream scientists, specifically geomorphologists (see chapter 3). As the broader scientific community—ecologists, water quality chemists—began to engage stream restoration, the claimed benefits and results of stream restoration came under increasing scrutiny. The academic community along with state and federal scientists began systematically studying restoration projects and raising questions about whether restoration as a practice was able to deliver on its presumed goals and ambitions, most notably the recovery of water quality improvements or aquatic insect community recovery. However, much of this science has not distinguished between restoration projects done for mitigation versus those for traditional mechanisms such as grant funding. That is, the engagement of the science community has been through the practice of restoration generally, not through mitigation banking specifically. Thus, scientists' critiques have been primarily of stream restoration as a whole, not of mitigation banking in particular.

Regardless of the focus of scientists' critiques, however, they have been largely ineffective once guidance documents are in place. Every scientist we interviewed described their input being ignored. For example, when a Southeastern state developed a new assessment technique for evaluating streams, they disregarded the critiques of a respected aquatic ecologist they asked to beta test it, who recounted:

> I was part of the beta testing of XX method, and honestly didn't think it was very good. I really had some heartburn and wrote a blazing response and I haven't really heard much about where—I think it is going to be approved. . . . [M]y position was that we are in a great position to really collect some data, some real data, and [the new method] is . . . very qualitative, very subjective. And I just really hope that at this point we could have come up with something better. . . . I think they were so invested in the process that they couldn't stop. They couldn't just say, "Well, it didn't work. Let's just not do it." They had to have something, and this is the product.[26]

Another stream scientist described being given funds to evaluate a particular agency's projects, but then being ignored when the subsequent evaluations were negative:

> I would say that [the agency] was pretty eager to have us doing evaluation of their projects. They gave us a little bit of money that got us started. But then there's . . . no feedback. . . . [W]hen they find out that something isn't working, it's not really clear that anything happens at that point.[27]

Landowners

> "Hey, I got a cow farm. Let's do a mitigation bank."[28]

All stream mitigation banking projects must be located somewhere. While this may seem like a mundane observation, it is surprisingly salient to the feasibility of mitigation banking as a whole because finding appropriate project sites is perhaps the most significant obstacle bankers face.[29] Private landowners are not required to provide land for mitigation bankers. Even when they agree to do so, they rarely sell land outright; easements are more common so that the landowner retains the ability to access the land and use it for other purposes (e.g., hunting, fishing), and to ensure that the mitigation project does not compromise the traditional uses of the land. For instance, a farmer will want to ensure that a mitigation project does not negate their ability to clean culverts for roads that go over restored streams.

Sometimes landowners contact mitigation banking firms. Most of the time, however, it is the other way around. As one mitigation banker described it:

> We sometimes get a phone call from a landowner, [who] says, "I've heard about this mitigation stuff. Could you please come out and look at my land." Most of the time we look quickly at Google Earth, and it's got like 20 acres and 400 feet of a stream, and we're like "Yeah . . . no." But every now and then we get a landowner that actually brings a project to the table. So that's the one extreme. And then the other extreme [is when we have found a site and are trying to convince the landowner to work with us. We have an employee [who is] . . . really good at tracking down who's who. He'll call neighbors, find out who Joe Smith is. "Oh, he lives in Delaware and his cousin farms the property. And his cousin hangs out at Joe's bar at 6 o'clock every night." So he'll go up there and go to the bar and find cousin Joe and . . . find out who the guy is in Delaware that he really needs to talk to. Other times, you can find their phone number and give them a call. Or you drive up to the site and he's out there on his tractor, and you say, "Can I have a minute?" It's amazing: most people are really nice, and totally willing to give you a few minutes to talk and hear you out. You don't get near as much, "Son, I've got a gun. Get off my property" as you would think you would. But you get a lot of immediate no. Like they hear you for a minute and they're like, "Nah, nah, not interested in that."[30]

The goal of private landowners is to extract profit from their property at the least cost possible to themselves, and with the least encumbrance of their future land rights. They are unaffected by, and thus unconcerned with, the questions of equivalence and uncertainty at the heart of stream mitigation banking. But even with landowners the motivation is not entirely financial. Particularly when parcels have been in a family for some time, there are emotional attachments that can either support or undercut landowners' willingness to sign on for a proposed project. For example, a mitigation banker described a "stream that was blown out, that needed restoration; a no-doubter. But there was one spot where for 50 [feet] it was fairly stable. But once you start restoring a whole system it's really hard to leave one piece out, and there was this tree that hung over it with a swing and [the landowner's] grandkids would swing into this pool."[31] In this case, the landowner didn't raise the issue of preserving the swimming hole until it was too far into the process to stop, but in other cases, loss of a special stretch of stream can be a dealbreaker, regardless of the potential profit.

Investors

> You go to the National Mitigation Banking Conference [these days], and there are more investors than practitioners. A lot of business meetings and discussions about return on your investment, not how to build a good mitigation site. It's a big industry.[32]

Investors play a crucial but largely unrecognized role in mitigation banking. Their primary goal is to generate at least market-rate return on their capital, so financial uncertainty is their central concern. While "impact investors" committed to alternative/green investing opportunities have begun to invest in (i.e., finance) mitigation banks, most of the capital for stream mitigation banking is provided by investors who are far less interested in environmental than in financial returns or investing in alternative opportunities to diversify their portfolios.[33] As one mitigation banker told us, investors are

> guys that come in with private equity type money or they build a fund for ecosystem services. They want to see at least the projection for their returns to be anywhere from 15–25%. . . . [I]f you show 'em a pro forma that says, "Hey investor, we're gonna need peak equity investment of $1.6m, and over the 7-year period of this project we're projecting your rate of return is gonna be 12.7%," they're gonna be like, "No thanks. On a risky market like mitigation banking?!?"[34]

There are a wide variety of investors in mitigation banking. For small, relatively simple projects with short turnaround times (and thus less risk to capital), mitigation bankers have often obtained capital via loans from local financial banks. In this debt-financing approach, investors are shielded from the potential risks of mitigation banking: the mitigation banker must pay back the loan and interest regardless of whether he makes a profit. Traditional loans thus carry far lower interest rates than the equity finance model (discussion follows). The ability of a mitigation banker to secure such a loan is dependent on whether the investor understands the mitigation industry business model sufficiently to have some level of confidence that the loan will be repaid. Because of the novelty of mitigation as an industry, many financial banks won't provide loans. Those that have made loans, however, are often willing to make a loan again in the future, as their familiarity increases their confidence. In fact, familiarity can come from a range of interactions between financial banks and mitigation banks. One mitigation banker noted that a local bank was more willing to finance a mitigation project after being required to purchase stream credits itself:

> The traditional challenge of mitigation banking is the [financial] bank ain't going to understand it. . . . I mean they ain't ever done one of those. . . . [But we work with a financial bank that] had to pay a nutrient fee [for a new building] and they were aware of [mitigation requirements], some of the senior management. . . . They're a small commercial [financial] bank here in [my state] and they're building their new headquarters and they'd had to pay some 24,000 dollar thing [to compensate for their impacts]. I think it [that fee] went to us now that I [think about it], you know?[35]

Other mitigation bankers noted that they received investments from local investors, friends, family, or colleagues.

There are also more sophisticated larger investors who invest in big mitigation banking projects or provide the capital for multiple mitigation projects. Larger projects typically have long development or construction times, or both, and thus carry significant financial risks, which makes it more likely that mitigation bankers will have to rely on equity financing for projects. In equity financing, the investor gets a portion of the economic return from the mitigation bank, but also is exposed to all the risk of the venture as well. From the mitigation banker's perspective, bringing in an outside investor can reduce the financial risk of a mitigation bank, but it also greatly dilutes the potential profit. As one mitigation banker described it:

> You bring in an investor for one project, they'll either reimburse what you got to that point (in this case everything we had pretty much done), give you that. You know, there's usually some other money, it's not just your costs. You'll get a little . . . I guess you could call it profit at that point. But then when it [the mitigation bank] starts producing money every penny goes back to those people until they're paid back, right? When they're paid back then you start splitting the proceeds.[36]

In addition to small-scale local investment and larger equity investors, investing funds dedicated to mitigation banking have begun to emerge, most notably the fund raised by Ecosystem Investment Partners—$200 million—to be deployed in mitigation banking. In this approach, the investment fund is used to capitalize mitigation bank projects whether these are developing projects de novo or buying out existing (or partially developed) mitigation banks. The goal of the fund is to raise and then deploy capital on projects that can generate return for the investors. This means that the fund manager must identify projects that will not only be profitable, but that match the timeline for fund investors, often five to seven years.

Sources of Uncertainty for Actors

> If you don't have standards, then the ability of private capital to come in and start developing banks in expectation of future markets is really limited, because there's, it's so much risk. So standards are crucial to that, and quality standards to the long-term public acceptance of compliance of mitigation and offset programs as a realistic and viable compliance alternative. And if you don't have standards, the public will lose trust and we'll get those nasty reports in *Newsweek* and all the other places and while you may have had some people make . . . a lot of money, the effect on the environment will—we won't realize all of the opportunity that we have right now to drive dollars that would otherwise be spent badly into being spent well.[37]

As this quote and the first half of this chapter illustrate, there are forms of uncertainty, and thus risk, for all of the actors in mitigation banking. If things go well, then investors and mitigation bankers can make money, permittees can proceed with projects, regulators can be confident of compliance, and the environment can be restored. But when things go awry, there can be a cascade of consequences; in such cases, there can be significant winners and losers. There are multiple sources of uncertainty embedded throughout the mitigation process, and many are interrelated. Here we consider regulatory, financial, implementation, reputational, ecological, and random uncertainties.

Regulatory uncertainty affects several groups of actors in different but highly interrelated ways. The regulatory uncertainty for permittees is that compliance with the CWA will be so unpredictable, time-consuming, or expensive that it substantively raises their costs or derails the entire project. Similarly, for bankers, regulatory uncertainty describes the possibility that regulators will take a long time to negotiate a Mitigation Banking Instrument or even refuse to approve a proposed bank, thus costing the mitigation bankers a great deal of money by extending the period of time before they can recoup their upfront costs, or simply rendering those costs unrecoverable. The risks associated with this uncertainty are greater if there are no specified standards guiding what is required in an MBI for approval, or if those standards are ambiguous.

Regulators are confronted with the flipside of these concerns: they face uncertainty as to how their two key partners in mitigation—permittees and bankers—will work under the constraints that regulators believe they need to impose. If permittees or bankers feel that they are being treated unfairly, then regulators face the risk of accusations of regulatory overreach or of litigation for arbitrary and capricious enforcement. Since part of their mandate is to make stream mitigation work for the regulated public, regulators are highly motivated to minimize regulatory uncertainty by making the process of CWA compliance as standardized and clear as possible. As one regulator in the Midwest put it:

> [Now] there's a set process and there's a little more certainty. . . . People are more likely to take the risk if they know: "Okay, there's not just this black box and we don't know if this is gonna take five years." . . . [I]t's still time consuming, but at least they have a better idea of how it's gonna go.[38]

In fact, the desire for certainty in the approval process discourages both bankers and regulators from proposing project types or approaches that fall outside accepted standards of practice. A regulator in the Southeast described this dynamic to explain why it has been so difficult to expand success criteria beyond physical stability to address chemical and biological factors:

> If you go to a new technique there's a certain risk of explaining it, and if you have somebody who is very versed in chemistry or aquatic biology, that's a very easy thing for them to do. But if you have a project that's administered by people that it's not their field or discipline . . . , that's very frightening.[39]

Similarly, a scientist described presenting data that mitigation projects were not creating ecological lift, and having a senior regulator override the presentation by saying that no permits had been delayed, sending the clear message that avoiding regulatory uncertainty was the most important criteria for success:

I got up and gave a presentation about . . . how we had yet to see a single restoration project in the state with demonstrable improvements in biological condition or any kind of ecological function. . . . This was a total of something like 35 or 40 evaluated projects. So a pretty comprehensive—and I was very careful in my tone and I talked a lot about how difficult it is and how we've really got to begin to get creative and then immediately after that, the director of [the lead agency] . . . began his presentation by saying that [his agency] was a complete success because [since] they had begun there had never been a single DOT [Department of Transportation] permit that had been slowed down by the mitigation requirement. And I said, "Oh, I guess I understand what the major criteria for this is."[40]

For bankers and investors, multiple sources of uncertainty can create *financial uncertainty*, which is another crucial consideration. The costs of developing a mitigation bank are primarily upfront, while the returns typically are several years in the future. This long timeline exacerbates the unavoidable uncertainty about what price credits will bring when they are finally released, or if there will be any demand for them at all. As one banker described the financial uncertainty he faces, "a lot of money is gonna go into something and then you *hope* you're gonna get it back. You're pretty sure. . . . [Y]ou hope you're gonna get it back fairly soon, but it could be longer." He continued:

Starting to do mitigation banks is getting tougher because you're putting out money a lot earlier, a lot more of it, it's much more at risk, and then you're waiting to get your credit release. Then you're waiting to sell those credits. . . . When you're doing mitigation banking the cost of capital, the risk cost is so much more.[41]

There is also a tremendous amount of uncertainty about the science and technology of restoration (see chapter 3), which leads to *implementation uncertainty* that the stream restoration project at the center of a mitigation bank might fail to meet the success criteria specified in the MBI. For regulators, this would be a disaster, as a failed project is very clearly not equivalent to the ecosystem services and functions provided at impacts sites. For bankers, project failure forces them to choose between losing credits (and thus profits) or going back to the project to make costly repairs.[42] Bankers seek to control implementation uncertainty in part by carefully assessing where they locate their projects: part of bankers' liking for headwater sites (discussed in more detail in chapter 7) is that such sites allow bankers to control what is flowing into their project. The greater the control, the less the potential for project failure, and thus implementation and reputational uncertainty (discussion of the latter follows).

> **Banker #1:** If we have an unprotected stream coming in, that immediately is a big risk point for us.
>
> **Banker #2:** Case in point [is] our XX project, you know. Adjacent upstream landowner built a pond, . . . and a totally huge amount of sediment came in and took out one of our trib[utarie]s. And there's really no recourse. We lost all the credit for that tributary. And the landowner, I'm not sure if was ever decided whether they did anything wrong, illegal or not. That's kind of a moot point. What happened, regardless: something occurred off-site and took out our stream.[43]

By contrast, larger streams are obvious sources of uncertainty and associated implementation risk because of that lack of control. Larger streams are more powerful (as a function of discharge) and can physically degrade very quickly. Also, they will be more heavily affected by tributaries and adjacent activities, as compared to small streams where much of the entire contributing watershed might be owned, and thus controlled, by the same landowner. As one banker succinctly put it, higher uncertainty and risk of failure are an inevitable part "of doing the big streams: . . . a lot more flow, a lot more shear stress, a lot more uncertainty on stability."[44]

Bankers and designers also try to minimize *reputational uncertainty* by going to great lengths to avoid project failures or other actions that might cause regulators to distrust them. Designers must maintain their reputations within the mitigation banking community to ensure they continue to get work, and bankers must maintain their reputations to reduce regulatory uncertainty for future projects. Indeed, this is one of the interesting aspects of a regulatory market: credit providers care more about their reputation with regulators than with their customers (permittees). As one banker explained it, the IRT "trusts and respects what we do and so that goes a long way. If they [the IRT members] discover that you tried to . . . cut a corner or get around a rule and they lose that trust, I mean that sets you back *years*, so we never want to do that."[45] As the same banker noted in a later interview, they save their reputational capital for moments when they want to propose an action that "we believe in, . . . but we know it's a little iffy for the IRT because it's hard for them to go outside their box. But if we've . . . never tried to push it, if we've never tried to get one over on them, then they're more likely to just have that trust in us. And so I feel like you save your political capital for that."[46]

Compensatory mitigation is supposed to ensure equivalence between the ecosystem damaged and the one restored, and yet it's not clear that we are any good at restoring fluvial systems. There is thus substantive *ecological uncertainty* about whether projects might fail to provide environmental improvement, or even cause degradation (see chapter 3). This is very much on the minds of many participants in mitigation banking. For regulators and scientists, ecological failure to meet their goals for stream mitigation banking undermines the whole premise of market-based approaches to environmental protection. For bankers and designers, ecological failure has a somewhat broader impact, carrying not only environmental, but also financial and reputational consequences. For investors, the consequences of ecological failure are primarily financial.

Where bankers, regulators, and designers depart from scientists is in how potential ecological degradation is measured: channel stability. As discussed earlier and in chapter 3, channel stability is used as a proxy measure for ecological degradation in stream mitigation banking. The result is an imperative to avoid physical change to the channel. For example, when we showed a mitigation banker two figures, one of which showed a view from above of the planform (i.e., alignment) of an unrestored stream, and one of which showed the planform of a stream restored for mitigation purposes, he immediately noted the potential for erosion (and thus channel instability) in the unrestored stream:

> When I look at that [pointing to the two big irregular bends at the end of the unrestored stream plan] I look at the potential for erosion and a cut through. And that's something that we would get dinged [for] with the IRT. This is a lot less risk averse than that [pointing to the large radius, very even meander bends on the mitigation figure] because [of] erosion. It's just a shame that you can't, that everybody views erosion as just a terrible thing when it's a completely natural thing with streams. Again, until the success criteria gets shifted to where that is not a big deal, you're going to see people staying away from it, which makes all the sense in the world.[47]

The key thing to note here is that the banker is well aware that a dynamic channel would be preferable, ecologically speaking, but cannot put that awareness into practice because of the current regulatory emphasis on stability. The banker could propose a project that would incorporate channel

The Actors in Stream Mitigation Banking

instability and associated ecological benefits, but this would introduce considerable regulatory uncertainty as the MBI would have to be based on new success criteria. And because of the novelty of the approach, the banker would be uncertain that the designer could actually achieve the stated goals of known/acceptable levels of channel migration and controlled instability. These regulatory and implementation uncertainties are simply too risky for a mitigation banker to take on when the existing approach already carries significant uncertainty.

From the point of view of regulators and scientists working for government agencies, the risk of ecological failure is particularly concerning, because their primary mission is environmental protection. Regulators will thus intervene if in their evaluation the ecological risk (and thus the uncertainty of achieving equivalence) is too high:

> If we feel like it's [the proposed sinuosity] inappropriate for whatever reason, then we can say, "Well, we're not going to approve it because we think it's too great a risk." There's a gray area in there where we may think it's too much, but that's where we let them go forward with it. It's their risk to make a successful project. . . . Then there's this kind of black area, where we know it's not appropriate. And there's risk to us, too, because we're investing time and money in the mitigation plan to try to get compensatory credits on the market that we can use. So we don't want to approve a project we know has problems. So there's this kind of scale in there where we would say, "Hey, you might want to look at this. We think it's too high."[48]

The last form of uncertainty is a whole group of unpredictable aspects that are unavoidable in stream mitigation banking. These are the *random uncertainties* that participants in mitigation banking have to account for in their decisions in some way, from mercurial landowner behavior to extreme weather events such as hurricanes or droughts. We talked to one banker in early October 2015 when heavy rains had deluged the Southeast:

> We have a project in construction right now in XX. In our rain gauge, which is there at the site, we have 24 inches of rain in the last five days. The project is 50% done in construction. It's been underwater to the point that you don't even know if the channel is still in existence. I mean, it's [the water has] been 300 [feet] wide, probably 6 [feet] deep over the floodplain, for the last five days. When the water finally recedes we're gonna go out there and see what's left. I mean I'm taking it lightly right now but it's frightening. It could be . . . $50,000–100,000 that we need to put back into the project just to get back to where we were.[49]

Conclusion

Collectively, the actors involved in stream mitigation banking make choices that create the practice of stream mitigation banking. There are significant trade-offs among the forms of uncertainty they face: *it isn't possible to minimize all types of uncertainty at the same time.* Instead participants in stream mitigation banking have to choose which sources of uncertainty to try to counter and which to ignore, which has direct consequences for the equivalence between impact and restoration sites. For example, a mitigation banker described prioritizing financial uncertainty over ecological uncertainty in deciding how strongly to stabilize the banks of a new project:

> There's also the stability thing which is, I *think*, in the ecological interests of the . . . site, . . . [and] is also in our economic interests. We do not want to return to it [to a restored site to repair damage]. We do not want it to look ugly, right? . . . The biggest problem now . . . is gun-shy engineers probably giving you the right sinuosity but building a plank road down the thing . . . literally with logs running down the whole thing, you know? . . . And we just got another like that down there and we told them. . . . "[C]ool it, man. We'll take the risk." We'll take the risk of it blowing out before we'll take the expense of the armoring. . . . Cause the armoring is very, very . . . expensive.[50]

In creating a particular stream mitigation bank, in a particular place, over a particular time period, the actors make choices about which types of uncertainty to emphasize, and thus about whether ecological equivalence will be prioritized or not. A series of events, actions, and decisions have to be made as part of any mitigation bank. These are what take mitigation banking from theory to practice, and it is to those realities that we now turn.

6 How Mitigation Banks Work, and the Biography of a Bank

The actors involved in mitigation banking, described in chapter 5, do not all interact and negotiate simultaneously. Nor do they have parallel interests. What happens when these different actors, with their disparate motivations, try to mitigate damage to streams?

In this chapter, we answer that question sequentially, explaining what is involved in creating a mitigation bank step by step. To do so, we present the biography of a bank first in concept, and then in practice through the story of a specific bank (the Hawthorne Stream Bank) from the perspective of the mitigation banker who proposed it. As bankers set in motion and carry through the development of a stream mitigation bank, they are the ones present for every step of the process.

This chapter follows the general sequence of these major steps:

1. Regulators create a market by developing necessary policies and guidance documents.
2. The mitigation banker locates a site for the bank.
3. The banker develops and gets regulatory approval for a formal agreement with the regulators: the Mitigation Banking Instrument.
4. The banker finds the capital needed to implement the project.
5. Working with a designer, the banker constructs the project and begins monitoring its success.
6. The banker markets the credits to potential buyers in order to generate revenue.

Precursors to a Bank: The Regulatory Foundations of a Market

A mitigation bank is created as part of a regulatory market; thus, the regulations for credit demand and supply are the key precursors to any mitigation bank. If a U.S. Army Corps of Engineers district is consistently and strictly enforcing Section 404 of the Clean Water Act and requiring in-kind compensation for stream impacts, then there will be a large credit demand and a thick market. If not, there will be limited demand for mitigation banking. To draw from our car inspection metaphor in chapter 2, this would be similar to whether or not a state regulatory office requires each car to be inspected every year (high credit demand), or if the office only requires some subset of cars to be inspected every few years (low credit demand). A regulatory market's activity is set by the rigor of regulatory enforcement.

Similarly, the regulations and practices need to be in place for the creation of credits. As one banker explained, a particular state did not yet have mitigation guidelines, and without rules, "it [is] really hard to work there. I know some people who are trying to start banks there, and I've said to them, 'With one stroke of a pen they can change whether your product is a good one or not. Do you understand that?' . . . Rules are everything."[1]

The term "rules," however, is not necessarily an accurate description of how stream markets are regulated; rather, standard operating procedures and other guidance documents are developed and accumulated in a particular Corps district, forming the basis of the local stream market gradually and cumulatively. These guidance documents for stream mitigation banking typically include high levels of flexibility, leaving as much room for professional judgment as possible. In interviews, staff members at federal and state agencies across the United States described working on either a "case-by-case" or "project-by-project" basis so that they could reward good projects appropriately, even if they did not strictly pencil out according to the current guidance documents. In the words of one Corps of Engineers staff member:

> The whole point of these guidelines . . . was to allow our project managers to make an assessment and not be boxed in and say, "Okay, you've met the definition of Enhancement 1, therefore you get [only] this much credit." . . . [A]s opposed to looking at that project and saying, "Wow, this thing has some attributes that I really like, one of which perhaps could be that the watershed is in good shape. And so, I know that by restoring habitat, I'll probably be providing

some uplift in benthic macro-invertebrate population, diversity, and what not. Okay!" So the whole point of those ranges was to allow project managers the flexibility to reward better projects with more credit.[2]

A key part of maintaining that flexibility for regulators comes from not finalizing guidance documents. Some Corps of Engineers staff reported deliberately leaving guidance documents or evaluation procedures in draft form so that they could be tinkered with as needed. Other Corps districts simply never published formal guidance documents at all, sticking with much less formalized guidelines, which result in explicit case-by-case negotiation of projects. For example, one Corps staff member corrected us when we mistakenly referred to the guidance documents he worked with as a "rule":

> It's not a rule. You know we've made a point all along that it's a procedure. It's an accounting procedure. It's not a rule, it's not guidance. You don't look there to see, uh, if mitigation is absolutely needed or not needed. It is a method for calculating the pluses and minuses—once we determine that stream mitigation should be used, is this a suitable method to use? You know there may be cases where somebody proposes a really great project that—if you run it through the numbers in the matrix, it just won't pencil out in terms of providing a lot of mitigation, but you know the benefits are there. An example might be removal of an irrigation diversion dam; that is a big [issue] here. You know the linear footage, the square footage. You know that the highest function rating you could give that size of a project might not pencil out to much of a credit, but it could be an expensive project and it could be a project that opens up, you know, hundreds or thousands of miles of tributaries to fish that need to move through the area. And if that's the case you do what makes sense and you allow that to be.[3]

The same staff member went on to describe the guidelines in their district as a living document:

> It's not perfect and it's intended to be a living document . . . Oh, it even says that on the front—"subject to periodic review and modification." Look at that [*laughs*]. So . . . it wasn't intended to be static at all and to know everything. It's a procedure, and where people have unique situations and it seems this won't apply or they run through it and they say, "We just can't get it to pencil out but this is a great project," we have that discretion to do what makes sense in the watershed.[4]

While these fluid definitions of restoration success benefit regulators, they can be a challenge to mitigation bankers. When considering a new potential stream market or creation of a new bank in an existing market, mitigation bankers must assess whether the approach they have applied in previous bank projects or in other markets will likely be successful and profitable. If regulators develop only informal standards, it creates a high level of regulatory uncertainty for bankers, who may then decide not to enter the market; interestingly, regulatory uncertainty also spikes in the rare cases where regulators develop stringent criteria for mitigation projects, as bankers may decide that they cannot meet them. Unsurprisingly, bankers often choose to work in a particular state or district for many years, increasing their familiarity with the regulations and the regulators themselves. This familiarity is one of the main ways that bankers can decrease uncertainty associated with fluid regulatory documents.

The balance any guidance document strikes between the needs of regulators and the needs of the market must then be tailored to the actual environmental conditions of the streams being regulated. As one Corps of Engineers staff member lamented:

> Things are never the same. No two streams look the same, no two streams function exactly the same. And so, for any [Corps of Engineers] district out there, including us . . . to try to put together something that's predictable to the providers [mitigation bankers] and try to provide guidance to them and also . . . provide something that satisfies our own program requirements is exceptionally difficult. Very, very difficult.[5]

All of these are ongoing considerations for a mitigation banker in assessing a current or potential new mitigation market: What are the official policies? What are the unofficial expectations? How rigorously are they being enforced to create credit demand? How are they affecting stream mitigation banks so far? What of their experiences from other districts will translate to this new district, or even from a previous project to a new stream project in the same district? These are foundational questions for a stream mitigation market (because it is a regulatory market), and a banker needs answers to all of them to evaluate the potential of a particular watershed, let alone a particular project site.

Locating a Bank: Finding Land

Once a mitigation banker decides that the necessary regulatory conditions are present in a state or Corps district to create a potential market, they will need to find a place to do an actual project. Mitigation bankers spend inordinate amounts of time scouring maps, monitoring transportation construction plans, digging through real estate records, and simply driving roads to see prospective sites. A mitigation banker may focus on a general area because of known, or suspected, credit demand there, or may search more broadly to find unusual opportunities.

A key factor for site location is the *service area*: the geographic area within which credits produced by a new mitigation bank will be accepted as compensation for impacts.[6] Service areas are typically part of the regulatory guidance and standard practices that regulators develop as part of setting up a market. Therefore, bankers know in advance roughly what size service areas they can expect as they consider different locations for banks. Service areas are typically specified via the U.S. Geological Survey's Hydrologic Unit Codes (HUCs), which are the national delineation of watersheds. HUCs are nested by scale: two-digit HUCs describe major river basins, and there are just eighteen in the continental United States. By contrast, there are tens of thousands of fourteen-digit HUCs, which delineate local watersheds (of 1–10 km^2). In most Corps districts, the maximum size of service areas is specified at the scale of eight-digit HUCS, of which there are more than two thousand in the United States.[7]

Larger service areas are very much in mitigation bankers' interests: the bigger the service area, the greater the potential number of permit applicants in search of mitigation credits. But the bigger the service area, the lesser the ecological connection between the stream to be damaged by development and the stream to be restored, and thus the more implausible the equivalence between the two. Regulators thus are juggling competing imperatives to make the mitigation market function and to protect environmental quality. Bankers and regulators do agree that the ideal service area is one in which there is high credit demand because this means there have been many impacts requiring compensation, and credits generated can be sold quickly and profitably.

In addition to being located in a service area with high credit demand, an ideal site for regulators and bankers is a stream that is visibly in terrible condition. As one regulator put it, "That's what we're looking for, is can you show a measurable difference, and what's the beginning quality of the stream."[8] A regulator from a different state made a similar point:

> What it will come down to is the [ecological] value of the mitigation bank. . . . [T]hey're not all gonna be equal: a mile of stream here is not gonna be worth the

same amount as a mile someplace else. [*In terms of function?*] Mm-hmm. And a lot of that will be based off of just the site conditions: slope, floodplain access, I mean all sorts of things that are going to affect that.[9]

Site selection, from the regulator's perspective, is an early mechanism to exert at least some control over ensuring equivalence and addressing uncertainty. Small service areas increase the potential similarity between the restoration site and the impacted site. Similarly, by pushing the banker to find a very degraded stream, any restoration activity is more likely to generate some ecological benefits, which reduces uncertainty about the efficacy of the mitigation banking project. As the same regulator succinctly said, "[With] a mitigation bank, site selection is everything."[10]

Because regulators prefer obviously degraded streams, bankers driving backroads looking for potential restoration opportunities search for clear visual evidence of degradation. As one mitigation banker described his site selection process:

> Sometimes, we literally are driving through a watershed because we're going to another site, and we're like, "*Man.* Good god, that looks *wrecked.*" And we get all excited. When I drive anywhere I'm always looking, and even if it's just a couple of thousand feet of like, cows, and big banks collapsing out, I get super excited, and I'm like, "Wow. How can we make this a project?"[11]

In terms of immediate visual impact, agricultural sites, preferably dairies, are the gold standard. When we asked the designers at a firm that frequently helps with site selection what their criteria were, their clear preference was for agricultural sites. As one put it, "Yes, if it's in the middle of an ag field, it's a no brainer."[12] Or as a mitigation banker put it:

> The best sites are typically cattle operations where the cows aren't being fenced off from the streams. Because you have nutrients, you have fecal [matter], you have everything. Sedimentation. And that is the kind of site that we prefer . . . because that's the one that's going to provide us with the greatest functional uplift. . . . I mean . . . that by far is the best kind of site to find.[13]

Beyond the ecological and service area factors, mitigation bankers must also consider the particular people with whom they will be working. For instance, they must consider whether regulators in a particular Corps district will be likely to approve a particular type of design, or whether there is some level of animosity between them and certain regulators. Bankers will also need to become familiar with the stream restoration designers working in a particular area, if there are any; otherwise, they may have to bring in designers from elsewhere despite the risk that these designers will be unfamiliar with the stream types at the potential project site.

The mitigation banker must keep all of this in mind as they select a specific site and develop some agreement with the landowner. Any mitigation bank must eventually have a permanent conservation easement to ensure that future uses of the land do not undermine the restoration. For a stream, a buffer area (typically 50 to 100 feet on either side of the stream) will be part of the required easement. Thus, any landowner is facing a future in which they still own the land outright, but may not use it in all the ways they have in the past. The banker will ensure this future by coming to some agreement with the landowner, whether through a formal option to use the land for a mitigation bank, profit-sharing of the eventual bank, or some other agreement to allow the use of the land in the future for a bank. Additionally, if it is a large or unique site (e.g., in a dense urban setting), the option or agreement may be quite expensive.

Because of the difficulties of finding an appropriate project site, many bankers base their mitigation projects on the particulars of a site rather than finding a site that fits a particular stream restoration design. For instance, the length of a project is not part of the starting conception; rather, a banker will base their proposed project length on the site characteristics available. That is, a banker does not go out saying they will create a 2,750-foot-long mitigation bank; rather, they find a likely property and then start conceptualizing what projects could be done based on that property's characteristics.

Specifying the Bank: The Mitigation Banking Instrument

With a site selected, mitigation bankers will begin developing their formal proposal to regulators for what they will do at the site, and what they expect in return: these characteristics are spelled out in what will eventually be the Mitigation Banking Instrument.[14] MBIs must be consistent with regulatory procedures and practices, and thus the banker will develop them so that they speak to relevant policies and regulatory guidance that exist at the time and in that district. Because of the need to comply with existing regulations and practices, one might expect MBIs to be standard. In fact, because each bank is unique (i.e., a product of a unique history and the particularities of local conditions) and each banker has developed their own way of doing business, MBIs can be surprisingly bespoke. Some bankers consider their MBIs to be proprietary, as they reflect significant investment of time from legal teams, and include nuances that the particular banker has found effective in negotiating with regulators in the past.

From the regulator's perspective, the MBI must ensure that the eventual mitigation bank fulfills the goals and mandates of the Clean Water Act, and it must be consistent with the locally applicable guidance documents. From the mitigation banker's perspective, the MBI also articulates the proposed number of credits that the mitigation bank can generate (if it is restored successfully), and thus, the potential revenue they will be able to obtain from the proposed bank. Effectively, then, the MBI is the mechanism through which individual mitigation banks are regulated, and thus is the crucial moment at which the needs of the market (bankers) are negotiated against the needs of the state (regulators).

MBIs specify several key attributes of the mitigation bank: the service area, the specific site location, what will be built, the success criteria, the monitoring plan, and the credit release schedule. Bankers need specificity about each of these in order to clarify what they will get out of the proposed bank, including how many credits the site will eventually generate; regulators need them as a form of assurance that if the project gets built, it will fulfill their needs for compliance (i.e., ensure equivalence).

Because of the MBI's importance, it can take months or years to prepare. Typically, the banker will develop the MBI in phases, beginning with a conceptual plan and prospectus; this preliminary phase allows the regulators a chance to provide early-stage responses to the banker, drawing attention to aspects of the project that might cause problems during the more formal review process. In general, the closer the project hews (in terms of size, location, and design) to what the regulators expect to see, the easier it is for them to approve the project and associated MBI from start to finish. The regulator will provide comments on the prospectus, and will also send out the prospectus for public comment. From there, the banker will develop a Draft MBI and submit it to the regulator, who then has a set period of time to review the instrument, including discussion with other agencies (typically via the Interagency Review Team), and internal decision-making within the Corps district as the lead agency. The regulator provides the banker with a notice of whether the Draft MBI will be approved, and if so, the banker submits the formal MBI.

All of these steps in the process and components developed for an MBI (see table 6.1) are time-consuming and expensive. While each aspect can be negotiated with regulators ("case-by-case basis" language is ubiquitous in stream mitigation policies and guidance documents), it is not typically in the banker's best interest to develop a plan that pushes the limits of acceptability, and then step backward if the regulator rejects it. That is, bankers do not develop a project incrementally (or iteratively) toward something that is just at the margin of regulatory acceptability because the submission and review process is lengthy, and because the regulators have limited capacity (and tolerance) to review submissions. This means that there is very limited opportunity for "discovery" or optimization, or even innovation, in stream mitigation banking: bankers attempt to minimize regulatory risk, and they do this by proposing projects that are likely to be quickly and readily approved.

Channel Design, Success Criteria, and Monitoring Plan

As part of the MBI submission, the banker must specify what exactly will be constructed at the site. This requires engineering specifications before the project can be approved, including precise dimensions of the stream, size of gravel and cobble to be used for the bed and banks, exact geometric layout of the stream to be built on the site, where fencing will go, and how road crossings will be rebuilt. It is at this phase that the central role of the designer emerges. In some cases, the mitigation banker will have designers on staff; in other cases, the banker will reach out to a stream designer they have worked with before, or may request proposals from a number of designers. The eventual banker-designer team will identify what can be done on the chosen site and, just as important, what is likely to be approved by the regulator.

It is important to note that what is articulated in the success criteria in the MBI is what the mitigation bankers are required to produce, tangibly, at their selected restoration sites. This is the central part of a mitigation banker's agreement with regulators: if the constructed stream has the characteristics laid out in the MBI's success criteria, then the regulators will agree to release credits for the banker to sell. Thus, the plans and specifications for a stream design developed as part of the MBI will be based on the typical success criteria of MBIs in that Corps district. The restoration project is designed to meet regulators' expectations.[15]

Table 6.1

Timeline for an MBI in the Wilmington District

Timing	Event	Number of days for response from regulators	Additional actions required of regulators
Phase 1	Optional preliminary review of draft prospectus	30	District Engineer provides copies of draft prospectus to IRT and will provide comments back to the mitigation bank sponsor within 30 days
Mitigation bank sponsor prepares and submits prospectus			
Phase 2—Day 1	Complete prospectus received by District Engineer		
Phase 2—Day 30	Public notice must be provided within 30 days of receipt of a complete prospectus	30	
Phase 2—Day 60	Thirty-day public comment period	30	
Phase 2—Day 90	District Engineer must provide the mitigation bank sponsor with an initial evaluation letter within 30 days of close of public comment period	30	District Engineer distributes comments to IRT members and sponsor within 15 days of close of public comment period
Sponsor considers comments, prepares and submits Draft MBI			
Phase 3—Day 1	Complete Draft MBI received by IRT members		
Phase 3—Day 30	Thirty-day IRT comment period begins 5 days after District Engineer distributes Draft MBI to IRT members	30	
Phase 3—variable	District Engineer discusses comments with IRT and seeks to resolve issues	60	Within 90 days of receipt of complete Draft MBI by IRT members, District Engineer must notify the sponsor of the status of the IRT review

Table 6.1 (continued)

Timing	Event	Number of days for response from regulators	Additional actions required of regulators
Mitigation bank sponsor prepares final MBI			
Phase 4—Day 1	Final MBI received by District Engineer and IRT		
Phase 4—Day 30	District Engineer must notify members of intent to approve/not approve final MBI within 30 days of receipt	30	
Phase 4—variable	IRT members have 45 days from submission of final MBI to object to approval of instrument and initiate dispute resolution process	15	
Phase 4—Day 45	FINAL MBI APPROVED/NOT APPROVED, or DISPUTE RESOLUTION PROCESS INITIATED		
TOTAL REQUIRED FEDERAL REVIEW PROCESS (PHASES 3–4) MUST BE LESS THAN OR EQUAL TO 225 DAYS			

Source: U.S. Army Corps of Engineers—Wilmington District 2018.

Based on preliminary designs and the general sense of approval or concern from the regulator, the designer will develop the specific blueprints and construction plans that will go through public comment, and eventually be approved by the regulator as part of the MBI. These specific designs are the core of what the banker is asserting they will be able to deliver.

Determining whether or not the restored stream fulfills the success criteria is based on the data collected as part of the *monitoring plan* articulated in the MBI. Such plans specify what must be monitored at the mitigation bank site, and for how long, to demonstrate the effectiveness of the project. In most Corps districts, data collection includes post-construction surveys of the channel to ensure that what was built matches what was proposed in the MBI (i.e., the stream dimensions constructed should be commensurate with what was presented in the design documents included in the MBI). While the primary focus across the United States is on the physical dimensions of the channels, bankers in many Corps districts are required to monitor the survival of planted riparian vegetation. In some cases, bankers are required to monitor other biological or chemical attributes, such as instream fauna (e.g., benthic macroinvertebrates) or dissolved oxygen. Importantly, not all of these monitoring data are used to determine whether the restored site has met its success criteria: the physical characteristics of the stream and limited aspects of riparian vegetation are typically success criteria; with the exception of stem counts of riparian vegetation, biological or chemical attributes are almost never formal success criteria.[16]

For mitigation bankers, the costs of monitoring are necessary but (a) take away from their long-term revenue stream, and (b) increase the chances for greater scrutiny by regulators. Thus, bankers tend to propose monitoring plans that fulfill some minimum requirement, but little beyond that. In contrast, from the regulators' perspective, increased monitoring requirements are a way to inform their overall program and approaches to restoration and mitigation. For instance, while benthic macroinvertebrates may not be considered as part of success criteria, regulators may require mitigation bankers to monitor such attributes to understand whether different types of restoration or locations of projects might be more effective. These expanded measurements beyond success criteria alone are important for regulators if they are to adaptively manage their overall regulatory programs.

Credit Release Schedule

MBIs also specify how many credits can be sold at what points in time during the project's completion and subsequent monitoring for compliance. This is the *credit release schedule*. Although it would be more ecologically rational, and preferable from a regulatory standpoint, to forbid bankers to sell credits until a restoration project is completed and monitored for compliance with success criteria, this is not feasible from the perspective of the market. Mitigation banks require a great deal of investment up front to acquire property rights, commission a restoration and monitoring plan, and pay for construction. In addition, the monitoring period to ensure banks meet their success criteria is anywhere from three to seven years, depending on the Corps district. If the entire cost of a mitigation bank—from site location to full monitoring—had to be fully financed up front, the interest payments would likely double the costs of the project (not to mention the difficulty of finding an investor willing to wait that long for any return).

An accelerated credit release schedule allows mitigation bankers to amortize the costs of project finance as different benchmarks are met. A portion of the potential credits are released for sale as soon as the MBI is approved by the regulators, which creates revenue bankers can use to repay land acquisition and design costs. This enables bankers to pursue financing for project construction with limited financial liabilities for the project, and a legal document in hand demonstrating that their project has regulatory approval. Subsequent credit releases in the years following construction allow bankers to repay these loans, and eventually to generate profits.

Many characteristics of credit release schedules are specified in the guidance documents for the Corps district, and regulators are unlikely to vary from the published schedule. However, there is significant variation in release schedules from one Corps district to another. For instance, in the Fort Worth District, more than 50 percent of credits are released when the MBI is approved, while in the Chicago District only 10 percent are released (figure 6.1).

Just as service areas are an attempt to ensure equivalence spatially, credit release schedules are a mechanism for ensuring equivalence temporally.

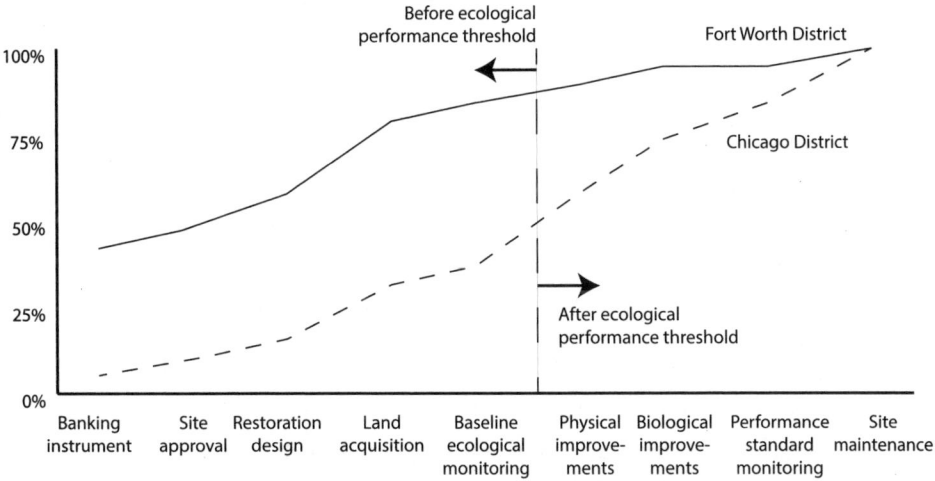

Figure 6.1
Comparison of credit release schedules (ca. 2010) in the Fort Worth and Chicago Districts of the Corps of Engineers. *Source:* BenDor, Riggsbee, and Doyle 2011.

The more regulators require to be done early in the process, the better the match in timing between when new habitat is developed and old habitat destroyed. Yet regulators must balance their desire for equivalence with bankers' needs (i.e., the market) to reduce uncertainty and risk: pure temporal equivalence (all project construction and monitoring completed prior to impacts) would place too much risk on bankers and disincentivize creating banks. Just as the definition of credits and service areas is a compromise between equivalence and the markets, so are credit release schedules.

Financing a Bank: Finding Money

For a mitigation banker, all of these elements of the MBI must be developed and assembled in advance of selling credits, and therefore in advance of revenue. This is the entrepreneurial part of mitigation banking: it requires aspects of the project to be done speculatively. It is in this phase that elements of project finance become relevant, because the mitigation banker needs some sources of capital while all of this work is being conceived and completed. Accordingly, one of the first things that a mitigation banker must do is assess their need for finance in the project development phase and, if capital is needed, identify investors.[17]

Mitigation bankers often have multiple projects at different stages of development and completion, creating the potential to finance new projects with revenue from completed projects. Not all bankers are willing to roll their profits from one bank into another, however, as it intensifies the financial implications of regulatory uncertainty. If the new project is not approved by regulators, the bankers may no longer have the capital available to develop an alternative project.[18]

If the mitigation banker does not want to risk revenue from a previous project on an uncertain future project, or if revenue from a previous project is not available, bankers must find external investors. This is not as easy to do as it might seem: investors rarely put capital into investments they do not understand. Home mortgages, for instance, are very well known to many investors, allowing them to assess the risk of providing a loan to different types of borrowers for different geographic areas or mortgage types. This enables homebuyers to choose from multiple investors (i.e., financial banks) seeking their business, which creates competition and drives down interest rates. Obtaining finance for a mitigation bank is entirely different.

How Mitigation Banks Work, and the Biography of a Bank

There are relatively few mitigation banks, and the industry itself is based on nuances of a federal law that few investors understand. Moreover, the regulatory guidance and market for credits (and thus mitigation banks) can vary tremendously from one Corps district to another, so that an investor's experience in one district could be relatively uninformative in another. Thus, there are not many investors willing to finance a mitigation bank.[19]

The ideal situation for a mitigation banker is to find an investor who understands the industry and can price the capital (via interest rates) commensurate with the actual risk. If the investor is not familiar with mitigation, they are likely to perceive the risks as much higher than they are, and to set the terms of the investment accordingly.[20]

Building a Bank: Conservation Easements, Construction, and the Monitoring Period

With a site selected, a Draft MBI approved, and money in hand, the mitigation banker can finally implement and build the project. Two things then happen that significantly increase the financial uncertainty and risk for the mitigation banker. First, for the MBI to go formally into effect, the banker must exercise the option (or other agreement) to put into effect a permanent conservation easement on the bank site. That is, the MBI becomes official only when the conservation easement is finalized legally with the landowner. This requires the banker to make a payment, often a large one, to the landowner (or exercise another type of agreement), placing the land under easement. Second, the banker must hire a construction firm to build the restored stream, also at considerable cost.

From there, the banker (often in collaboration with the designer) will oversee construction of the stream restoration project, with a significant interest in ensuring it is built in close agreement to what the MBI proposed. The constructed stream is then surveyed (via an "as-built survey"), along with any other required monitoring, and this first round of monitoring data is delivered to the regulator. So long as the constructed site characteristics match what was specified in the MBI, a second tranche of credits is released for the banker to sell to permittees.

The mitigation banker will then be responsible for monitoring and maintaining the site as stipulated in the MBI's monitoring plan, typically for three to seven years. The monitoring commonly includes channel surveys, riparian vegetation surveys, and any additional data collection required by the MBI. Required maintenance is also specified in the MBI, and can include ensuring riparian plant survival, excluding livestock via fencing, and maintaining the reconstructed form of the channel.

There are many things that can go wrong with a stream restoration project during this time period. Vegetation may not thrive, or may be killed by pests. A flood may cause the erosion of channel banks or sedimentation in the channel bed. The regulator could decide any change in channel characteristics means the project is falling out of compliance, and thus a portion of the credits would not be released for sale. In such cases, the banker must decide whether it is more cost effective to go back to the stream to do post-construction maintenance work or to accept the loss of those credits. For instance, on a 2,000-foot-long stream restoration project, the regulator may determine that erosion has led to 200 feet of the restored stream not meeting success criteria. The banker must then make a financial and risk-based decision whether to remobilize equipment to repair the erosion, or give up the potential revenue of those 200 feet (i.e., 10 percent of total project returns).

Each year of the monitoring period, the banker delivers monitoring reports, and the regulator reviews them and releases another set of credits. In the final year, the banker and the regulator will conduct a close-out site review; if the site is still meeting success criteria, the regulator will release all remaining credits. At that point, the banker is freed from any requirements for reconstruction or channel maintenance.

The final disposition of the stream itself depends on the property owner. If the site is on public land, then the banker may simply provide a financial package for ongoing maintenance of the site. If the site is on private land, then the property owner will be required to maintain whatever is articulated in the easement contract. Finally, if the banker owns the land, they may seek to transfer it to another entity, such as a public resource agency or an environmental land trust, or retain direct ownership going forward.

It is worth noting that the credits released at site close-out are indistinguishable from those released at the initial stages of the project (e.g., at the MBI signing). All mitigation banking credits are fungible in that each one equally fulfills the compliance obligations of a permittee. It is also worth noting that bankers' profits (if any) come during the later stages of the project. Because of the need for pre-project finance to cover land acquisition, design, and construction costs, much of the revenue generated from credit sales immediately following the MBI and project construction goes to repaying investors or compensating contractors (e.g., design and construction firms). *Bankers thus have considerable interest in ensuring that the close-out of the project results in full credit release.* This creates an incentive for bankers to maintain projects as opposed to letting them evolve or degrade in any way. However, after close-out, the banker has no further financial incentive to maintain the project.

Finding Buyers

All along the way, mitigation bankers are either assessing the market for credits, or marketing credits. This begins during project conception by identifying areas that already have, or are likely to have large credit demand. But as the project develops and credits are released by the regulators, the bankers will market those credits to permittees. This process is not simple.[21] Mitigation bankers typically have relationships with different types of likely credit buyers, and often develop those relationships prior to the credits being available for sale. For instance, there are often large organizations that bankers know in advance will have significant demand for credits, such as a department of transportation, a large-scale land developer, or a water resource authority/utility. This scale of buyer can often single-handedly justify a banker initiating a project in the first place. If such a buyer exists, then the banker benefits from having a known market for most or all of the generated credits, and the permittee benefits by having a known supply of credits, reducing their regulatory uncertainty. Because of this mutual benefit, bankers may sell credits to large buyers at a relatively reduced rate. The credit price for permittees with more limited market demand typically is greater on a per-credit basis. If credits are sold quickly, then the revenue generated allows the banker to repay loans quickly, as well as generate profits for themselves or any external investors (e.g., figure 6.2). The worst case end point for mitigation bankers is to have credits for which there are no buyers.[22]

Biography of a Bank

The mitigation process outlined in this chapter is generalized. Every stream mitigation bank goes through these steps, but none in quite the same way,

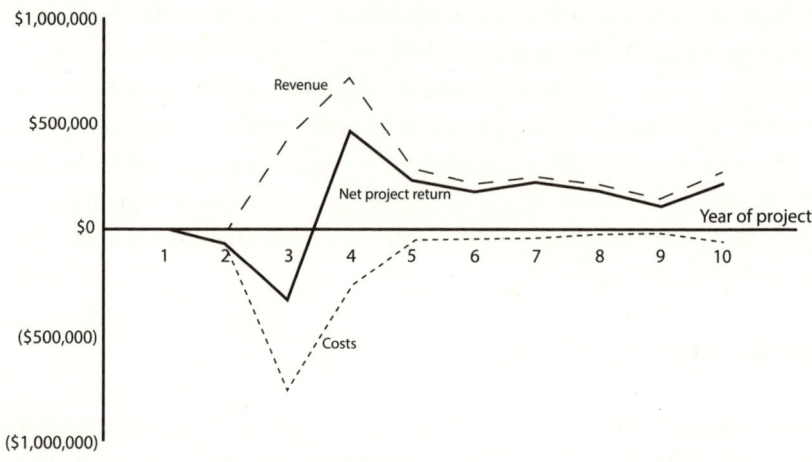

Figure 6.2
Costs and revenue of an existing stream mitigation banking project, based on financial information provided by the mitigation banker who developed the project, December 17, 2018. Costs and revenue for years 1–3 are actual, and for years 4–10 are projected based on the assumption that all released credits can be sold immediately. The project was financed with $1.2 million in year 0; if credits can be marketed as projected (i.e., sold in their entirety in the year they are released), the $1.2 million investment will generate an internal rate of return of 15 percent (based on repayment agreements the mitigation banker made with the investor).

even if they are located in the same Corps district. To illustrate how this works in practice—the negotiations and decisions that shape actual mitigation banks—we present the detailed biography of a particular bank: the Hawthorne Stream Bank, developed by The Enhancement Bank (TEB).[23] Both are pseudonyms, and we have made a few changes to the site description in order to maintain their anonymity. TEB is one of the larger mitigation banking firms in the Southeast, with increasing presence in other regions.

The Hawthorne Stream Bank originated, like many other banks, in a series of long-term conversations with landowners in a region of interest to TEB because it looked like it could be a good market for stream credits. As the project manager noted, "It's all about the site, and working with the landowner is really a ten-year relationship." Many landowners in rural areas find out about mitigation banking from another landowner who has done a mitigation project: "They'll hear about it at Walmart or especially talking about things at church; that's how landowners first learn about [mitigation] banking." This was the case with the Hawthorne Stream Bank: there were several small mitigation projects that had been finished in this rural area by different mitigation bankers, and TEB had even done a very small bank in the same watershed. This gave them confidence that there was at least some demand for credits and, based on their projections for development, likely very large demand in the future. Because of this, TEB was looking for a big project site—something on the order of thirty-thousand feet—and they had been diligent about maintaining relationships with several landowners who were interested in their land being used for a mitigation bank.

In late 2012, TEB noticed that the smaller mitigation banks in the area were selling credits almost immediately after they were released. This indicated high credit demand, and TEB began looking actively and intensively for sites. This was more complicated than usual because the size of bank they envisioned was unlikely to be found on a single parcel of land. Instead, it would require working with multiple landowners on adjacent or nearly adjacent sites with the right characteristics. Eventually, TEB found eight different landowners willing to partner with them, each of whom had ideal sites with substantial lengths of visibly beat-up streams.

Securing land rights with eight different landowners, however, took TEB more than three years. This, in and of itself, increased the costs and risks of the project because TEB had to provide semi-annual payments to each landowner in exchange for agreeing to allow TEB to eventually develop a mitigation bank on their property. For the landowners, this meant that they began receiving money immediately, but would lose some of their land for farming and/or have to change some aspects of their property (e.g., road access, stream crossings) at some unknown date in the future when the restoration work actually began. This created uncertainty for the landowners, and the longer the project dragged on (i.e., the longer the time from signing on for their land to be used to when stream restoration actually began), the more difficult it was for TEB to keep them happy. That made TEB's regular meetings with the landowners, to keep them appraised of the overall project development and timeline, as important as the early payments.

In early 2015, with all the needed land rights secured, it was time for TEB to make significant decisions about how to finance the Hawthorne Stream Bank project. When TEB developed the earlier, smaller project in the area, they had been in a gap period financially: their other mitigation banks were not generating significant revenue, so they could not finance the smaller bank themselves. Instead, they brought in a private equity partner for the smaller project. This partner paid TEB cash up front, and in return received a significant portion of the financial return of future credit sales. This is the financial trade-off of any mitigation banker taking on external finance: an additional investor spreads some of the financial risk for a mitigation banker, but that diffuses the economic returns.[24]

For the Hawthorne Stream Bank project, the timing was better. TEB had other projects that were in different stages of completion and were generating revenue. TEB could thus use those profits as the startup capital for the new project. This is a far riskier approach: if the Hawthorne Stream Bank was a bust, then TEB would lose profits from it as well as from the earlier projects they had used to finance it. However, if the Hawthorne Stream Bank worked as well as TEB hoped, and if they could finance the project solely themselves, they would not have to share the eventual profits. TEB decided on this self-financed approach, which would mean internalizing all the risk, but also all the profits.

TEB also had to decide in 2015 just how large a project to push forward. They had identified and paid for rights at eight different sites, all of which were viable, and all of which were located in a heavy credit-demand region. TEB decided to go big by developing an umbrella bank instrument: a single MBI for the eight different project sites. This was a high-risk and high-reward strategy, just like the decision to not bring on a financial partner. The rationale for the big umbrella bank was that if they could secure all eight sites and the associated credits generated, they would be able to minimize any likely competition in the service area; once word got out that there was a surge of credits coming online, it would be less likely that another banker would move into the basin. This would increase TEB's certainty that they would be able to sell the credits they generated.

From a purely market perspective (that of the mitigation banker), a single, mega-bank made the most sense. However, a mitigation bank is only viable if it successfully runs the regulatory gauntlet. Because of the size and complexity of the proposed Hawthorne Stream Bank, this was not going to be a run-of-the-mill mitigation bank. TEB thus engaged the regulatory agencies early in the process by developing a prospectus, or as the project manager described it, "an MBI lite." The prospectus went to the regulators (i.e., the Corps and Interagency Review Team) and let them know what TEB was thinking in terms of the proposed sites and type of restoration activity. The prospectus also had the benefit of going on public notice, so that any other mitigation bankers considering projects in the area would become aware of the project being developed.

After the public comment period and a review by the regulator, TEB received an Initial Evaluation Letter, which served as a type of agreement in principle. This was the chance for the regulator to identify potential issues of concern that would need to be addressed in the final MBI. For this mega-bank, the regulator requested that TEB reduce the number of project sites from eight to four. Quite simply, the regulator did not have the bandwidth for a project as large and as complicated as what was being proposed; they were unsure that they would have the resources and time to keep up with the scale of the project. This demonstrates how regulatory markets are a partnership between credit providers and regulators: the mega-bank was ideal for the banker but not feasible for the regulator. And so they had to negotiate what worked for both.

Up until this point in the process (before submitting a Draft MBI), TEB could have walked away from the Hawthorne Stream Bank project, let their agreements with landowners expire, and absorbed their losses. However, once TEB decided to develop a Draft MBI, there were more serious costs involved. In the project manager's words, "Then you got to pull the trigger on the science." That is, they would have to hire engineers and designers, as well as all of the teams that collect relevant data that feed into the design, plans, and blueprints. At a minimum, TEB estimated that to develop a Draft MBI for one of the project sites would cost about $50,000, so the costs for the four sites the regulator was willing to include in the MBI were starting to add up. As the project manager put it, "You start dribbling money, which at some point starts to be become real dollars." And this Draft MBI would still have to go through review and potential revision by the regulator, which could bring additional costs.

At some point, TEB would reach a point of no return where the amount of time and money invested was large enough that they would have to complete the project to generate revenue to compensate for their investments. For the Hawthorne Stream Bank, TEB estimated that price point was at around $750,000. Once they crossed that threshold, they had to go through with the project because their firm could not absorb that scale of loss.[25]

Based on their assessment of profit potential, and of all the risks and uncertainties involved, TEB decided to move forward with developing a Draft MBI. This meant that they had to identify and contract with designers to do the actual design work, and continue to make payments to all of the landowners to keep the agreements for work on their land (each time for six to twelve months). In this case, TEB chose a stream designer they had worked with many times in the past, and who they were very confident could do the work quickly and effectively. With the plans in hand, TEB developed a Draft MBI and submitted it to the regulators, who then had ninety days to review it and provide comments.

During the review of the Draft MBI, the regulators and the TEB project manager did a formal site visit. Site visits have multiple functions: they give regulators a chance to actually see the site, but they also give the entire project group a significant amount of time to talk through the details, and to negotiate trading ratios (see chapter 4). As the Hawthorne Stream Bank's project manager put it, "all the deal-making happens in the field, mainly about the trading ratios." After the field visits for the four sites included in the Hawthorne Stream Bank, and further review of the Draft MBI, the regulators requested a few adjustments and then filed a notice of their intent to approve the MBI. TEB revised the MBI based on comments from the regulator, and then submitted the final version. At that point, the regulator had another forty-five days to either approve, not approve, or initiate a dispute resolution process. All of these time periods add up. TEB had already invested a considerable amount of money, and the delays also began to weigh on their relationship with landowners.

The submission of the final MBI is the trickiest time for a mitigation banker, but that was particularly the case for the Hawthorne Stream Bank because TEB was working with multiple landowners. By the time the final MBI for the Hawthorne Stream Bank was submitted, TEB was "hundreds of thousands of dollars in the hole," and the landowners had yet to receive their final (and largest) payments. One of the key elements of the final MBI was the requirement for permanent conservation easements on the land. This is typically a large amount of money, especially for a project the size of the Hawthorne Stream Bank. For this project, TEB said that by the time they got the easements finalized, which allowed the final MBI to go into effect, they were "well over a million dollars committed" in terms of money and time spent on the project. This was the critical moment, because at that point TEB was legally and financially on the hook to build the Hawthorne Stream Bank.[26]

Happily for TEB, however, the final approved MBI triggered the release of 15 percent of the credits to infuse capital into the project and push the construction phase forward. For the Hawthorne Stream Bank, the first release of credits was in the summer of 2017, fully five years after TEB began formal negotiations with landowners. But the size of the project meant that the initial release of credits was considerable: just over 2,200. With credits in North Carolina selling at the time for up to $500 each, this initial release of credits represented over $1 million in potential revenue. And to TEB's relief, the demand for those credits was immediate: they were able to sell credits within two weeks of their release. This gave TEB "walkin' around money; not enough to buy new cars, but enough to pay our bills." They were able to recoup all of the money they paid the landowners and to contract with designers and construction firms (an additional cost of just over $1 million, which would then be paid in full after the next tranche of credits was released). Construction was completed in the winter of 2018, and the finished site was monitored for the first time; this triggered the release of an additional 2,200 credits. If all of those credits could be sold, then TEB would be near the point of financially breaking even. Credit sales generated by annual monitoring would then generate revenue during the winter of 2019.

As TEB pointed out, the money from these initial sales of credits looks like profit, and some of it will certainly go to refilling the firm's coffers. But a substantial amount of the potential revenue from Hawthorne Stream Bank is spoken for because it will finance their next project, mostly likely the other four sites that were part of their initially conceived bank in the region.

Conclusion: What Would We Expect the Hydroscape to Look Like after All These Negotiations?

As this chapter and the previous one show, the process of creating even a single mitigation bank is the result of a complex set of eco-social relations. Regulators, mitigation bankers, permittees, and others must consider trade-offs among different forms of ecological and social uncertainty, as well as policies, questions of equivalence, financial concerns, and the ecological particularities of rivers and streams. These negotiations—formal and informal—occur for each mitigation bank created, and thus each stream restored. Over time, these restoration projects accumulate. The existing hydroscape is reshaped as all of the individual actions since the birth of stream mitigation banking in the late 1990s are integrated over space and time. What does this hydroscape look like, and whose signature does it bear?

7 The Streams That Mitigation Banking Creates

How do streams restored under the auspices of this market for ecosystem services manifest the tensions and trade-offs among concerns about equivalence, and the range of uncertainties inherent in stream mitigation banking: regulatory, financial, ecological, implementation, reputational, and random? How have the day-to-day practices of creating and maintaining the mitigation banking market reshaped the hydroscape?

To answer these questions, we compared the physical form of streams restored to create mitigation banks with those restored for other purposes, and then compared both with a random sample drawn from the vastly larger universe of unrestored streams. In all, we compared 186 streams, a significant dataset on the physical form of streams in the United States.[1]

We concentrated our research in the U.S. state of North Carolina, a hotspot for stream restoration and where stream mitigation banking originated. The sheer prevalence of mitigation projects in North Carolina makes it unusual among states implementing stream mitigation banking. North Carolina also stands out for the high level of consensus among its regulators and designers about what a restored stream should look like—the state is one of the national centers of Natural Channel Design, a widely accepted approach to stream restoration (see chapter 3). But in many other ways, stream mitigation projects in North Carolina are representative of the vast majority of such projects across the United States, with many Corps districts' guidance documents modeled after the one created for the Wilmington Corps District.[2]

Some of our geomorphic data on channel form were mined from required monitoring reports on stream mitigation banking projects, and other data came from surveys of unrestored streams. It is important to note that stream reaches in the latter category were in no sense pristine; presumably all of those surveyed had been affected by human actions directly or indirectly. The only thing stream reaches in this category share is that there has been no attempt to restore them.

Defining Stream Credits in North Carolina

To understand how restored streams in North Carolina came to take the forms that they do, we need to first understand how stream mitigation developed in North Carolina, as every state grafts restoration into their landscape and hydroscape in particular ways. The modern stream restoration movement in North Carolina began in the early 1990s through state Soil and Water Conservation Districts and local citizen groups in the mountainous, northwestern corner of the state, a region of cold-water streams with resident trout populations. This restoration work was largely grant-driven. Meanwhile, water-quality-driven restoration work up through the mid-1990s (e.g., compensatory mitigation and projects funded by the state's Clean Water Trust Fund) had been focused largely on wetlands, with impacts to streams addressed via wetland restoration, if at all. However, there was a growing sense among regulators in North Carolina that this focus on wetlands was problematic, and that they needed to address the growing, unmitigated impacts to streams. As a result in 1998 North Carolina became the first state to require that impacts to streams be mitigated in kind (by restoring other streams), which introduced a major source of demand for stream restoration projects (see chapter 3 for a review of this history).

When Dave Rosgen taught his first stream restoration short course in North Carolina in 1996, participants were planning to use grants to fund stream restoration. The nascent stream restoration community immediately embraced Rosgen's approach, and grant funding from the EPA was used to send local, state, and federal agency staff to Rosgen's subsequent courses.[3] Practitioners within North Carolina, particularly several housed in the agricultural extension branch at North Carolina State University, began to experiment with stream restoration based on Natural Channel Design and to teach short courses on it locally. This produced a core group of restoration practitioners and regulators with a clear, shared sense that Natural Channel Design was the best way to restore streams. Thus, when stream mitigation took root, Rosgen's approach (including his stream classification system) made sense as the basis for defining and inventorying stream credits: by that point, the state's stream restoration community knew it well.[4] In particular, the state agency overseeing compensatory mitigation of stream impacts associated with public infrastructure was staffed with practitioners well versed in Natural Channel Design. The very large number of stream impacts this agency was tasked with mitigating created significant demand for streams restored using this approach, increasing its credibility.[5] Thus, from the earliest days of stream mitigation in North Carolina, in the late 1990s, stream credits were defined by linear feet of a particular Rosgen stream type.

The ubiquity of Natural Channel Design at the time stream mitigation banking took off had another important consequence. The core technique of Natural Channel Design is to physically reconfigure degraded channels. Therefore, while compensatory mitigation for streams can include preserving existing high quality streams (referred to as *preservation*) or less intensive manipulation of channel conditions such as fencing out cattle or planting riparian vegetation (referred to as *enhancement*), the guidelines in North Carolina privileged full channel reconfiguration, the only activity defined as *restoration* (also noted in chapter 4). As defined in North Carolina's mitigation regulations, preservation produced the lowest number of credits on a given site, and enhancement carried a medium number of credits. The maximum number of credits was only available if mitigation bankers reconfigured the existing channel. Regulators thus created a powerful economic incentive for full reconstruction rather than preservation or enhancement. Because many Corps districts have adapted mitigation guidelines from the Southeast Division rather than developing their own policies from scratch, that is true across much of the United States.[6]

This particular way of defining the ecosystem services at the heart of stream mitigation banking has three important consequences: it narrows equivalence to the point of removing uncertainties about the environmental efficacy of mitigation banking; it takes most of the other forms of risk and uncertainty discussed in chapters 5 and 6 off the table; and it creates perverse economic incentives.

First, defining stream credits based on Rosgen's stream classification radically narrows the range of criteria that must be evaluated to determine equivalence between the stream reach damaged by development and the one restored for mitigation. Instead of having to compare the biological, chemical, and physical particularities and interconnectivities of the two sites, stream mitigation banking in North Carolina calls out a relatively narrow range of physical characteristics, dramatically reducing the possible axes of difference. The physical characteristics are then lumped into a small set of scale-neutral ranges (the core of Rosgen's classification-based approach), further dampening the possibility that differences between impact and restoration sites would rule out equivalence.

Equivalence is thus reduced to criteria that are relatively easy to measure and control. Biology and chemistry, not to mention more complex physical characteristics (e.g., groundwater connectivity) are excluded from consideration because channel form is considered an adequate proxy for them ("build it and they will come"; see chapter 3). This highly simplified equivalence makes mitigation look simple, and effectively takes concerns about ecological uncertainty (discussed in the previous chapters) off the table.

Second, in narrowing equivalence and thus eliminating concerns about ecological uncertainty, the definition of stream credits removes or sharply reduces most of the other forms of uncertainty discussed in chapter 5. As long as a mitigation banker in North Carolina proposes and builds a channel that maintains its specified physical form over the monitoring period for the mitigation bank, they will have:

- Eliminated *regulatory and reputational uncertainty*, because they are conforming to the accepted standard of practice;
- Almost entirely eliminated *implementation and ecological uncertainty*, because designers in North Carolina have learned how to produce stable channels, and stability is considered the proxy for physical, chemical, and biological health;
- Reduced the physical component of *random uncertainty*, because the stabilization measures used are sufficiently robust to survive even extreme weather events; and thus
- Reduced their *financial uncertainty* considerably.

The only substantial sources of uncertainty mitigation bankers in North Carolina still face, given how regulators define stream credits, are finding and acquiring rights to appropriate sites, and finding buyers for their credits. For their part, North Carolina regulators' uncertainties and risks are also drastically reduced, as are those of permittees, investors, and designers. In fact, the only actors whose uncertainties are not dramatically reduced with this simplified credit definition are scientists since they do not consider stability to be a proxy for the overall chemical, biological, or physical health of a stream.

And third, the definition creates two clear economic incentives for where mitigation bankers do their work and how they design their projects. The first incentive is that mitigation projects will be preferentially located in small streams. Rosgen's classification system is scale-neutral, meaning that streams in the same category can be fairly different sizes. Restoring a small stream in most cases is far cheaper than restoring a larger one based on simple logistical challenges of working in larger systems (e.g., more earth moving is required, larger flows must be diverted to allow construction work), thus producing higher profits for bankers. So defining stream credits by Rosgen classification creates the incentive to restore the smaller streams in a particular category. This preference for restoring smaller systems is reinforced by the fact that in any stream network, the majority of stream length is accounted for by the smallest streams: if you were to randomly put your finger on a map, you would be far more likely to be on (or near) a very small stream than a large river. Thus, impacts from permittees should, on average, be affecting smaller streams rather than larger ones (figure 7.1), another reason we would expect stream mitigation banks to preferentially locate to smaller streams.

North Carolina's definition of stream credits by the linear foot resulted in the second incentive, to maximize the sinuosity of restored channels far beyond what might be found in streams restored for nonmarket purposes (e.g. for grants, recreation in parks, etc.). A stream designer can alter just about any physical aspect of a stream channel, including sinuosity (figure 7.2). Increasing sinuosity would increase the total length of restored stream, thus maximizing the credits generated from a given property. Altering sinuosity (or any other physical feature) beyond what a site would naturally accommodate in order to increase the number of credits generated, and thus profits, is referred to in mitigation banking as *credit chasing*.

However, among other consequences, dramatically (or over-) increasing stream sinuosity also increases the potential for project failure. Highly sinuous curves increase hydraulic force on the outside of meander bends, thus increasing the chances that they will erode rapidly (figure 7.2).[7]

These purely market-based incentives created by how stream credits were defined in North Carolina (and in the many Corps districts whose

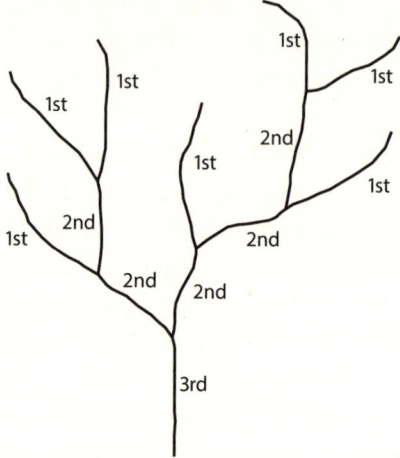

Figure 7.1
Stream order designation in a watershed, according to the Horton-Strahler approach. (For a description and set of schematic examples of different stream orders, see Knighton 1998, 9–12.) Typically, the smallest "fingertip" tributaries are designated as order 1; the junction of two streams order x forms a downstream reach of order $x + 1$. For instance, where two 1st order streams join, the downstream reach is designated a 2nd order stream (or similarly, where two 2nd order streams join, the downstream reach is designated a 3rd order stream). However, where a 1st and 2nd order stream join, the downstream reach remains designated a 2nd order stream. One limitation of the typical stream-ordering approach is what to do with intermittent tributaries; now these are often designated as "0th order" streams.

policies and practices draw from that definition) made a particular set of undesirable material outcomes very likely: lots of small, highly sinuous streams restored for mitigation that failed in extreme weather events. What actually happened was surprisingly counter to these incentives built into how stream credits were defined, however, for reasons chapters 5 and 6 help us understand.

What Actually Got Built

The first of these incentives suggested that we would find a disproportionate percentage of mitigation banking projects in the smallest drainage basins to take advantage of lower costs. To test this, we compared the drainage basin

The Streams That Mitigation Banking Creates

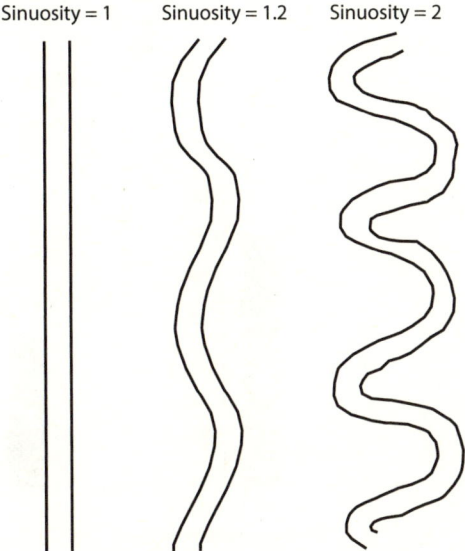

Figure 7.2
Sinuosity is the ratio of stream length divided by straight-line length. A perfectly straight channel will have a sinuosity of 1; a stream that takes twice the length of a straight-line path will have a sinuosity of 2. Taking a perfectly straight stream and rebuilding it with a sinuosity of 1.2 will increase the stream length, and thus the number of stream credits the site produces, by 20 percent; increasing the sinuosity to 2 will double the stream length and credits.

size of streams restored for mitigation banking to that of streams restored for other purposes, and also to the frequency of occurrence of drainage basins of different sizes across the North Carolina landscape (as revealed by our random sample).

It turned out that a large number of mitigation banks did indeed locate on small, headwater streams (figure 7.3), although the percentage of mitigation projects on headwater streams (0–1 km^2) was nearly representative of the percentage of headwater streams present on the landscape in general. The largest group of mitigation projects, however, were located on somewhat larger, second order streams. While the economic incentive to restore small streams was clearly visible, the effect was not as strong as we expected.

A much clearer finding was that streams restored for non-mitigation purposes, such as those funded by grants, were skewed toward larger streams

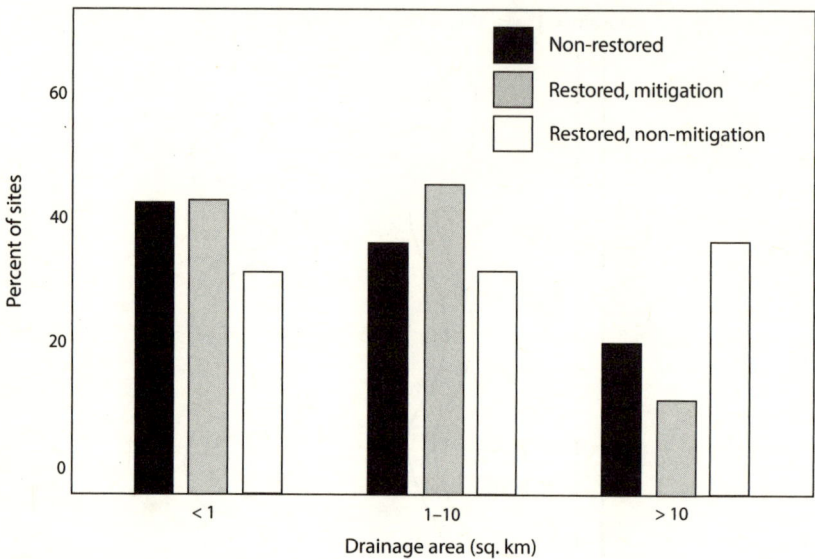

Figure 7.3
Project location in the watershed. The smallest category typically corresponds with 0th, 1st, and in some case 2nd order streams; the middle category (1–10 km^2) typically contains 2nd and smaller 3rd order streams; the largest category (> 10 km^2) typically contains 3rd order and above streams.

(figure 7.3). Most likely, this was because restoration project managers had the site handed to them; funding was available to restore a particular stream at a particular place (e.g., a county park, or conservation land), whereas finding a site for the mitigation bank was part of the project. We might think of this as the result of restoration for mitigation being "we need to restore *a* stream" and grant-based restoration being "we need to restore *that* stream."

While mitigation bankers were siting projects somewhat consistently with economic incentives, what they built in terms of sinuosity was notably inconsistent with economic incentives: bankers were not chasing credits by increasing sinuosity (figure 7.4). While there were statistically significant differences between the typical sinuosity of streams restored for mitigation and non-mitigation purposes, those differences were not large (1.24 for mitigation vs. 1.18 for non-mitigation). That is, if 1,000 feet of stream was restored, then a typical non-mitigation restoration project would generate a stream that was 1,180 feet long, whereas a mitigation project would generate one

The Streams That Mitigation Banking Creates

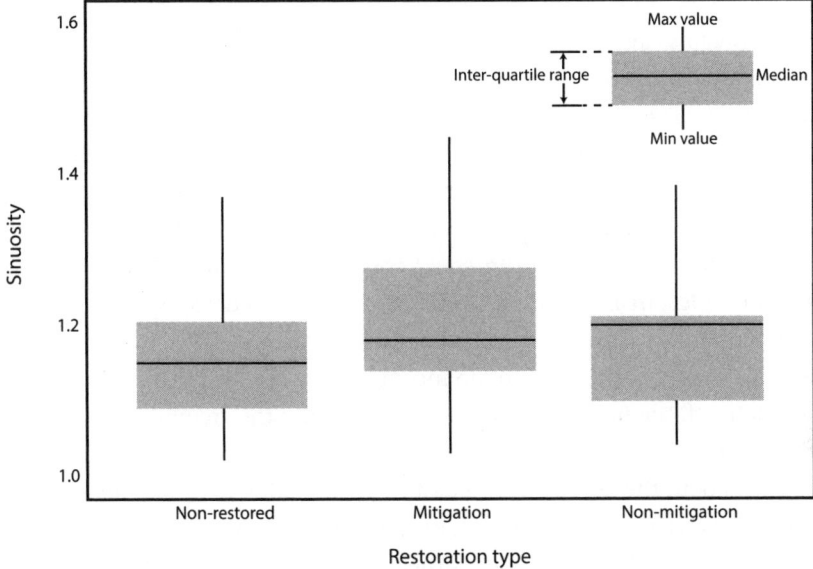

Figure 7.4
Sinuosities of stream reaches by type of restoration. Each box and whisker shows the range of sinuosities for all stream reaches of a particular restoration type; the horizontal lines indicate median value, the boxes indicate inter-quartile range, and the whiskers indicate range of values (maximum and minimum).

1,240 feet long, generating only an additional 60 feet of stream length. Based on stream mitigation credit prices during this period of time (approximately $300 per credit, or linear foot of stream; as of this writing, prices are substantially higher than when the projects surveyed were originally constructed), the slight increase in sinuosity used for mitigation vs. non-mitigation would only have increased revenue by $18,000. If mitigation bankers were changing their design to produce additional revenue, they were not generating much. For comparison, if stream designers had used a sinuosity of 1.50, which would have been at the upper range of a reasonable design,[8] it would have generated $96,000 in extra revenue for the same 1,000 feet of stream. Thus, overall, our data suggest that streams were not being designed differently for the market than they would have been otherwise.

What was going on here? Why were the very clear economic incentives built into the definition of stream credits in North Carolina not visible on the hydroscape? Perplexed, we went back to our interviewees to ask.

The preferential siting of mitigation projects on 2nd rather than 1st order streams (figure 7.3) turned out to be a rational response to aspects of the stream mitigation banking regulatory market not visible in the credit definition alone. In setting up the market, regulators allowed mitigation projects to compensate for impacts to streams of roughly comparable size: the order of the mitigation stream can be within their own stream order and those immediately above or below. That means that while a mitigation project on a 2nd order stream could compensate for impacts to 1st, 2nd, and 3rd order streams, a mitigation project on a 1st order stream could only compensate for impacts to 1st and 2nd order streams. Thus, while bankers were following a clear economic incentive in how the mitigation market was defined, the incentive was not visible if only the credit definition was considered.

How about the lack of credit chasing by designing over-sinuous streams (figure 7.4)? Here the ubiquity of Rosgen's Natural Channel Design approach to restoration in North Carolina turned out to be key. Restoration designers were, to a person, adamant that they used the same design approach (Natural Channel Design) for any project, regardless of whether it was funded via mitigation or grants. In the words of one designer:

> When it comes down to core design work, if you take two sites: Farm A and Farm B. They are both cattle farms, they are both 500 acres, they both have 12,000 feet of streams on them, and one is funded via mitigation and one is funded via grants. When it comes down to how are you going to look at the existing conditions, you know, assuming the goal is ultimate restoration as much as possible and assuming the budget is fairly reasonable on both, then our goal is going to be go to through the same design process that we would go through with any site . . . and ultimately aim for the same end result, which [is] the highest level of lift that we can accomplish on it.[9]

There were several reasons for this refusal to pursue the obvious economic incentive to make channels more sinuous. First, the designers, like almost everyone else in the stream restoration community, care deeply about stream health and would see a design that obviously degraded a stream reach in order to maximize profit as professionally and environmentally unacceptable. Second, because the broader stream restoration community in North Carolina (including not just designers but also funders, regulators, and others) strongly espoused Natural Channel Design, any proposed project that visibly departed from that approach's specified ranges

The Streams That Mitigation Banking Creates 131

of sinuosity would be obvious credit chasing, and thus subject to immediate regulatory crackdown, with long-term implications for that restoration designer's professional reputation. And finally, credit chasing via increased sinuosity would likely result in very visibly failing restoration projects. In one designer's words:

> I've seen people try to maximize their length.... You know, if credit is tied to footage, then add as much footage as they can and put in a lot of sinuosity. However, I think you have to weight that with if you get too far outside of your design parameters... you risk failure. To me that risk is not worth the reward of the additional credit. Nature will let you know if you make that mistake! (*laughs*) You'd have to go back and make that repair [or lose the credits].... The market kind of has a way to self-correct itself... if you're being a little greedy on the front end, as far as trying to push the site beyond what credits it can really yield.[10]

Our interview data made clear that for a range of reasons, including the risk of visibly violating professional norms, mitigation bankers were not altering their designs to maximize sinuosity (and thus the number of credits) in response to the economic incentives inherent in the definition of stream credits in North Carolina. Instead, bankers were maximizing channel length, and thus profits, within the market rules by restoring tributaries in the distal headwater reaches of a watershed.

This first became apparent in interviews, when both mitigation bankers and restoration designers pointed us to the physical implications of the real estate market and the difficulty and expense of procuring mitigation sites. As described in chapters 5 and 6, there are significant economies of scale in developing longer restoration projects, so mitigation bankers strive to offset the upfront costs of obtaining rights to any property (not to mention design work and permitting) by producing a larger number of credits. For example, one mitigation banker explained:

> To do a mitigation project, you have got to do a mitigation plan, you have got to do all your monitoring, you have to got to do your permitting, you have got to get a conservation easement. All these things have a lot of fixed cost to them, and so you really need your project to be of a certain size... so you can spread those fixed costs over more credits or more length.[11]

In the most upstream reaches of a watershed, there will be many small, 1st order streams in a fairly small area (and likely a larger number of 0th order intermittent streams), but far fewer larger 2nd order ones; that is, there can be many 1st order streams and possibly a 2nd order stream. But it is less likely that there will be a 3rd order stream, and if one is present, its length will likely be quite limited. From a mitigation banker's perspective, that means that unlike downstream reaches of a watershed, in the headwaters there could be many small streams on a single land parcel (making the process of developing a mitigation bank much easier and less expensive since bankers would only need to negotiate with one landowner). Mitigation bankers made use of this simple physiographic feature by restoring not only the main stem of a stream, but also any available tributary (e.g., figure 7.5).[12] Basically, any flowing waterway on a parcel of land would be a restoration target for a mitigation banker, and working in the headwaters ensures many more opportunities in a small area.

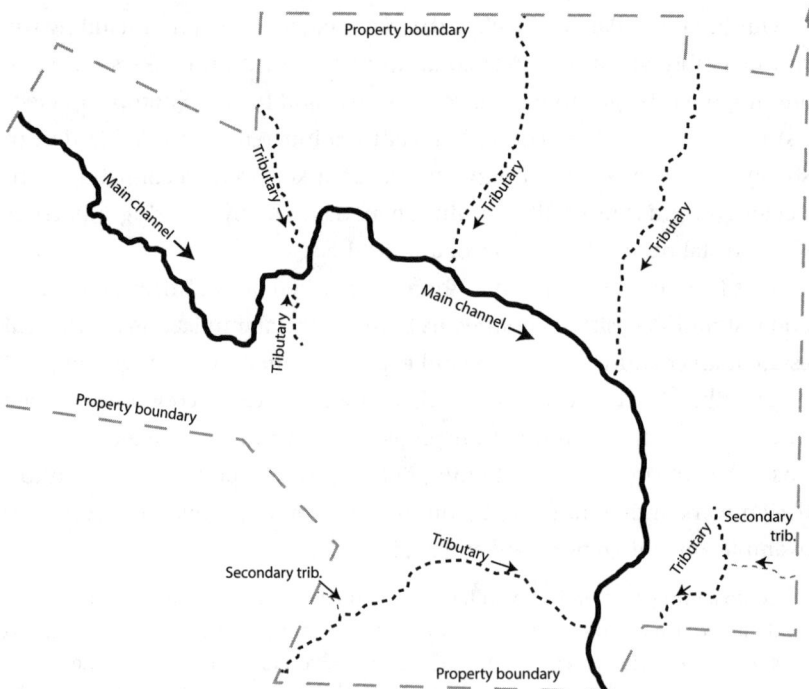

Figure 7.5
Site map for a mitigation banking project, showing restoration of the main channel and the tributaries. Note that all restoration work stopped at the property boundary, and that tributaries and secondary tributaries on the property were restored up to the edge of the property boundary.

The Streams That Mitigation Banking Creates

In contrast, non-mitigation restoration projects almost always concentrated exclusively on a particular stream and ignored any tributaries that fed into the project reach. The particular streams of interest for non-mitigation projects tended to be larger streams than were typically the focus for mitigation projects; non-mitigation projects restored the biggest, highest-order stream and ignored everything else. In contrast, by restoring so many of the small tributaries on a site, mitigation bankers maximized project length, and thus credits and profits. But bankers did so through careful site selection (and maximizing use of available streams and tributaries on that site) rather than through maximizing sinuosity. This was, in effect, a different form of credit chasing, one that conformed to the market rules for stream mitigation banking.

When we showed these results to our interview subjects in a subsequent round of fieldwork, they confirmed this as an obvious and accepted facet of mitigation projects. The surprise for them was that non-mitigation projects did not address tributaries! As several people noted, if you want to control what happens in the reach of stream you are restoring, geomorphically and ecologically, you are better off controlling everything that flows into it. Looking at a version of figure 7.5, for example, one mitigation banker said:

> I want to get everything [mainstem and tributaries]. I want at the end of the day, when I'm done with that project, I want to say every linear foot of stream or close to it, is under protection, or is being fixed. Because if you just do that one [main stem] site and you leave this trib and this trib and this trib [*pointing to tributaries shown in the figure*], you've got stuff coming right [in], you don't have control. I mean that's my goal, on every project we can. Now a lot of times you're too far down in the watershed and there's no way. But for mitigation projects, that's a big reason why we somewhat start up towards the headwaters, because you really want to have control of what's coming onto your main site. Partially because it feels like a better project [ecologically], it feels more holistic.[13]

This banker is quite right: restoring streams should be more effective when the upstream watershed is also restored. This could be a fortuitous ecological consequence of economically rational decisions (although for reasons we will discuss, the actual effect is likely to be far less positive).

These were all reasons for working in the headwaters of a watershed and increasing sinuosity somewhat (yet apparently not too much). But they do not explain the most striking feature of the mitigation hydroscape: the symmetrical sine wave channels with which we began this book.

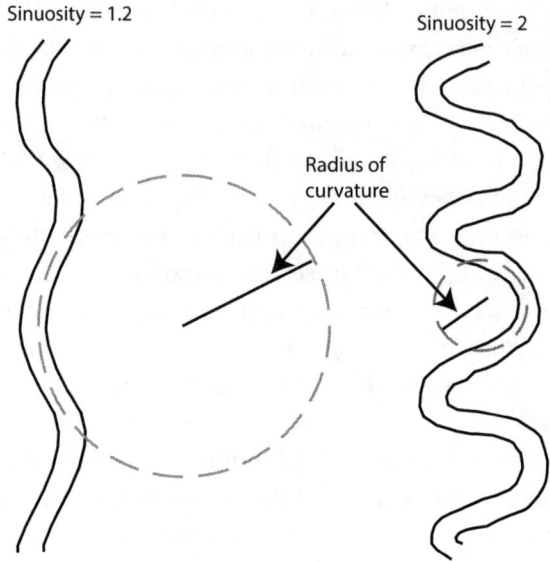

Figure 7.6
Radius of curvature is a measure of the tightness of a meander bend. A large radius of curvature indicates a sweeping meander bend and typically is associated with a low sinuosity channel. A low radius of curvature indicates tight meander bends, and thus, higher sinuosity. Most natural channels will have many different sizes of meander bends, and therefore a wide range of radii of curvature in a single stream reach.

Sine Waves and Stability

One of the most characteristic features of a river is its meandering, sinuous form. Scientists have come up with all manner of metrics to describe and quantify the features of a meander. The *radius of curvature* describes the relative tightness of a meander bed in a river or stream (figure 7.6). A sharp bend has a small radius of curvature, while a gradual bend has a large one. What we found was that while unrestored streams had a very broad range of variation in radii of curvature, typically stretching over multiple orders of magnitude, streams restored for any purpose typically had much less variation, with radii of curvature that stretched across only one or two orders of magnitude (figure 7.7). This is a quantitative way of saying that unrestored streams have meander features that vary a lot; they are messy. In contrast, streams restored for mitigation typically had little variation. Moreover, the curves put in restored streams were very similar for the

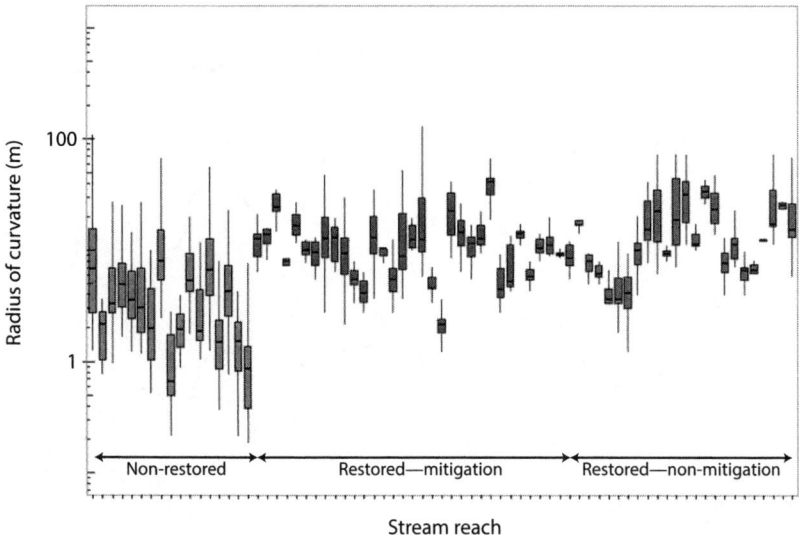

Figure 7.7
Radii of curvature within individual project sites (note logarithmic scale on y-axis). Each box and whisker shows the range of radii within a particular stream reach with the horizontal line indicating median value for the entire stream reach, the box indicating inter-quartile, and whiskers indicating range of values (maximum and minimum). Note that non-restored stream reaches generally had lower median values than restored streams, and much broader range of values overall.

entire reach whether they were restored for mitigation or non-mitigation: they all looked the same. Streams restored for any reason were far more uniform than unrestored streams, dominated by large gradual curves. The end result was that restored streams had more in common with sine waves than with the far more unpredictable and highly variable forms of unrestored streams (figure 7.8).

What explains such homogenized stream forms? Unlike with the similarities in sinuosity in streams restored for mitigation and non-mitigation purposes, the answer does not lie in Natural Channel Design.[14] Instead, there are relatively idiosyncratic reasons that came up in our interviews. For example, it is difficult to draw irregular curves in AutoCAD, the engineering software that is used by most design firms. Also, the engineers sheepishly admitted that they preferred symmetry aesthetically, and because it made it easier to calculate some important parameters in their analysis and designs:

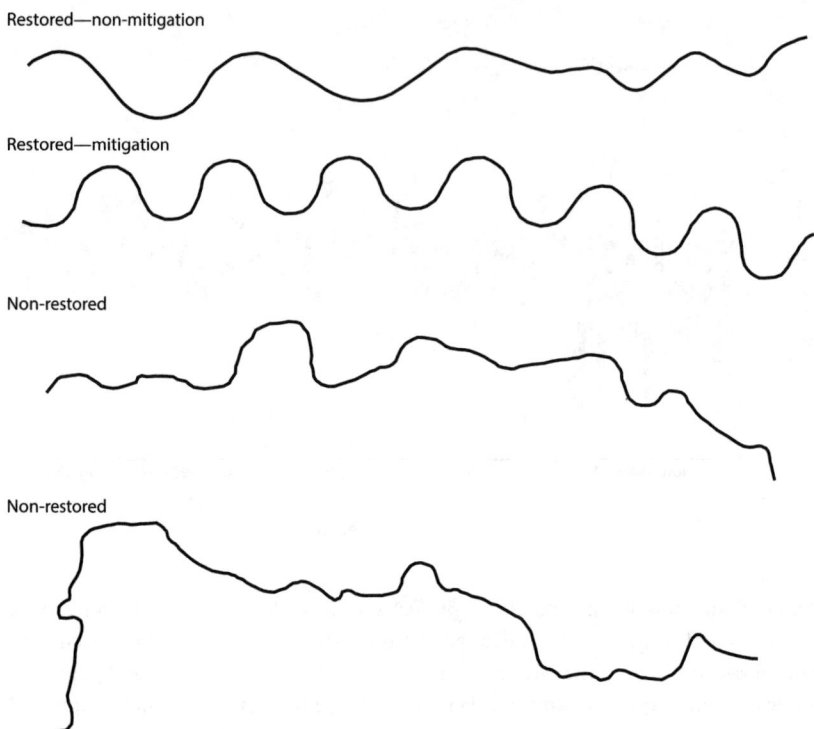

Figure 7.8
Channel center-lines of two restored and two non-restored channels. Note the regular pattern of the restored channels, and the unregular pattern of the non-restored channels. There was a bridge crossing in the lower portion of the restored, non-mitigation channel (where the straighter section of channel appears).

it is easier to say that the shear stress of a particular design is 7 than it is to say that the shear stress varies from one bend to the next. But these reasons apply just as much to streams restored via grant money as to streams restored for mitigation.

For mitigation banks in North Carolina, however, the economic incentives not only encouraged, but also overdetermined these exceedingly uniform channels because the success criteria for mitigation projects were defined in terms of physical stability; to earn their credits, channels restored for mitigation needed to stay where they were put.[15] That meant that the only ball off which bankers could not take their eye was channel stability. And of all the channel forms that optimize stability while increasing stream length, homogenization of sweeping, uniform meander bends is perhaps the easiest and most certain.[16]

In interviews, bankers consistently emphasized the fact that mitigation projects in North Carolina were monitored for seven years (or five years for some of the earlier projects). If a channel eroded significantly during that window, the regulator certifying the bank would reduce the number of credits that the project could generate, and fewer credits would mean less profit. Sharp and irregular curves are more likely to erode and migrate.[17] By contrast, broad, smooth, regular curves are, from a purely hydraulic perspective, more stable. This incentive for stability led to the hydroscape we found: gradual, sometimes disconcertingly symmetrical curves with structural controls on the outside of meander bends to more firmly hold them in place.

This is notably inconsistent with the natural dynamics of rivers and streams. Meanders imply (somewhat tautologically) the movement of meandering. Yet the very movement that creates the channel form is considered (via the regulations that set up the mitigation banking market) to be a sign of failure. In designing meanders that simultaneously prevented movement and ensured stability, this political-economic system led to oddly homogenous streams: an artificial hydroscape bearing the signature of regulation rather than natural processes. Stream designers knew that this inconsistency existed, yet they had a powerful economic incentive to create a channel that did not move:

> What is stable, and what is . . . the channel migrating naturally at some space and time across the landscape in its sort of natural range? . . . [I]f you have credits at risk, then you probably have a little bit more fear of those credits being dinged because, "Oh my gosh, there's some erosion!" Or, "There's some aggradation!" Or whatever would happen if you . . . tried to go the high end of the range [of sinuosity] and you actually got outside of it and you caused a little instability in that bank, or a little bit of aggradation in that riffle, or whatever the consequence of the geomorphic response to it would be.[18]

The economic incentive for channels that were explicitly designed to not move came from the requirements of regulators who, ironically, were likewise aware of this potential overemphasis on stability. As one said in an interview, "mitigation . . . in North Carolina is based on a lot of geomorphic measurements and otherwise to gain stability. Stability equals success."[19] Expanding on this blunt declaration, another regulator explained:

When we wrote these [stream mitigation guidelines] we didn't have ... good watershed assessment tools, we didn't have good stream assessment tools. And so a lot of decisions were made purely based on what the stream appeared to look like, stability-wise, ... as a kind of proxy. And that can work in a lot of cases. So for example, you go out and look at a channel and it's deeply incised ... so it's not connected with the floodplain ... and it has lots of erosion ... at least in the early days and still somewhat today is—people use that as a basis for saying, "Wow, we can make that stream better."[20]

From the bankers' and designers' point of view, this meant that stability was the only target that mattered:

So the bar in North Carolina pretty much up to current [times] ... was that the channel ... is going to be stable and for that monitoring period it's not going to move. There's going to be zero bank erosion, there's going to be no migration, there's going to be no incision. And so with those success criteria in mind I think there very well could be a tendency to design more conservatively.... It's how conservative you want to be is really the way I would phrase it, and where you've got success criteria and you or your client want—it really doesn't make a difference because it's your reputation either way—but when somebody is financially on the line for that system performing and somebody is going to have a scorecard in year five or seven when you did it or didn't do it, you know, that adds quite a bit of scrutiny to the process.[21]

Returning, then, to the central question of this chapter, to what extent do the economic incentives built into the stream mitigation market shape the hydroscape created?

In some ways, mitigation bankers were not following the most obvious economic incentives built into stream credit definitions in terms of how they design their restored streams. Homogenization and sweeping meander bends, to take one notable example, produced relatively few credits compared to how many could be generated by maximizing sinuosity. This apparent departure from economic rationality was because bankers were responding not just to credit definitions, but also to the rules of the mitigation market overall (which is why chapters 5 and 6 did not focus only on how stream credits are defined).

The entire portfolio of uncertainties conditioned the particular ways bankers behaved. As noted in chapter 6, any Mitigation Banking Instrument proposing an artificially high sinuosity would have faced additional scrutiny from regulators, and if it was too high the proposed design would simply be rejected (*regulatory uncertainty*), costing the banker a great deal of extra money to redesign the project (*financial uncertainty*). If somehow the project was approved, chances were very high that the suspect meander bends—with higher sinuosity and associated erosion potential—would fail (*implementation uncertainty*) if a significant storm happened to occur soon after construction (*random uncertainty*), producing what to a regulator would be obvious ecological degradation and thus reduced credits (*ecological and financial uncertainty*). This would in turn tarnish the reputation of the banker as being overly profiteering and the designer as being incompetent, setting them up for additional scrutiny on any future projects from regulators now highly suspicious of their motives (*reputational uncertainty*). Given that bankers were able to maximize credits in other ways that kept them firmly within the market rules (by restoring tributaries as well as main stems, and by focusing on channel reconfiguration rather than less interventionist approaches), there was little point in courting the risks associated with pursuing the economic incentive to create over-sinuous channels.

Thus, what initially appeared to be a perplexing failure by stream mitigation bankers to behave with economic rationality was instead a rational, if nuanced, response to the overall market rules and to the way questions of equivalence and uncertainty were handled in stream mitigation banking. And the end result of what was built on the hydroscape—eerily uniform, sweeping meander bends along streams, and many tributaries, clustered in the headwaters of rural areas—was likewise a system designed to pass the particular tests set by regulators while still generating profits.

Conclusion: The Market Matters

With these data, what can we say about the physical impacts of the way regulators in North Carolina have chosen to define stream credits, and thus manage equivalence and uncertainty? The increased project length resulting from the restoration of both main stem reaches and tributaries in stream mitigation projects (as opposed to stream restoration projects funded through other sources) appears at first glance to be highly positive. According to ecological theory, both of these things are more likely to produce a positive ecological impact; headwater streams are critically important for water quality throughout a watershed,[22] and there are ecologies of scale (i.e., processes should accrue disproportionately with the size of restoration project).[23] This could suggest that stream mitigation banking (as an instrument of aquatic ecosystem restoration) is actually better for the ecological health of fluvial systems than previous forms of non-market-based environmental management because it shifts restoration to headwaters and results in larger restoration projects.

There is a very substantive caveat here, however: *it is not at all clear that current stream restoration practices actually work* (see chapter 3). To date, most types of stream restoration (with notable exceptions such as the removal of dams, culverts, and other human-built barriers), have had limited success for ecological recovery.[24] Channel stabilization and reconstruction, the restoration approach privileged by the fossilization of late 1990s stream restoration science in mitigation market rules has produced a worrisome lack of measurable response. Channel reconfiguration appears to be surprisingly ineffective for improving water quality, flood attenuation, or macroinvertebrate communities, among other characteristics.[25]

There are many reasons for this lack of effectiveness. Most notably, while channel instability can exacerbate ecological degradation, channel stability cannot, in and of itself, improve the ecological condition of a stream because any stream is a product of its watershed. That is, any stream integrates its upstream watershed, which means that hydrologic and ecological impacts across the watershed will dominate any given stream reach, no matter how perfectly it has been reconfigured. In addition, many of the ecological gains we expect from restored streams—reduced water temperature, nutrient retention, attenuated hydrographs—require considerable lengths of stream to achieve over significant periods of time, far beyond current practice. Even relatively long restoration projects by today's standards (e.g., up to a mile) are insufficient to produce significant ecological improvements, let alone in measurable amounts. In sum, restoration typically has been unsuccessful in ecological terms because even a relatively long reach of restored stream is minor in comparison to the scale of watershed disturbance or length of stream network.

This complicates the ability of markets for ecosystem services to improve actual stream health. If the types of restoration privileged in mitigation banking were effective for generating ecological outcomes, then there would be benefits to longer project lengths and restoring tributaries. But they are not. *Rather than improving conservation outcomes, market-based approaches to streams are simply expanding the scope of an ineffective management practice.*

At least in the case of stream mitigation banking, the consequence of implementing an ecosystem service market is continuity not radical change. Implementing an ecosystem service market is doing very little to streams that was not already happening to them anyway, in terms of the hydroscape produced. Market-based approaches have not stopped development that damages fluvial systems, which is continuing despite the explicit intention of the Clean Water Act to prevent it. Further, while there are notable differences between stream restoration conducted for market and non-market purposes (e.g., location), it is not clear how much those differences matter given the overall uncertainty of restoration practice. The homogenization of channel form, which has only gotten likelier with mitigation banking, is more consequential for stream ecosystem health. Credit markets for streams thus appear to be intensifying trends that were in place under an earlier command-and-control implementation regime for the Clean Water Act rather than marking an inflection point that sends environmental conservation off in a significantly new direction, as advocates for ecosystem service markets suggest.

One clear lesson from this empirical work is that when markets are used as an instrument for regulation, the metrics (including not only credit definitions but also the broader infrastructure of market rules that support them) through which regulators address issues of equivalence and uncertainty really, really matter. Most everyone involved in stream mitigation banking—regulators, bankers, designers, and scientists—was aware that channel stability was at best an inadequate measure of the health of naturally dynamic systems, and at worst actively counter-productive. Yet stability remained the centerpiece of the regulatory market, so stability-maximizing streams were what got designed, permitted, and constructed.

The good news is that if the metrics changed, it is very likely that stream mitigation banking practice would change, too. As one scientist pointed out:

> If the regulatory agencies would ask the consulting firms that actually go out there and do the work to pay attention to specific goals [things could change]. . . . [Consultants] are smart people. I mean they know what they are doing. If they were given those types of challenges, streams could be built and those goals could be met, but in the past those regulatory agencies have just kind of dwelt on things like Natural Channel Design and reattaching the stream to its floodplain and blah, blah, blah, blah. That is just not what the stream is. It is much, much more than that.[26]

The scientist went on to say:

> My big gripe is that here in North Carolina and perhaps in the Southeast we are not good at goal setting. If we tell a construction company that their goal in this project is to improve water quality and we monitor for it and we actually look at nutrient levels or whatever, we can do that. If we told the construction company we want to build a small stream in the mountains here in North Carolina and make the stream so that it supplies habitat for the reproduction of brook trout, they will do it. They will do that, but you got to tell them. You got to set that goal, because if you don't do that—if you are not creative about goals than it is just the same old mitigation game.[27]

This then indicates the primacy of the metrics, which convert the goals of MES into tangible material outcomes. Using markets only affects the practice of restoration insomuch as regulators allow it. Instead of stability, regulators could demand that markets produce restored streams that provide specific services that actually improve stream condition and function, even if they are more difficult to achieve (e.g., nitrogen retention, or diverse fish populations), but this would dramatically decrease the potential for a robust market in stream credits. Thus, stream regulators adapted their demands to the reality of mitigation markets through the use of highly simplified, proxy-driven metrics.

This has had profound consequences on stream ecosystems. Once the metrics were set, markets scaled up approved practices dramatically, with initial guidance documents adapted and adopted across much of the United States. Most important, the market delivered exactly the commodity required by regulators: in this case, stable streams. Credit producers (e.g., mitigation bankers) found ways to increase the profitability of creating stable streams, such as restoring not just the main stems, but also tributaries. But market participants did not alter their practices to increase ecological lift because there was no incentive to do so. *In a regulatory market, whatever regulators deem to be the goal —via metrics—is what gets delivered.*

If regulators want some other end result from the ecosystem service market for streams, they will need to change the metrics, but that may be easier said than done. As a different scientist ruefully observed:

> It's really hard for regulators . . . [to] change anything. The box is so small, that restoration is allowed to operate in. . . . [W]hy did these regulations get locked in in such a restricted way so quickly? It's kind of an amazing, um—you think about how hard it would be to get a set of regulations that you're really promoting in place. How did that happen in this case? And it's now so hard to change them.[28]

Stream mitigation regulations are hard to change because there are many forces reinforcing the status quo. First, keeping success criteria centered on stability creates a metric that is relatively simple and fast to measure and monitor, thus accommodating the very real time and funding constraints that regulators face. If credit definitions and success criteria expanded to include diversity of aquatic insects, for example, it would require far more skill, money, and time to measure compliance: to sustain equivalence, regulators would need to require assessment of insect diversity from impact sites as well as restoration sites. Such data would have to be collected, synthesized, reported, and inventoried, dramatically increasing the costs for impactors and bankers, and the effort of regulators across multiple programs. Moreover, regulators themselves argue that they are already stretched too thin with other responsibilities to give stream mitigation the attention it deserves. As one regulator in North Carolina explained in an interview:

> There's only so much time we can spend on each project. Our project managers may be looking at four or five sites in a day, and each site may have eight to ten streams that they're having to evaluate. . . . You try to imagine running an assessment that requires you to take our [survey] rods and tape measures and it's just not even . . . it's not going to happen.[29]

Or as another North Carolina regulator put it, "We defined rapid as taking no more than fifteen minutes. Because that is how much time we have."[30] If regulators are hard-pressed to complete even the most basic physical measurements of a channel, how would they find the additional time required to inventory and track an expanded range of success criteria, and adapt those criteria over time if needed? Simple considerations of practicality thus support the modest scope and blunt measures of current metrics.

The second force keeping the current system in place is that unlike most stream attributes, channel stability can be generated in isolation. With sufficient structural reinforcement, a restored stream can be made stable even if the upstream watershed is unstable and dynamic. Almost any other stream attribute, even one that is relatively straightforward to measure (e.g., water temperature or dissolved oxygen), would be far more difficult to control given the hydrologic connectivity of streams. Bluntly, improvements at any mitigation project are at the mercy of everyone upstream. Years of effort to improve species richness in a particular stream reach, for instance, might be wiped out by a farmer allowing cattle to graze in an upstream reach for a week, which would remove riparian vegetation (thus increasing stream temperatures) and release enormous amounts of fine sediment, both of which would decimate the viability of downstream aquatic communities. Similar changes due to urbanization (increased pollutants and thermal changes due to paved surfaces) would negate improvements driven by downstream restoration projects.

If mitigation bankers cannot control the external forces that affect the characteristics of their site, they cannot control whether they will be able to meet their legal success criteria and produce stream credits they can sell. This drastically increases the uncertainty for a mitigation banker, likely preempting their willingness to enter the market altogether. As one scientist noted, "It's a whole lot harder to have success when you have to go beyond making a shape on the landscape. It's just hard to do. It's *really* hard to do" (*laughs ruefully*).[31] Fixing a stream physically in place through the liberal use of rock, rootwads, and aggressive geoengineering is something that mitigation bankers can ensure at the individual site level, increasing their certainty that their success will depend largely on actions under their own control.

The third powerful force making it difficult to change stream mitigation banking metrics is this: once you open the door to a fuller accounting of equivalence, where do you stop? The slope is slippery, and it goes down a long, long way into measures of equivalence so nuanced that no site could ever really compensate for another, and no market could function (as discussed in chapter 2). Even assuming you could find a legally and scientifically defensible place to stop part way down the slope, how would you then cope with the resulting uncertainty, which would rise in lockstep with the complexity of the measure of equivalence? It is not at all clear that the market in stream credits could function with more nuanced credit definitions.[32]

Given these very substantive barriers, why is expanding the metrics of stream credits even being considered? The simple answer: because most actors involved would benefit. Scientists could increasingly specify what aspects of streams are functioning at both impact and compensation sites; conservation advocates could use greater precision to argue that what was being lost was not being fully compensated (thus reducing impacts altogether), or could make compensation increasingly expensive; and regulators could articulate with greater certainty how they were strictly and precisely enforcing the demands of the Clean Water Act. Meanwhile, more precise metrics would increase the number of categories of stream credits (e.g., temperature, nitrogen retention, dissolved oxygen), which would increase the number of potential markets for mitigation bankers (thicken the market), thus drawing in bankers and investors alike; this would increase the demand for designers who could custom-design streams for the myriad functions being bought and sold.

The primary force pushing back on expanding metrics is sheer practicability: regulatory capacity, uncertainty about upstream changes, and the potential proliferation of hair-splitting metrics in the future all are powerful sources of uncertainty protecting the status quo. And this is one of the most significant lessons from the robust market for stream mitigation: *once it is set up and operating, an ecosystem service market is very difficult to change.*

There are multiple actors, many of them strange bedfellows indeed, who advocate for the status quo even though it does not optimize any of their particular interests. Scientists certainly would not look at the streams produced by mitigation banking and view them to be natural, or functionally restored. Bankers might want the streams to be far more sinuous to generate more credits, and regulators would want them to be clearly recovering functions of interest, particularly water quality. While no one considers the streams restored under mitigation banking ideal, almost all the actors involved can live with them. And with no concerted effort to change it, mitigation banking continues to produce regulated, negotiated, physically stable, and homogenous streams.

The limitations of relying so strongly on stability are broadly apparent. All the participants in stream markets recognize the shortcomings of the existing system, but they have failed to push forward any changes that would benefit their particular interests. The question now is whether the crucial issues laid out in this chapter can be addressed in a way that allows the market in stream credits to continue functioning. In the final chapter of this book, we explore what this failure to act means not only for stream mitigation, but also for the feasibility of MES as an approach to environmental conservation.

8 Conclusion: Can Markets for Ecosystem Services Fix Conservation?

Markets for ecosystem services, along with other market-based approaches to environmental protection at the root of the nascent restoration economy, have been a central part of conservation and restoration thinking for decades. Scattered academic and think tank research in the 1970s and 1980s coalesced in the late 1990s into an influential intellectual and policy framework that recast markets as environmental saviors. What was less clear was exactly how markets would do that. The core assumption of this framework was that if natural ecosystems were economically valued, they would be better protected via preservation or, in many cases, restoration. But this left some big issues unaddressed, three in particular.

First, the MES paradigm focused on the mechanism for improved conservation—markets—but had (and still has) startlingly little to say about the *ecological goal* beyond generalities of preventing ecosystem loss. What did proponents of MES hope to achieve? To restore previous ecological structures and functions? To maximize ecosystem services? To create new ecosystems better suited to changing climates and increasing human impacts? To prevent extinctions? The entire enterprise was premised on markets amplifying the amount of restoration without addressing what that restoration should achieve biophysically.

A second crucial but overlooked issue was *economic*: how the practicalities of creating an ecosystem service market might distort its intended function. MES are regulatory markets: they do not spontaneously emerge; they are created, and with a great deal of intentionality. In the case of regulatory markets, that intentionality is focused on how to increase the efficiency of regulation. That focus on efficiency can produce some decidedly odd results that can undermine the economic (and environmental) goals of MES.

That brings us to a third consequential issue omitted from MES discussions then (and now): the scope of *regulation* needed for MES. Contrary to the assertions of MES advocates, does the introduction of markets actually alter what is protected by environmental regulation? Using MES requires converting ecosystems into something that can be sold. Regulators must develop approaches that ensure equivalence between the traded commodities so that the impacted ecosystem attributes are offset by the restored ecosystem attributes. Yet market forces also play a substantial role because no one will be willing to produce the commodity for sale in an ecosystem service market if there is too much uncertainty. Thus, to use markets, regulators must adapt their regulatory approach to draw in market participants, creating potential for the use of markets to alter which aspects of the environment have regulatory protection.

None of these issues were addressed clearly in early or even more recent work on MES, yet together they set the parameters for how well or poorly any particular ecosystem service market accomplishes what advocates claim it can do: better incentivize the conservation and restoration of the environment and its ecosystems. In the section that follows we examine how these three interrelated issues—ecological, economic, and regulatory—shape the environmental impacts of stream mitigation banking, the particular ecosystem service market we have followed throughout this book. We then return briefly to the examples of conservation banking and carbon sequestration introduced in chapter 2. We conclude with a discussion of what this means for MES as an approach to environmental conservation, and consider how stream mitigation banking might proceed from here.

What Markets for Ecosystem Services Do to and for the Environment?

The ecological results of stream mitigation banking are not inspiring. Current practices do a fine job of minimizing uncertainty and simplifying equivalence (and thus of facilitating the market). But because market rules in North Carolina and most of the United States fossilize a 1990s focus on channel form and stability, stream mitigation banking does not encourage approaches to restoration likely to maximize genuine ecological improvement. Instead, current market rules encourage weirdly symmetrical channels that produce little to nothing in the way of biological and chemical restoration, or even of broader physical improvements beyond channel

Conclusion

stability; impacts to the watershed upstream are nearly impossible to undo with downstream stream restoration, and a fairly robust and growing scientific literature now documents this reality.[1]

In most of the United States, the ecosystem service market for streams did not create a system of incentives in which high-functioning natural streams were protected (due to higher credit ratios for channel reconfiguration than for preservation of existing high-quality streams), nor did it create a system that produced dynamic, near-natural streams. Rather, this regulatory market created a system that enabled the further ecological degradation of existing natural (and already degraded) streams, and compensation for those impacts with the creation of stream types unlikely to provide much in the way of environmental improvement.[2]

In economic terms, mitigation banking seems a far cry from the (relatively) free market visions of its early proponents. As discussed in previous chapters, stream mitigation banking is based on credit definitions that have been highly simplified in part because of a lack of regulatory capacity to monitor more complex ecosystem attributes. By contrast, mitigation bankers would prefer a broader range of definitions so that they would have more kinds of credits to sell.[3] Further, there is no incentive for bankers to innovate in an attempt to produce better environmental outcomes because their customers are in the market to buy regulatory compliance, not ecological improvement. And contrary to the expectations of market proponents, mitigation banking does not produce less costly or more nimble discharge of regulatory obligations; the big advantage of mitigation banking is that it provides permit applicants the certainty that they will be able to comply with Section 404 of the Clean Water Act by writing a check, as discussed in chapter 4.

Finally, our analysis of stream mitigation banking suggests strongly that regulatory coverage has been reduced in order to make markets more robust. The Clean Water Act explicitly calls for protection of the biological, chemical, and physical condition of waters of the United States, but mitigation banking has narrowed this down to physical stability because that is easiest kind of credit for bankers to produce and regulators to monitor. That regulatory move greatly increases the appeal of producing stream credits for mitigation bankers, but it reduces the attributes of aquatic ecosystems being protected. The highly simplified credit definitions and success criteria across most of the United States create a robust market, but reduce the extent of regulatory protection under the Clean Water Act and its ecological efficacy.

Returning to our discussions of conservation banking and carbon sequestration from chapter 2, there are some notable similarities. Like mitigation banking, conservation banking uses very blunt metrics, leading to highly uncertain environmental outcomes. For example, by defining credits for red-cockaded woodpeckers based on acres of suitable habitat rather than number of breeding pairs, this ecosystem service market detaches endangered species protection from the species itself, and rests instead on the far less certain ecological improvement of providing habitat that individuals of that species could, in theory, use. However, because conservation banking is far more reliant on preservation of existing habitat than on restoration of degraded habitat, there is a much higher chance than in stream mitigation banking that the preserved habitat will have a wide range of secondary ecological benefits, even if the target species does not utilize it. In terms of the potential for distortion of regulatory markets, conservation banking is very similar to stream mitigation banking: neither operates as a "free" market because regulatory capacity and incentives to innovate are lacking.

Regulatory markets for carbon sequestration provide an instructive contrast, but also some notable parallels. The highly complex credit definitions mean that they are far more likely to produce what they are intended to produce: specified amounts of carbon sequestration with clear linkages to the permanence of that sequestration. These definitions have little to say about other environmental attributes (e.g., habitat for forest-dwelling animals), however, leading to the weirdly uniform pine plantations described in chapter 1, which likely have far fewer of the secondary benefits of natural forest ecosystems. As in stream mitigation and conservation banking, there is little incentive to innovate because buyers are in the market for regulatory compliance, not ecological improvement. But in the case of carbon markets, there seems to be far less impact from constraints on regulatory capacities. Finally, unlike either stream mitigation or conservation banking, the market for carbon sequestration does not seem to have produced any narrowing of environmental protection to enable a robust market. As a direct reflection of this, the market has not expanded to the degree initially envisioned or expected.

Advocates of MES assumed that increased economic valuation of natural ecosystems would lead to their preservation, or to the restoration of near-equal ecosystems. However, with the possible exception of conservation banking, markets for ecosystem services neither preserve nor produce the ecosystems they were intended to protect; they preserve or produce only the narrowly defined characteristics of those systems that are identified and captured by the metrics that regulators use at the time.

Because of this, MES incentivize and capitalize the creation of very particular ecosystems. Stream mitigation banking capitalizes the creation of stable, eerily uniformly meandering streams; such streams may harbor fish and invertebrates, but they may not. Conservation banks capitalize the creation or preservation of aspects of forests thought to be important for woodpeckers, which in turn leads to forests with particular characteristics that may harbor breeding pairs of woodpeckers, but they may not. Carbon markets capitalize the creation of tree plantations that sequester carbon, which may provide habitat for additional forest-dwelling fauna, but they may not.

The point is this: any ecosystem service market capitalizes the creation of whatever particular attributes regulators prioritize, which results in the creation of ecosystems containing those attributes. It appears that functional MES lead to the creation of bespoke, somewhat unnatural ecosystems. Thus, a critical finding of our research is that the MES paradigm has not led us where its advocates thought it would. *MES neither preserved nor restored nature as we understand it: complex, dynamic, interconnected, stochastic, and—frankly—messy.*

What Then Shall We Do?

Any scientist or environmentalist will likely find the current state of markets for ecosystem services highly unsatisfactory. Stream mitigation banking is producing fluvial systems that are not only starkly unnatural in form, but also provide little if any ecological benefit to offset the loss of streams impacted in development projects. To one of us (Lave), this suggests that MES have failed and should be discarded as a conservation approach; the other (Doyle) thinks that this outcome reflects how the regulators are implementing the market, and is not necessarily the fault of the market itself. We agree, however, that because stream mitigation banking is not going away any time soon, we must figure out how to do it better. We see two very different ways to move stream mitigation banking forward: increasing equivalence, or increasing uncertainty.

The first option would be to abandon the project of restoring natural conditions in favor of *maximizing equivalence* between a few key ecosystem services, or perhaps just one, at the impact and mitigation sites. This option typically yields what are referred to as *designer ecosystems*, or *function-specific ecosystems*.[4] Instead of wincing at the artificiality of obviously human-modified landscapes and hydroscapes, we would embrace artificiality and relinquish the idea of restoration as recreating the ecosystems that development destroys. The principles and practices for creating designer and function-specific ecosystems are still being developed, but this first option offers a much higher certainty of producing at least some limited environmental benefit than current stream mitigation practices do.

There are already examples of designer streams. For example, a range of stream designs has been developed for increasing the retention of nutrients, particularly nitrogen.[5] Whether through the growing practice of two-stage ditches or using flow-through wetlands (effectively converting a stream into a broad swale), these streams look far from natural, but are highly efficient at this particular ecosystem function. Another technique has been focused on designing stream features to force water into the hyporheic zone to either decrease water temperature or increase removal of pollutants. While still somewhat experimental, this can be done by installing artificial riffles or weirs (i.e., blockages) across the channel with particular dimensions and spacings, as well as by lining the subsurface portion of the riffles with rubber to force flow deeper into the subsurface.[6] A more extreme case could be the manipulation of the community of microorganisms to increase rates of desired biochemical processes, such as degradation of particular organic compounds.[7] This narrow focus on increasing equivalence by restoring a limited function or set of functions obviously is more complicated with ecological as opposed to chemical functions. It is impossible to produce breeding pairs and natural recruitment of juveniles of endangered salmon, for example, without addressing a wide range of stream attributes. But we can dump hatchery-raised fish into a stream reach and hope for the best.[8]

This first option of engineering stream characteristics around a particular function (e.g., temperature), and particularly using non-native materials (or beings, as with hatchery fish), is clearly moving stream restoration away from attempts to recreate the natural and instead toward the intentionally designed. The core rationale the techniques described above share is their insistence that rather than failing at attempts to recreate complex, dynamic

Conclusion

interconnected ecosystems, we would be better off doing what we're good at: exerting control to ensure at least some function-specific outcomes, and thus to increase equivalence between streams impacted and those restored under mitigation banking.

What would it look like to refocus stream mitigation banking—the science, policy, and market—on producing designer streams? In place of the current relatively homogenous credit definitions across the United States, it would involve developing a range of exactingly specified credit definitions, each of which would be focused on replacing a particularly important ecosystem service (or small set of services). Instead of treating channel form and stability as a proxy for general ecological uplift, regulators would specify the one or two ecosystem services mitigation banking projects needed to produce. In effect, it would be a low-risk, low-reward strategy. After all, it is likely easier (and also cheaper, given how expensive channel reconfiguration projects are) to design a flowing body of water in order to generate equivalent invertebrate habitat or temperature reduction if you are not being held to the standard that it needs to have anything else in common with an unmodified stream, or if you are not expected to produce both functions at the same site, but rather maximize habitat in one reach of stream, and optimize temperature reduction at another. Thus, we would be more likely to see actual ecological improvement than under mitigation banking today, but only within a very narrow range, and potentially only for a very specific set of attributes. The end result would likely be an accumulation of widely divergent stream types peppering the landscape: a 1,500-foot-wide swale (that optimizes nitrogen retention) flowing directly into a 2,500-foot reach of rubber-lined cascades that optimizes water temperature reduction. Watersheds would become heterogeneous at the entire network scale as these varied types of homogenous reaches were pieced together like function-optimizing Lego blocks.

The second option we envision would be to *maximize uncertainty* by rejecting the weirdly unnatural ecosystems that MES currently produce, and trying to create the conditions for messy, dynamic, complex ecosystems. Instead of exerting substantial human control to meet carefully specified credit definitions, this uncontrolled option would embrace and increase uncertainty in the hopes that more natural systems, and their attendant ecosystem benefits, might duplicate a wide range of conditions and functions lost at impact sites.

As with designer ecosystems, there are already precursors of this uncontrolled option in stream restoration, but it is almost nonexistent in mitigation banking. For example, some restorationists argue for the creation of self-forming channels, a form of restoration whereby an oversized valley is excavated and a channel (or in some cases a wetland) is allowed to form entirely on its own; the system is controlled only at its most extreme margins (e.g., at the edges of the valley), but otherwise is allowed to adjust itself to whatever form and function are possible. Bill Zeedyk has long promoted a slightly more interventionist form of stream restoration in the arid Southwest, in which brush is used to provide minimal guidance for a reconfigured channel, but the water is for the most part allowed to create its own path. Both of these forms of restoration have the advantages of being very inexpensive and of ensuring that the aquatic system that develops is in dynamic equilibrium with upstream conditions because it is shaped by them.[9] Another form of restoration that embraces uncertainty is to remove infrastructure, particularly dams, and then allow the channel to adjust on its own. This has benefits similar to those of self-forming channels, while also greatly improving ecological conditions by reactivating upstream/downstream mobility for water, sediment, organisms, and nutrients. In these cases, an initial intervention is followed by observation and adaptive management if needed rather than intensive ongoing maintenance or direct intervention that nails the river in place.

What would it look like to refocus stream mitigation banking on these far less structured forms of restoration and to accept the much higher levels of uncertainty that accompany them? As with the designer ecosystem option, the uncontrolled option would involve walking away from the current set of guidance documents that specify mitigation banking practices across the United States. But instead of developing a set of very narrow restoration techniques, each designed to produce equivalence to a particular ecosystem service, this option would encourage a relatively unrestricted period of experimentation and minimalistic adaptive management specific to the disparate physiographic regions of the United States. The goal would be maximizing the self-determination, complexity, and functionality of fluvial systems rather than meeting a narrow set of goals.

For anyone familiar with how stream mitigation banking works today, it is a stretch to imagine putting this highly uncertain and fairly chaotic option into practice. Notably, of the three forms of uncertainty-embracing stream restoration described earlier, only dam removal has been used—and only rarely—to produce stream mitigation credits. There is some movement on this front, however: as of this writing, dam removal has been approved to create stream credits in a number of districts and the Corps of Engineers recently issued a nationwide approval for other states and districts to experiment with dam removal for mitigation.[10]

The reason for this reluctance to adopt the second option of uncontrolled restoration may be that while projects intended to relinquish human control reduce upfront costs, they also create messy, dynamic, complex systems that dramatically increase the uncertainty of project outcomes. In contrast to the current mitigation banking system, these would be high-risk, high-reward projects: they would have far more potential than the stream mitigation banks approved today to actually restore ecosystems, but also far more likelihood to fail, leaving bankers with no credits to sell and regulators with no mitigation to offset permitted impacts. Thus, it is not clear whether bankers and regulators (not to mention investors, designers, and landowners) would be willing to go this route. If they did, we might (ironically) have something far more like the dynamic and innovation-driving markets that MES proponents initially imagined, but with regulators as the customers, choosing among mitigation banking approaches based on their ecological outcomes.

These two options are in effect binary: we can maximize equivalence, certainty, and human control to produce a narrow set of environmental gains, or we can maximize uncertainty and natural complexity by letting streams be streams. The latter has the potential to produce something ecologically real by helping jumpstart nature's ability to restore itself, but also to fail spectacularly. We believe the same binary choices apply to any ecosystem service market. For conservation banking, for example, this is the difference between zoos and captive breeding programs on the one hand, or removing remaining human populations and re-wilding the Great Plains by introducing proxies for extinct mega-fauna on the other. To produce the environmental benefits that MES are intended to provide, we have to choose between regulating radically more or radically less.

Notes

Acknowledgments

1. That first conversation was an interview for Rebecca's dissertation which ended up lasting several hours, ranging way off our original topic, and turning into a strategy session for writing a grant for this project.

1 Introduction

1. Monoculture-based tree plantations are increasingly used for forest restoration. In the 2011 Bonn Challenge, which aimed to restore 350 Mha of forest by 2030, 45 percent of all commitments involved planting of monocultures (Lewis et al. 2019).

2. Mitigation banking is the most market-like approach to compensatory mitigation of the three mechanisms: mitigation banking, Permittee Responsible Mitigation, and In Lieu Fee programs (all are described in more detail in chapter 4).

3. As of December 2018, there were 3,408 mitigation banks in the United States, while there were only 950 in 2010. We estimate, conservatively, that a third of those in 2018 would be stream-only banks, although the number is likely much larger than this. Also, many mitigation banks have both wetland and streams as part of a single bank.

2 Market-Based Approaches to Conservation

1. Author interview, August 30, 2011.

2. Using mitigation for compliance with the Clean Water Act has generated some innovation. Most generally, the innovation of using a "bank" of credits for compensating across multiple impact sites was an early innovation (see chapter 4). In addition, alternative forms of mitigation have been developed in highly competitive markets like North Carolina, and these have included dramatically different

approaches such as dam removal (described at the end of chapter 8; see Corps of Engineers 2018).

3. For discussions of regulatory capacity, see Gardner et al. 2013 and Rayment et al. 2014. For debates about durability, see Walker et al. 2009; McKenney and Kiesecker 2010; Bull et al. 2013; Gardner et al. 2013; and Quétier, Regnery, and Levrel 2014. For discussion about social equity, see BenDor and Brozovic 2007; BenDor and Stewart 2011; Gardner et al. 2013; FERN 2014; and Rayment et al. 2014. For more on additionality, see McKenney and Kiesecker 2010; Gillenwater 2012; Bull et al. 2013; and Quétier, Regnery, and Levrel 2014. Finally, for concerns about time lags, see Maron et al. 2012; Curran, Hellweg, and Beck 2014; and FERN 2014.

4. Conservation easements are legal constraints on property use applied to a specified land area to increase or sustain its environmental conservation values.

5. The specific ecosystem services that are regulated or required/desired to be offset change through time with new science or attention of regulators. In the stream case, *hyporheic exchange* (the mixture of surface water with shallow groundwater) was not mentioned in earlier goals for stream restoration, but became a desired outcome of stream offset programs in the 2010s. See Cochran and Logue 2011.

6. The literature on offsets is extensive. For good starting points, see Robertson 2006; Walker et al. 2009; Quétier and Lavorel 2011; Bull et al. 2013; Curran, Hellweg, and Beck 2014.

7. See discussions in Quétier and Lavorel 2011; Maron et al. 2012; Bull et al. 2013; and Curran, Hellweg, and Beck 2014.

8. See, for example, ten Kate, Bishop, and Bayon 2004; Kiesecker et al. 2010; Quétier and Lavorel 2011; Gardner et al. 2013; and Pilgrim et al. 2013.

9. See Lave, Doyle, and Robertson 2010 for a detailed discussion of how stream credits are defined.

10. For more on credit release schedules, see chapter 6 and BenDor, Riggsbee, and Doyle 2011.

11. Given that the legality of such easements is only just beginning to be tested in the courts, it is not clear whether they will actually protect compensation sites over the longer term. In any case, literal perpetuity is unlikely. Even the longest-lived human institutions (e.g. the Catholic Church) have been in existence for fewer than 2,000 years; U.S. property law, which unlike the legal systems in many other countries allows the unbundling of different use rights, is an order of magnitude younger. As one report ruefully notes, "perpetuity is an awfully long time" (ten Kate, Bishop, and Bayon 2004, 66).

12. For a useful discussion of restoration and novel ecosystems, see Hobbs and Suding 2009.

13. For reviews of which stream restoration techniques seem to be working and which do not, see Palmer, Menninger, and Bernhardt 2010; Bernhardt and Palmer 2011; and Wohl, Lane, and Wilcox 2015.

14. See, for example, White et al. 2012.

15. See discussions in Moilanen et al. 2009; McKenney and Kiesecker 2010; Quétier and Lavorel 2011; and Curran, Hellweg, and Beck 2014.

16. For a strong critique of trading ratios, see Moilanen et al. 2009.

17. For an early review of potential issues with credits based on afforestation and reforestation, see Lecocq and Chomitz 2001.

18. See Dutschke and Angelsen 2008.

19. For a useful introduction to afforestation and reforestation credits, see Pedroni 2005.

20. For a deeper introduction to why carbon markets have been so weak, see The Economist 2012.

21. Section 9 of the Endangered Species Act (ESA) prohibits the *take* of listed endangered species, defined broadly by the USFWS to include impacts that result in significant habitat modification or in degradation that kills or injures wildlife by "significantly impairing essential behavioral patterns including breeding, feeding, or sheltering." The ESA provides an exception to the prohibition on take when the USFWS authorizes a conditional permit issued under Section 10 of the ESA. To obtain a permit, an applicant must submit to the USFWS (for terrestrial and freshwater species) or the National Oceanic and Atmospheric Administration (NOAA) Fisheries (for marine species) a habitat conservation plan that minimizes and mitigates the impact of the take "to the maximum extent practicable." Terrestrial conservation banks are regulated by USFWS personnel, and marine and anadromous fish conservation banks are regulated by staff at the NOAA Fisheries.

22. Poudel 2017 provides a useful overview of the state of conservation banking.

23. DOI 2013, 9–11. This report provides another useful overview of conservation banking in the United States.

24. ELI 2008, 18.

25. Fox and Nino-Murcia 2005, 999. This article provides one of the earliest detailed overviews of conservation banking in the United States.

26. ELI 2008, 20.

27. For the drastic simplification of vernal pool credits, contrast Mead 1998, 275, with Mead 2008, 23; Fox and Nino-Murcia 2005, 999, explain that this kind of highly simplified credit is typical in conservation banking.

28. Bonnie and Wilcove 2008, 65.

29. Poudel 2017 provides a useful analysis of the U.S. market for conservation banking.

3 How Stream Restoration Was Born, and What Came of It

1. For more detail on the history of European settlers' impacts on streams, see Wohl, Lininger, and Baron 2017 and Doyle 2018.

2. For channelization statistics, see NRC 1992, 194; and Brookes 1988, 10, 18–19.

3. See Walter and Merrits 2008 and Wohl, Lininger, and Baron 2017.

4. See Jordan 2000 for one of the most cited and accessible justifications for ecological restoration.

5. For more on the history of restoration in the United States, see Egan 1990; Thompson and Stull 2002; Hall 2005; and Thompson 2013.

6. The most accessible publication from this era that describes the range of work they did is Van Cleef 1885.

7. Hubbs, Tarzwell, and Greely 1932 offers a summary of the University of Michigan work and some of the lessons learned.

8. For the effect of this work on conservation more broadly, see Clepper 1966, 64–68.

9. A good example of this is Clarence Tarzwell, who went from the University of Michigan program, to the U.S. Forest Service in Albuquerque, to the Tennessee Valley Authority, and applied the training he received at the Michigan School throughout: Tarzwell 1937.

10. On this approach being applied in California, see Ehlers 1956. For Wyoming, see Mueller 1954.

11. Thompson provides an excellent review of the early years of instream restoration people and projects, with great details of the designs in different period of time (Thompson 2005, 2006). The most detail and review are provided in Thompson and Stull 2002.

12. Thompson reviews some of these works as well as some of the careful research being done on their effectiveness (Thompson 2005, 2006).

13. Thompson 2006 is a thorough statistical review of the data available from this early phase of stream restoration. He compiles the available data and then does a rigorous meta-analysis of it, demonstrating limited efficacy of instream restoration.

14. Leopold, Miller, and Wolman 1964 was the first synthesis and clear presentation of hydraulic geometry equations, and this essential book represents the pivot from geomorphology as a descriptive science to a quantitative one.

15. Most hydraulic engineering texts began including chapters on hydraulic geometry in the 1980s; for example, see Chang 1988.

16. Author interview, December 12, 2011.

17. Quoted in Lave 2012, 42.

18. For more on the initial attempts at channel reconfiguration, see Lave 2012.

19. See Lave 2012 for an extended treatment of Rosgen and the controversy over his restoration approach.

20. Ibid., 83. The influence of Natural Channel Design continues in Harman and Starr's Stream Function Pyramid, much of which draws upon it.

21. FISRWG 2014.

22. Lave 2012, 30.

23. Ibid., chapter 5, for more detail.

24. For an overview of how river migration shapes landscapes, see Florsheim, Mount, and Chin 2008.

25. See Lave 2012, 60–62, for a more detailed discussion.

26. Ibid., 61; emphasis in original.

27. For an overview of these conflicts, see Lave 2009.

28. See Palmer, Menninger, and Bernhardt 2010, 205.

29. C. M. Tarzwell 1937. See also Chamberlain and Huber 1947 for description of restoration work and an evaluation of its efficacy in the mountainous region of North Carolina, and Thompson 2006 for the efficacy of this work generally.

4 How Markets, and Mitigation, Came to Be Accepted Forms of Environmental Regulation

1. We are grateful to Matt Kondolf for bringing this quote to our attention; see Brautigan 1967, 104–105.

2. For useful introductions to neoliberalism, see Mirowski 2009 and Brown 2015.

3. Robertson (2018), who unearthed these documents and brought them to our attention, provides additional detail.

4. Carter 1978.

5. See Carter 1980.

6. See U.S. Regulatory Council 1980, v, for more detail.

7. See Reagan 1981.

8. For more detail on Reagan's regulatory reform efforts, see OIRA 1998 and Weidenbaum 1997.

9. For more detail on regulatory reform under Bush Sr., see Hilts 1991.

10. Daniel Yergin describes this succinctly in *The Quest* (2011), 478–480.

11. See Clinton 1993.

12. For more information on Clinton's regulatory reform efforts, see National Performance Review 1995.

13. Dempsey and Robertson 2012, 758.

14. Norgaard 2010, 1219.

15. For early work by ecologists developing the concept of ecosystem services, see King 1966; Helliwell 1969; Odum and Odum 1972; and Ehrlich and Ehrlich 1981.

16. See Costanza et al. 1997.

17. Daily 1997.

18. Dempsey and Robertson 2012, 758–759.

19. For more extended treatments of this point, including very useful histories of the development of ecosystem service markets, see Gomez-Baggethun and Ruiz-Pérez 2011 and Dempsey and Robertson 2012.

20. See U.S. Congress 1958: Section 2(b). For the full text of the FWCA, see U.S. Congress 1958. For descriptions of the early decades of mitigation and the heartburn it caused USFWS and state wildlife agency staff, see Greenwalt 1979; Swanson 1979; and Short 1988.

21. For channelization statistics, see NRC 1992, 194; and Brookes 1988, 10, 18–19.

22. For a very helpful review of the history of CWA implementation, see Hough and Robertson 2009.

23. The CWA gains its authority as federal legislation through the Commerce Clause of the Constitution, and so interstate navigability for commercial purposes was the starting point. The Mississippi River, the Gulf of Mexico, the Great Lakes, and any significant waterway that could be used for commercial traffic clearly fell under the intent and scope of the Constitution and thus were readily regulated under the

CWA as waters of the United States; this is why the CWA jurisdiction is often hinged on "traditionally navigable waters."

24. The scope of Clean Water Act jurisdiction has changed with each related Supreme Court decision and with the introduction of new rules or guidance by federal agencies, and with each administration since that of George W. Bush. As of this writing, the Trump administration has reverted the Waters of the United States rule back to that used in 1986. See the recent review by Walsh and Ward (2019) for a very useful overview.

25. For an overview of the National Wetlands Inventory Project, which began in 1975, see Dahl 1990. Wilen and Bates (1995) provide an overview of the first twenty years of the project.

26. For instance, support of on-farm wetlands conservation in the 1985 Farm Bill, and the Emergency Wetlands Protection Act of 1986.

27. See https://www.epa.gov/cwa-404/memorandum-agreement for the full text of the MOA.

28. For an extended discussion of stream restoration in North Carolina, see Lave 2012.

29. Personal communication, regulator, October 15, 2018. See also Owen 2017. This shift was possible because the year before, in 1997, North Carolina revised its General Certification for Nationwide Permits to trigger review of any project impacting 150 linear feet of stream. The 2000 General Certification is the first time a North Carolina state document required compensatory mitigation for stream impacts in kind.

30. The Johns River Bank; personal communication, regulator, October 15, 2018.

31. For the next nine years—through the duration of the Obama administration, and in the aftermath of the 2008 Mitigation Rule—the EPA and the Corps of Engineers worked on what would become the Clean Water Rule, released in April 2015, rescinded in 2016, and then reformulated under the Trump administration. The Clean Water Rule and its subsequent revisions specified what types of features would be considered by federal agencies to be waters of the United States, and thus worthy of protection, and which ones were not.

32. See Houck 1989, 836, cited in Hough and Robertson 2009, 23.

33. National Research Council, 2001, 3.

34. In Lieu Fee programs function effectively as mitigation banks, but with important operational and financial differences. Operationally, ILF programs must be managed and operated—"sponsored"—by a government agency (e.g., municipality, state department of environment or transportation) or by an NGO (e.g., The Nature

Conservancy). Financially, an ILF program can accept fees in lieu of providing actual credits to offset regulated impacts. That is, if a permittee has generated fifty debits of stream ecosystem from their proposed development project, the permittee can either purchase fifty credits from a mitigation bank or can pay fifty credits' worth of fees to an ILF program. The ILF program accepts fees from many such permittees, and consolidates those fees until they are sufficient to generate the necessary compensatory mitigation to extinguish the debits associated with accepted fees. An important distinction, then, is the timing of compensatory mitigation: for mitigation banks, the credits must be produced in advance of accepting payment from a permittee; for an ILF program, the credits are generated after (sometimes many years after) the impacts. Importantly, ILF programs can either generate credits themselves (i.e., by designing and constructing restoration projects) or can purchase credits from mitigation banks. For an extended discussion, see Doyle and BenDor 2011 and Doyle 2018.

35. The U.S. Fish & Wildlife Service's 1988 report on mitigation banking (Short 1988) provides an excellent overview of its early history.

36. For more detail, see Soileau, Brown, and Fruge 1985 as quoted in Short 1988, iii.

37. Short 1988.

38. See Hough and Robertson 2009, 24–25, for a more detailed discussion.

39. For a more extended discussion of the issues with ILF programs, and how they differ from traditional mitigation banks, see note 33 above and Doyle and BenDor 2011.

40. For a review of how policy within the different Divisions and Districts of the Corps converges over time, see Doyle et al. 2013.

41. There is only one state that calls out channel movement as a positive future outcome: Montana. Their 2013 Stream Mitigation Procedure encourages "allowing room for future lateral channel migration." See https://usace.contentdm.oclc.org/utils/getfile/collection/p16021coll11/id/2675.

42. Federal Register, 40 CFR Part 230, Compensatory Mitigation for Losses of Aquatic Resources; Final Rule, April 10, 2008.

43. Instead of big yellow machines, restorationists such as George Palmiter and Bill Zeedyk used strategic placement of large woody debris to improve the health of rivers and streams while maintaining their dynamism. For more on George Palmiter's restoration approach, see Lave 2014a. For Bill Zeedyk's work, see Zeedyk 2006.

44. Typically, simply preserving an existing high-quality stream reach produces the lowest number of credits on a given site; regulators might award this 0.25 credits per linear foot of stream (i.e., preservation of 100 ft of stream produces 25 stream credits). Less invasive (but highly effective) enhancements, such as fencing out cattle or planting riparian vegetation along the streambanks that do not physically alter the

Notes

channel itself carry a moderate number of credits (e.g., 0.5 credits per linear foot of stream). To maximize the potential credits at a site, however, and receive a 1:1 ratio of credits per linear foot restored, mitigation bankers were required to reconfigure the existing channel.

45. There are exceptions to this. The Wilmington District briefly included biological requirements for mitigation banks produced via dam removal in the early 2010s. As of this writing, the Savannah District has the option of including biological and chemical criteria in Mitigation Banking Instruments, although so far this is rare, and the South Pacific Division of the Corps recently began including biological and chemical criteria in setting trading ratios. The Chicago District began including biological and chemical success criteria in 2019. It is not yet clear how these expanded requirements will affect the stream mitigation banking market.

5 The Actors in Stream Mitigation Banking

1. George Kelly, mitigation banker, December 18, 2018, during a presentation at the mitigation conference ACES, Washington, DC. This is something Kelly says frequently, and is quoted often in the mitigation banking community.

2. Whether ephemeral and/or intermittent streams are covered by the CWA, and thus require mitigation, has varied over time (see chapter 3).

3. Author interview with designer/scientist, July 9, 2012.

4. See, for example, Shabman, Scodari, and King 1994.

5. Robertson (2007, 508) makes this same point.

6. Author interviewer with scientist/designer, January 30, 2012.

7. Author interview with regulator, September 16, 2011.

8. Ibid.

9. Author interview with regulator, August 29, 2011.

10. Author interview with regulator, August 30, 2011.

11. For more discussion of service areas, see Womble and Doyle 2012.

12. Author interview with designer/banker, October 5, 2015.

13. Author interview with regulator, October 8, 2015.

14. Although it is worth noting that unlike most engineering projects (e.g., infrastructure) or architectural projects, stream restoration designers are not often legally liable if their projects fail unless they are licensed professionals and legally stamp and sign their drawings (i.e., officially designate that they take legal responsibility for the work). Such designation is not always needed for projects where public safety or property is not at risk.

15. For more on designers' motivations, see Doyle et al. 2015.

16. Author interview with designer, December 11, 2012.

17. Author interview with designers, December 7, 2012.

18. Author interview with scientist, November 19, 2012.

19. See discussion in Lave 2014b.

20. This is demonstrated by the fact that few studies of stream restoration designate or differentiate whether the stream was restored as part of a mitigation banking program or a grant program (e.g., Violin et al. 2011; Sudduth et al. 2011).

21. See, for example, Shields et al. 2003.

22. See Ibid. for an example of the emphasis on stability, and the tension between restoring for ecological purposes and designing for stability.

23. Scientists' lack of influence in stream restoration in the United States is discussed in depth in Lave 2012.

24. Author interview with scientist, December 5, 2012.

25. See, for example, Palmer and Filoso 2009; Sudduth et al. 2011; Violin et al. 2011; Palmer and Hondula 2014; and Miller and Kochel 2013.

26. Author interview with scientist, November 9, 2012.

27. Author interview with scientist, December 16, 2012.

28. Author interview with mitigation banker, November 16, 2012.

29. While currently it is far less common practice, mitigation projects can be placed on public lands. In that case, the landowner (e.g., municipal golf course, university campus, or state or federal park) is able to benefit from having ecosystem restoration done on their property "for free." Typically, public landowners have not charged mitigation banks for siting projects on their lands. Public landowners often provide additional services to mitigation bankers, such as contractual services, legal services, and even monitoring using personnel employed by the land-owning agency. Compensating for harm on public land raises serious issues of additionality, however, since presumably any public land is protected from development already, and would eventually be restored.

30. Author interview with mitigation banker, October 5, 2015.

31. Author interview with mitigation banker, October 5, 2015.

32. Author interview with regulator, October 8, 2015.

33. This is addressed in more depth in Spence et al. 2017.

34. Author interview with mitigation banker, October 5, 2015.

35. Author interview with mitigation banker, July 11, 2012.

36. Ibid.

37. Author interview with consultant, February 9, 2012.

38. Author interview with regulator, February 9, 2012.

39. Author interview with regulator, July 12, 2012.

40. Author interview with scientist, December 5, 2012.

41. Author interview with banker, October 5, 2015.

42. Making repairs not only requires bringing employees and construction equipment back to the site, but also obtaining a new construction permit, a time-consuming and costly process.

43. Author interview with mitigation bankers, October 8, 2015.

44. Author interview with mitigation banker, October 5, 2015.

45. Author interview with mitigation banker November 16, 2015.

46. Author interview with mitigation banker, October 5, 2015.

47. Author interview with mitigation banker, October 8, 2015.

48. Author interview with regulator, October 8, 2015.

49. Author interview with banker, October 5, 2015.

50. Author interview with mitigation banker, October 18, 2015. Because their reputations depend on it, mitigation bank designers are very, very good at designing stable channels. The project described was, in the words of the banker who developed it, "GROUND ZERO" for Hurricane Harvey in 2017. Even without the initially proposed "super armoring," the only damage to the twenty-mile-long project was a broken fence (personal communication with mitigation banker, December 20, 2018).

6 How Mitigation Banks Work, and the Biography of a Bank

1. Author interview with mitigation banker, July 19, 2012.

2. Author interview with regulator, September 16, 2011.

3. Author interview with regulator, August 11, 2011.

4. Ibid.

5. Author interview with regulator, September 16, 2011.

6. For more on service areas, see Womble and Doyle 2012.

7. See http://water.usgs.gov/GIS/huc.html for more detail on HUCs.

8. Author interview with regulator, May 3, 2012.

9. Author interview with regulator, February 10, 2012.

10. Ibid.

11. Author interview with banker, October 5, 2015. Note that the ideal site is not only physically impaired, but also has clear issues from nutrient pollution. This speaks to the fact that even though success criteria are almost solely focused on channel form, the goals for stream mitigation banking are broader.

12. Author interview with designers, December 7, 2012.

13. Author interview with banker, July 9, 2012.

14. While MBIs function as a contract between the banker and the regulator, regulators are quick to point out that they are not legal contracts or even agreements between the agencies and the mitigation bankers. MBIs are formally agreed on between the mitigation banker and an Interagency Review Team, which is comprised of relevant regulatory representatives from federal and state environmental agencies: the Corps of Engineers is the lead agency on any IRT (because the Corps implements the CWA), but other agencies will be relevant to the state and the particular project (e.g., U.S. Fish & Wildlife Service, state department of water quality, etc.).

15. There is some irony here in the relative backgrounds and expertise of the designers vis-à-vis the regulators. The majority of stream designers had engineering degrees or technical training, or both, specifically in stream restoration and hydraulic engineering, whereas the regulators rarely had training (beyond short courses) in river processes and engineering. Yet regulators are granted, and have taken, wide latitude to tweak and even alter restoration designs.

16. A number of Corps districts, such as Charleston, Ft. Worth, and Omaha, have expanded their guidelines in recent years to include "function-based" success criteria. These are typically proxies for desired functions (e.g., visual assessments of the extent of channel habitat for aquatic insects or fish rather than surveys to determine whether they are actually present). In a few districts, however, success criteria now include measured biological criteria, as in the Chicago District's June 2019 revised guidelines, which require streams restored for mitigation to meet the measured water quality (including temperature and dissolved oxygen) and biodiversity of fish and benthic macroinvertebrates of their specified reference reaches. As of this writing, it is not yet clear whether that will prove to be workable in practice.

Notes

17. This is also why mitigation banks differ markedly from In Lieu Fee programs; ILF programs are able to accept fees prior to developing mitigation projects. These fees build up the capital necessary for implementing projects, thus reducing, if not eliminating the financial uncertainty and risk associated with developing a mitigation project in advance of impacts and associated revenue.

18. This is also a reason why mitigation bankers note that their profit margins are not nearly what they appear; the actual "take home" from a sale of credits can often be largely routed right back into new projects. If those future projects do not turn out to be profitable, then the combination of projects is a loss.

19. This is changing, however. In June 2016, the global investment firm KKR made a "significant investment" in the mitigation banking firm Resource Environmental Solutions, LLC ("RES"). KKR has investments in the tens of billions of USD, and is known internationally for alternative asset classes (e.g., energy, infrastructure, real estate). Thus, its interest in mitigation banking drew the attention of the mitigation banking community as well as the alternative asset investing community (BusinessWire, "Resource Environmental Solutions Receives Investment from KKR," June 30, 2016).

20. Twenty years ago it was rare for commercial lenders to provide capital for a mitigation bank, but several mitigation bankers described ongoing relationships with their local bank as that bank developed understanding of the entire industry. One mitigation banker noted that they could now use an MBI as collateral for a loan from their local bank.

21. There is a federally maintained website—RIBITS—that tracks mitigation banks. This website could be used by a permittee in search of credits, although the site can be out of date and has not been entirely reliable.

22. This is again where ILF programs become quite relevant; an ILF program will be taking on fees as well as the obligation to procure mitigation credits. A mitigation banker might view an ILF program as a likely purchaser of the credits to be generated from a site. However, the ILF program will also have a fixed amount that they can (or may be willing to) pay based on the fees they have assessed. Thus, a banker selling credits to an ILF program will have a known revenue stream but a likely limited profit margin.

23. This section is based on author interviews with staff at The Enhancement Bank, October 17, 2018.

24. A different project manager at TEB discussed this with us in 2012, with the full quote in chapter 5: "You bring in an investor for one project . . ." (author interview, July 11, 2012). The project manager noted that once the project is completed, the outside investor ends up taking a large portion of the profits, thereby turning the mitigation banker into more of a consultant and construction manager than an entrepreneur.

25. This is a reality of mitigation banking. In the case of TEB, stepping away from this project would have meant the loss of $750,000 of existing investment, including the profits from the previously completed project. This level of loss would likely have meant not just the end of the Hawthorne Stream Bank project, but also potentially the entire firm. It would have taken too long to develop a pipeline of other projects that could generate financial revenue to pay salaries sufficient to justify the continuation of the firm. This gives a sense of the high-risk nature of mitigation banking.

26. The banker also noted that while this timing was tricky, all indications for Hawthorne Stream Bank were positive and this gave them confidence that the MBI would be signed. In other cases, the banker noted that the outcome was completely unknown until the day that the regulator actually decided to sign the MBI.

7 The Streams That Mitigation Banking Creates

1. For a full discussion of our geomorphic results, see Doyle et al. 2015. Some of our geomorphic data on channel form were mined from required monitoring reports on stream mitigation banking projects, and other data came from surveys of unrestored streams. It is important to note that stream reaches in the latter category were in no sense pristine; presumably all of those surveyed had been affected by human actions directly or indirectly. The only thing stream reaches in this category share is that there has been no attempt to restore them.

2. See Doyle et al. 2013.

3. Rosgen's approach may have been appealing to early restoration practitioners in North Carolina because of the similarities between the coldwater trout streams characteristic of the Front Range of the Rockies, where Natural Channel Design was developed, and the coldwater streams of the mountainous northwestern region where stream restoration got its start in North Carolina.

4. See Lave 2012, chapter 2, for a more comprehensive history of the use of NCD in North Carolina. It is worth noting that Rosgen was concerned about the use of his classification system as the basis of defining stream credits.

5. The state mitigation program is (and was) an In Lieu Fee program. It began as the Wetland Restoration Program in 1996, became the Ecosystem Enhancement Program in 2001, and as of this writing is the Division of Mitigation Services (DMS). Initially, DMS was responsible for procuring mitigation credits to offset impacts associated with state development activities, particularly those by the Department of Transportation; later, it was authorized to accept fees from and provide mitigation for private permittees as well. DMS can either develop projects itself or procure them from mitigation bankers (referred to as "full delivery"). Thus, DMS functions sometimes as a mitigation banker (when it develops its own projects) and sometime

Notes

as a credit broker (when it purchases credits from bankers and then transfers those credits to an entity with liabilities to mitigate). When DMS works as a broker, its staff select which mitigation projects to pursue for purchase. Thus, staff at DMS have had an inordinately large effect on stream mitigation design, as they exert selective pressure via which types of credits they are willing to purchase.

6. For more on the prevalence of particular ways of defining stream credits across the United States, see Doyle et al. 2013. The notable exceptions to this practice of privileging channel reconfiguration are in the Northeastern United States, where preservation of existing high-quality streams is favored.

7. Increasing sinuosity also decreases the slope of the stream because it effectively increases the length of the stream for a particular site. If the slope is decreased too much, the stream will not be able to transport its sediment load. Thus, an additional mode of failure for credit chasing via increased sinuosity would be systemic deposition of sediment, or aggradation.

8. Sinuosities between 1.2 and 1.5 are considered moderate by most ubiquitous classification approaches, e.g., chapter 2 in Rosgen 2006.

9. Author interview with designer, November 14, 2012.

10. Author interview with designer, December 7, 2012.

11. Author interview with banker, November 16, 2012.

12. In some areas, regulators also recognize "0th order" tributaries, which are ephemeral or intermittent streams that only flow occasionally. If such features are regulated, then mitigation bankers also have an incentive to restore those very small streams as well, as there would be demand elsewhere for them. Alternatively, bankers could restore 1st order streams and use them on the market to compensate for 0th or 2nd order streams. The Trump administration's redefinition of waters of the United States does not include ephemeral streams, placing the status of some 0th order streams in doubt, as it is not clear whether impacts to them would require mitigation.

13. Author interview with banker, October 5, 2015.

14. Natural Channel Design directs designers to develop their own ranges of radii of curvature for particular projects empirically by examining reference reaches in the area. By contrast, NCD specifies a fixed range of sinuosity to accompany each stream classification category.

15. There are some minor encouragements to homogeneity that are specific to mitigation banking. For example, landowners preferred straight boundary lines around the mitigation site, which is easier with homogenized meander patterns. And for mitigation bankers, it was easier to survey and cheaper to fence straight property lines that are possible only with regularized river forms. For regulators, it was easier

to monitor homogenized sites because any change in the physical form of the channel would be very obvious. But none of these would have been sufficient if the economic incentives had not overwhelmingly supported homogeneity, as we will detail.

16. It is worth noting that the emphasis on stability is another incentive to site mitigation projects in smaller, easier-to-control streams. Bankers could be more confident that neither upstream actors nor the energy of the stream itself would damage the project, resulting in loss of credits (and thus of profit). As one regulator pointed out to us in an interview:

> I think [there is] a tendency on the part of the mitigation providers . . . to focus on smaller streams because they're just less risky, you know. . . . [And] with the mitigation obviously, they're held to performance standards, . . . credit release is associated with that. . . . [O]n the large end, you know these large order, large-size tributaries, I think, providers specifically avoid those. Partly because there have been a couple projects in the past that have been very expensive, . . . that have had a lot of problems because of the size. It's harder to control your watershed when you're that big an area, and the forces you're dealing with are, you know, much greater. (October 8, 2015)

17. See Odgaard 1987 for an extended discussion of the relative stability/instability of different meander patterns.

18. Author interview with designer, October 21, 2015.

19. Author interview with regulator, July 12, 2010.

20. Author interview with regulator, September 16, 2012.

21. Author interview with banker, July 11, 2012.

22. For more on the role of headwater streams in water quality, see Peterson et al. 2001.

23. For more on ecologies of scale in stream restoration, see Bond and Lake 2003; Lake, Bond, and Reich 2007; Ardon et al. 2010; and Beechie et al. 2010.

24. There is a growing literature documenting the unpromising record of many stream restoration approaches. See Maron et al. 2012; Palmer and Filoso 2009; Bernhardt and Palmer 2011; Sudduth et al. 2011; Violin et al. 2011; and Nilsson et al. 2015.

25. For evaluations of channel reconfiguration projects in particular, see Tullos et al. 2009; Sholtes and Doyle 2011; Sudduth et al. 2011; Violin et al. 2011; and Palmer and Hondula 2014.

26. Author interview with scientist, November 9, 2012.

27. Ibid.

28. Author interview with scientist, December 5, 2012.

29. Author interview with regulator, July 9, 2012.

30. Author interview with regulator, July 10, 2012.

31. Author interview with scientist, December 6, 2012.

32. For discussion of the intractability of more complex regulatory markets, see Robertson 2006; Walker et al. 2009; and Robertson et al. 2014.

8 Conclusion

1. This literature is reviewed more thoroughly in chapter 7, but generally see Nilsson et al. 2015 and Bernhardt and Palmer 2011.

2. For a critical review of the efficacy of stream mitigation see Doyle and Shields 2012; they document that stream restoration, as practiced through reliance on channel realignment focused on stability, has not led to demonstrable improvements in physical, chemical, or biological integrity of streams.

3. Robertson 2006; Robertson et al. 2014.

4. For more on designer ecosystems, see Palmer et al. 2004 and Ross et al. 2015.

5. For a discussion of designing streams to maximize nitrogen retention, see Craig et al. 2008.

6. For improvement of water quality, see, for example, Herzog et al. 2018. There are a number of studies that are seeking to use stream design to reduce instream temperature (see Menichino and Hester 2014) and to retain organic contaminants (see Peter et al. 2019). Perhaps ironically, the rise in research about stream structures and temperature appears to be driven by a policy in Oregon that created a stream temperature trading program.

7. Bioaugmentation is the process of adding selected strains or mixed cultures into wastewater reactors to improve processing or removal of specific compounds. While this is limited to wastewater treatment bioreactors, it is not altogether unlikely that such approaches could be applied to natural systems over time; see Herrero and Stuckey 2015.

8. There is a long and convoluted history of stream restoration being conflated with fish stocking, which has long-term implications for both being perceived as producing "restored" aquatic ecosystems. Thompson (2013) gives a remarkable history of this for New England.

9. Public agency staff in Ohio, including at Ohio State University agricultural extension, are among those promoting self-forming channels as a restoration approach; see https://agditches.osu.edu/channel-designs/self-forming. A good introduction to

Bill Zeedyk's approach can be found in Zeedyk 2006 (http://altarvalleyconservation.org/wp-content/uploads/pdf/75-Induced_Meandering_Field_Guide.pdf). For more on George Palmiter, see Lave 2014a.

10. In September 2018, the Corps of Engineers released a much-anticipated policy that set clearer guidance for using dam removal for compensatory stream mitigation (Corps of Engineers 2018). This type of guidance typically is the precursor for expanding mitigation activities. As of this writing, dam removal is permitted in the Kansas City, Little Rock, Omaha, Wilmington, and New England Corps districts, and in Montana, Ohio, and Pennsylvania.

References

Ardon, M., J. L. Morse, M. W. Doyle, and E. S. Bernhardt. 2010. "The Water Quality Consequences of Restoring Wetland Hydrology to a Large Agricultural Watershed in the Southeastern Coastal Plain." *Ecosystems* 13:1060–1078.

Beechie, T. J., D. A. Sear, J. D. Olden, G. R. Pess, J. M. Buffington, H. Moir, P. Roni, and M. M. Pollock. 2010. "Process-Based Principles for Restoring River Ecosystems." *BioScience* 60:209–222.

BenDor, Todd, and Nicholas Brozovic. 2007. "Determinants of Spatial and Temporal Patterns in Compensatory Wetland Mitigation." *Environmental Management* 40 (3): 349–364.

BenDor, Todd, and Audrey Stewart. 2011. "Land Use Planning and Social Equity in North Carolina's Compensatory Wetland and Stream Mitigation Programs." *Environmental Management* 47 (2): 239–253.

BenDor, Todd, J. Adam Riggsbee, and Martin W. Doyle. 2011. "Risk and Markets for Ecosystem Services." *Environmental Science and Technology* 45:10322–10330.

Bernhardt, Emily, and Margaret Palmer. 2011. "River Restoration: The Fuzzy Logic of Repairing Reaches to Reverse Catchment Scale Degradation." *Ecological Applications* 21:1926–1931.

Bond, N. R., and P. S. Lake. 2003. "Local Habitat Restoration in Streams: Constraints on the Effectiveness of Restoration for Stream Biota." *Ecological Management and Restoration* 4:193–198.

Bonnie, Robert, and David S. Wilcove. 2008. "Ecological Considerations." In *Conservation and Biodiversity Banking: A Guide to Setting Up and Running Biodiversity Credit Trading Systems*, ed. Nathaniel Carroll, Jessica Fox, and Ricardo Bayon, 53–68. New York: Earthscan.

Brautigan, R. 1967. *Trout Fishing in America*. New York: Mariner Books.

Brookes, A. 1988. *Channelized Rivers: Perspectives for Environmental Management*. Chichester, UK: John Wiley & Sons.

Brown, Wendy. 2015. *Undoing the Demos: Neoliberalism's Stealth Revolution*. Cambridge, MA: MIT Press.

Bull, Joseph, K. Blake Suttle, Ascelin Gordon, Navinder J. Singh, and E. J. Milner-Gulland. 2013. "Biodiversity Offsets in Theory and Practice." *Oryx* 47 (3): 369–380.

Bureau of Fisheries. 1935. *Methods for the Improvement of Streams*. U.S. Department of Commerce, Bureau of Fisheries, Memorandum I-133, January 1935.

Carter, Jimmy. 1978. Executive Order 12044: Improving Government Regulations.

Carter, Jimmy. 1980. White House Memorandum for the Heads of Executive Departments and Agencies.

Chamberlain, T. K., and W. W. Huber. 1947. "Ten Years of Trout Stream Management on the Pisgah." *Progressive Fish Culturalist* 9:185–191.

Chang, H. H. 1988. *Fluvial Processes in River Engineering*. Malabar, FL: Krieger Publishing Company.

Clepper, H. 1966. *Origins of American Conservation*. New York: Ronald Press Company.

Clinton, William. 1993. Executive Order 12866: Regulatory Planning and Review. Edited by the White House. Washington, DC.

Cochran, Bobby, and Charles Logue. 2011. "A Watershed Approach to Improve Water Quality: Case Study of Clean Water Services." *Journal of the American Water Resources Association* 47 (1): 29–38.

Corps of Engineers. 2018. Regulatory Guidance Letter: Determination of Compensatory Mitigation Credits for the Removal of Obsolete Dams and Other Structures from Rivers and Streams. RGL No. 18-01, September 25.

Costanza, Robert, Ralph d'Arge, Rudolf de Groot, Stephen Farber, Monica Grasso, Bruce Hannon, Karin Limburg, Shahid Naeem, Robert V. O'Neill, Jose Paruelo, Robert G. Raskin, Paul Sutton, and Marjan van den Belt. 1997. "The Value of the World's Ecosystem Services and Natural Capital." *Nature* 387:253–260.

Craig, L. S., M. A. Palmer, D. C. Richardson, S. Filoso, E. S. Bernhardt, B. P. Bledsoe, M. W. Doyle, P. M. Groffman, B. A. Hassett, S. S. Kaushal, P. M. Mayer, S. M. Smith, and P. R. Wilcock. 2008. "Stream Restoration Strategies for Reducing River Nitrogen Loads." *Frontiers in Ecology and the Environment* 6:529–538.

Curran, Michael, Stefanie Hellweg, and Jan Beck. 2014. "Is There Any Empirical Support for Biodiversity Offset Policy?" *Ecological Applications* 24 (4): 617–632.

Dahl, T. E. 1990. *Wetlands Losses in the United States 1780s to 1980s*. Ed. U.S Fish & Wildlife Service. Washington, DC: U.S. Department of the Interior.

References

Daily, Gretchen C., ed. 1997. *Nature's Services: Societal Dependence on Natural Ecosystems*. Washington, DC: Island Press.

Dempsey, Jessica, and Morgan M. Robertson. 2012. "Ecosystem Services: Tensions, Impurities, and Points of Engagement within Neoliberalism." *Progress in Human Geography* 36 (6): 758–779.

DOI Office of Policy Analysis. 2013. *Conservation Banking Overview and Suggested Areas for Future Analysis*. Washington, DC: Department of the Interior.

Doyle, M. W. 2018. *The Source: How Rivers Made America and America Remade Its Rivers*. New York: W. W. Norton.

Doyle, M. W., and T. BenDor. 2011. "Evolving Law and Policy for Freshwater Ecosystem Service Markets." *William and Mary Environmental Law and Policy Review* 36:153–191.

Doyle, M. W., R. Lave, M. M. Robertson, and J. Ferguson. 2013. "River Federalism." *Annals of the Association of American Geographers* 103:290–298.

Doyle, M. W., and F. D. Shields. 2012. "Compensatory Mitigation for Streams under the Clean Water Act: Reassessing Science and Redirecting Policy." *Journal of the American Water Resources Association* 48:494–509.

Doyle, M. W., J. Singh, R. Lave, and M. Robertson. 2015. "The Morphology of Streams Restored for Market and Non-market Purposes: Insights from a Mixed Natural-Social Science Approach." *Water Resources Research* 51 (7): 5603–5622.

Dudley, R. 2004. *Hydraulic-Geometry Relations for Rivers in Coastal and Central Maine*. U.S. Geological Survey Scientific Investigations Report 2004-5042.

Dutschke, Michael, and Arild Angelsen. 2008. "How Do We Ensure Permanence and Assign Liability?" In *Moving Ahead with REDD: Issues, Options and Implications*, ed. Arild Angelsen, 77–85. Bogor, Indonesia: CIFOR.

Economist. 2012. "Carbon Markets: Complete Disaster in the Making. *The Economist*, September 15.

Egan, David. 1990. "Historic Initiatives in Ecological Restoration." *Restoration & Management Notes* 8 (2): 83–89.

Ehlers, R. 1956. "An Evaluation of Stream Improvement Devices Constructed Eighteen Years Ago." *California Fish and Game* 42:203–217.

Ehrlich, P. R., and A. H. Ehrlich. 1981. *Extinction: The Causes and Consequences of the Disappearance of Species*. New York: Random House.

ELI. 2008. *Design of U.S. Habitat Banking Systems to Support the Conservation of Wildlife Habitat and At-Risk Species*. Washington, DC: Environmental Law Institute.

FISRWG. 1998. *Stream Corridor Restoration: Principles, Processes, and Practices.* Washington, DC: Federal Interagency Stream Restoration Working Group.

FERN. 2014. *Briefing Note 3: Biodiversity Offsetting in Practice.* Brussels: Food and Environment Reporting Network.

Florsheim, J. L., J. F. Mount, and A. Chin. 2008. "Bank Erosion as a Desirable Attribute of Rivers." *BioScience* 58:519–529.

Fox, Jessica, and Anamaria Nino-Murcia. 2005. "Status of Species Conservation Banking in the United States." *Conservation Biology* 19 (4): 996–1007.

Gardner, Toby, Amrei Von Hase, Susie Brownlie, Jonathan Ekstrom, John Pilgrim, Conrad Savy, R. T. Theo Stephens, Jo Treweek, Graham Ussher, Gerri Ward, and Kerry ten Kate. 2013. "Biodiversity Offsets and the Challenge of Achieving No Net Loss." *Conservation Biology* 27 (6): 1254–1264.

Gillenwater, Michael. 2012. *What Is Additionality?* Silver Springs, MD: Greenhouse Gas Management Institute.

Gomez-Baggethun, Erik, and Manuel Ruiz-Pérez. 2011. "Economic Valuation and the Commodification of Ecosystem Services." *Progress in Physical Geography* 35 (5): 613–628.

Greenwalt, Lynn. 1979. "Mitigation in Our Future." Paper read at The Mitigation Symposium, at Fort Collins, CO.

Hall, Marcus. 2005. *Earth Repair: A Transatlantic History of Environmental Restoration.* Charlottesville: University of Virginia Press.

Helliwell, D. R. 1969. "Valuation of Wildlife Resources." *Regional Studies* 3 (1): 41–47.

Herrero, M., and D. C. Stuckey. 2015. "Bioaugmentation and Its Application in Wastewater Treatment: A review." *Chemosphere* 140:119–128.

Herzog, Skuyler, Christopher Higgins, Kamini Singha, and John McCray. 2018. "Performance of Engineered Streambeds for Inducing Hyporheic Transient Storage and Attenuation of Resazurin." *Environmental Science & Technology* 52 (18): 10627–10636.

Hilts, Philip J. 1991. "At Heart of Debate on Quayle Council: Who Controls Federal Regulations?" *New York Times*, December 16.

Hobbs, R. J., and K. N. Suding. 2009. *New Models for Ecosystem Dynamics and Restoration.* Washington, DC: Island Press.

Houck, O. A. 1989. "Hard Choices: The Analysis of Alternatives under Section 404 of the Clean Water Act and Similar Environmental Laws." *University of Colorado Law Review* 60:773–840.

References

Hough, Palmer, and Morgan M. Robertson. 2009. "Mitigation under Section 404 of the Clean Water Act: Where It Comes From, What It Means." *Wetlands Ecology and Management* 17:15–33.

Hubbs, C., C. M. Tarzwell, and J. R. Greely. 1932. *Methods for the Improvement of Michigan Trout Streams*. Ann Arbor: University of Michigan Press.

Jordan III, William R. 2000. "Restoration, Community, and Wilderness." In *Restoring Nature: Perspectives from the Social Sciences and Humanities*, ed. Paul H. Gobster and R. Bruce Hull, 21–36. Washington, DC: Island Press.

Kiesecker, Joseph M., Holly Copeland, Amy Pocewicz, and Bruce McKenney. 2010. "Development by Design: Blending Landscape-Level Planning with the Mitigation Hierarchy." *Frontiers in Ecology and the Environment* 8 (5): 261–266.

King, R. T. 1966. "Wildlife and Man." *New York Conservationist* 20 (6): 8–11.

Knighton, D. 1998. *Fluvial Forms and Processes: A New Perspective*. London: Arnold Publishing.

Lake, P. S., N. Bond, and P. Reich. 2007. "Linking Ecological Theory with Stream Restoration." *Freshwater Biology* 52:597–615.

Lave, R. 2009. "The Controversy over Natural Channel Design: Substantive Explanations and Potential Avenues for Resolution." *Journal of the American Water Resources Association* 45 (6): 1519–1532.

Lave, R. 2012. *Fields and Streams: Stream Restoration, Neoliberalism, and the Future of Environmental Science*. Athens: University of Georgia Press.

Lave, R. 2014a. "Freedom and Constraint: Generative Expectations in the Stream Restoration Field." *Geoforum* 52:236–244.

Lave, R. 2014b. "Neoliberal Confluences: The Turbulent Evolution of Stream Mitigation Banking in the U.S." *Political Power and Social Theory* 27:59–88.

Lave, Rebecca, Martin W. Doyle, and Morgan M. Robertson. 2010. "Privatizing Stream Restoration in the U.S." *Social Studies of Science* 40 (5): 677–703.

Lecocq, Franck, and Kenneth Chomitz. 2001. *Optimal Use of Carbon Sequestration in a Global Climate Change Strategy: Is There a Wooden Bridge to a Clean Energy Future?* Washington, DC: World Bank.

Leopold, L. B., J. P. Miller, and G. M. Wolman. 1964. *Fluvial Processes in Geomorphology*. San Francisco: Freeman.

Lewis, S. L., C. E. Wheeler, E. T. A. Mitchard, and A. Koch. 2019. "Restoring Natural Forests Is the Best Way to Remove Atmospheric Carbon." *Nature* 568:25–28.

Lutz, K. J. 2007. *Habitat Improvement for Trout Streams*. Pennsylvania Fish and Boat Commission, Harrisburg, PA.

Malakoff, David. 2004. "The River Doctor." *Science* 305 (5686): 937–939.

Maron, Martine, Richard J. Hobbs, Atte Moilanen, Jeffrey W. Matthews, Kimberly Christie, Toby Gardner, David A. Keith, David B. Lindenmayer, and Clive A. McAlpine. 2012. "Faustian Bargains? Restoration Realities in the Context of Biodiversity Offset Policies." *Biological Conservation* 155:141–148.

McKenney, Bruce A., and Joseph M. Kiesecker. 2010. "Policy Development for Biodiversity Offsets: A Review of Offset Frameworks." *Environmental Management* 45 (1):165–176.

Mead, Deborah L. 1998. "Determination of Available Credits and Service Areas for ESA Vernal Pool Preservation Banks." In *Ecology, Conservation, and Management of Vernal Pool Ecosystems—Proceedings from a 1996 Conference*, ed. C. W. Witham, E. T. Bauder, D. Belk, W. R. Ferren, and R. Ornduff, 274–282. Sacramento, CA: California Native Plant Society.

Mead, Deborah L. 2008. "History and Theory: The Origin and Evolution of Conservation Banking." In *Conservation & Biodiversity Banking: A Guide to Setting Up and Running Biodiversity Credit Trading Systems*, ed. Nathaniel Carroll, Jessica Fox, and Ricardo Bayon, 9–32. New York: Earth Scan.

Menichino, G. T., and E. T. Hester. 2014. "Hydraulic and Thermal Effects of In-stream Structure-induced Hyporheic Exchange across a Range of Hydraulic Conductivities." *Water Resources Research* 50:4643–4661.

Miller, J. R., and R. C. Kochel. 2013. "Use and Performance of In-stream Structures for River Restoration: A Case Study from North Carolina." *Environmental Earth Science* 68 (6): 1563–1574.

Mirowski, Philip. 2009. "Postface: Defining Neoliberalism." In *The Road from Mt. Pelerin: The Making of the Neoliberal Thought Collective*, ed. Philip Mirowski and Dieter Plehwe, 417–455. Cambridge, MA: Harvard University Press.

Moilanen, Atte, Astrid van Teeffelen, Yakov Ben-Haim, and Simon Ferrier. 2009. "How Much Compensation Is Enough? A Framework for Incorporating Uncertainty and Time Discounting When Calculating Offset Ratios for Impacted Habitat." *Restoration Ecology* 17 (4): 470–478.

Mueller, J. W. 1954. "Wyoming Stream Improvement." *Wyoming Wild Life* 18: 30–32.

National Performance Review. 1995. *Reinventing Environmental Regulation*. Washington, DC: Office of the Vice President.

Nilsson, C., L. E. Polvi, J. Gardestrom, E. M. Hasselquist, L. Lind, and J. M. Sarneel. 2015. "Riparian and In-stream Restoration of Boreal Streams and Rivers: Success or Failure." *Ecohydrology* 8:753–764.

Norgaard, Richard B. 2010. "Ecosystem Services: From Eye-opening Metaphor to Complexity Blinder." *Ecological Economics* 69 (6): 1219–1227.

NRC. 1992. *Restoration of Aquatic Ecosystems: Science, Technology, and Public Policy.* Washington, DC: National Academy Press.

NRC. 2001. *Compensating for Wetland Losses under the Clean Water Act.* Washington, DC: National Academy Press.

Odgaard, A. J. 1987. "Streambank Erosion along Two Rivers in Iowa." *Water Resources Research* 23:1225–1236.

Odum, E. P., and H. T. Odum. 1972. "Natural Areas as Necessary Components of Man's Total Environment." *Transactions of the Thirty Seventh North American Wildlife and Natural Resources Conference* 37:178–189.

OIRA (Office of Information and Regulatory Affairs). 1998. *Report to Congress on the Costs and Benefits of Federal Regulations, Ch. 1: The Role of Economic Analysis in Regulatory Reform.* Washington, DC: Office of Management and Budget.

Owen, Dave. 2017. "Little Streams and Legal Transformations." *Utah Law Review* 2017 (1): 1–55.

Palmer, Margaret, Emily Bernhardt, Elizabeth Chornesky, Scott Collins, Andrew Dobson, Clifford Duke, Barry Gold, Robert Jacobson, Sharon Kingsland, Rhonda Kranz, Michael Mappin, M. Luisa Martinez, Fiorenza Micheli, Jennifer Morse, Michael Pace, Mercedes Pascual, Stephen Palumbi, O. J. Reichman, Ashley Simons, Alan Townsend, and Monica Turner. 2004. "Ecology for a Crowded Planet." *Science* 304 (5675): 1251–1252.

Palmer, M. A., and S. Filoso. 2009. "The Restoration of Ecosystems for Environmental Markets." *Science* 325 (5940): 575–576.

Palmer, M. A., and K. Hondula. 2014. "Restoration as Mitigation: Analysis of Stream Mitigation for Coal Mining impacts in Southern Appalachia." *Environmental Science & Technology* 48 (18): 10552–10560.

Palmer, M. A., H. L. Menninger, and E. Bernhardt. 2010. "River Restoration, Habitat Heterogeneity and Biodiversity: A Failure of Theory or Practice? *Freshwater Biology* 55:205–222.

Pedroni, Lucio. 2005. "Carbon Accounting for Sinks in the CDM after CoP-9." *Climate Policy* 5 (4): 407–418.

Peter, K. T., S. Herzog, Z. Tian, C. Wu, J. E. McCray, K. Lynch, and E. P. Kolodziej. 2019. "Evaluating Emerging Organic Contaminant Removal in an Engineered Hyporheic Zone Using High Resolution Mass Spectrometry." *Water Research* 150: 140–152.

Peterson, B. J., W. M. Wollheim, P. J. Mulholland, J. R. Webster, J. L. Meyer, J. L. Tank, E. Marti, W. B. Bowden, H. M. Valett, A. E. Hershey, W. H. McDowell, W. K. Dodds, S. K. Hamilton, S. Gregory, D. D. Morrall. 2001. "Control of Nitrogen Export from Watersheds by Headwater Streams." *Science* 292 (5514): 86–90.

Pilgrim, John, Susie Brownlie, Jonathan Ekstrom, Toby Gardner, Amrei von Hase, Kerry ten Kate, Conrad Savy, R. T. Theo Stephens, Helen Temple, Jo Treweek, Graham Ussher, and Gerri Ward. 2013. "A Process for Assessing the Offsetability of Biodiversity Impacts." *Conservation Letters* 6 (5): 376–384.

Poudel, Jagdish. 2017. "Economic Analysis of Habitat Conservation Banking in the United States." Ph.D. diss., Auburn University.

Quétier, Fabien, and Sandra Lavorel. 2011. "Assessing Ecological Equivalence in Biodiversity Offset Schemes: Key Issues and Solutions." *Biological Conservation* 144 (12): 2991–2999.

Quétier, Fabien, Baptiste Regnery, and Harold Levrel. 2014. "No Net Loss of Biodiversity or Paper Offsets? A Critical Review of the French No Net Loss Policy." *Environmental Science & Policy* 38:120–131.

Rayment, Matt, Rupert Haines, David McNeil, Mavourneen Conway, Graham Tucker, and Evelyn Underwood. 2014. *Study on Specific Design Elements of Biodiversity Offsets: Biodiversity Metrics and Mechanisms for Securing Long Term Conservation Benefits*. Report prepared for European Commission. London: ICF International.

Reagan, Ronald. 1981. Executive Order 12291. Washington, DC.

Riley, Ann L. 1998. *Restoring Streams in Cities: A Guide for Planners, Policymakers, and Citizens*. Washington, DC: Island Press.

Robertson, Morgan M. 2006. "The Nature That Capital Can See: Science, State and Market in the Commodification of Ecosystem Services." *Environment and Planning D: Society and Space* 24 (3): 367–387.

Robertson, Morgan M. 2007. "Discovering Price in all the Wrong Places: The Work of Commodity Definition and Price under Neoliberal Environmental Policy." *Antipode* 39 (3): 500–526.

Robertson, Morgan M. 2018. "Flexible Nature: Governing with the Environment in the Development of U.S. Neoliberalism." *Annals of the American Association of Geographers* 108 (6): 1601–1619.

Robertson, Morgan M., Todd BenDor, Rebecca Lave, Adam Riggsbee, J. B. Ruhl, and Martin W. Doyle. 2014. "Stacking Ecosystem Services." *Frontiers in Ecology and the Environment* 12 (3): 186–193.

Rosgen, David L. 1996a. *Applied River Morphology*. 2nd ed. Pagosa Springs, CO: Wildland Hydrology.

Rosgen, D. L. 2006. *Watershed Assessment of River Stability and Sediment Supply*. Pagosa Springs, CO: Wildland Hydrology.

Ross, M. R. V., E. S. Bernhardt, M. W. Doyle, and J. B. Heffernan. 2015. "Designer Ecosystems: Incorporating Design Approaches into Applied Ecology." *Annual Review of Environment and Resources* 40:419–443.

Shabman, L. A., P. Scodari, and D. King. 1994. *National Wetland Mitigation Banking Study: Expanding Opportunities for Successful Mitigation: The Private Credit Market Alternative*. Alexandria, VA: U.S. Army Corps of Engineers Institute for Water Resources, IWR 94-WMB-3.

Shetter, D. S., O. H. Clark, and A. S. Hazzard, 1949. "The Effects of Deflectors in a Section of a Michigan Trout Stream." *Transactions of the American Fisheries Society* 76:248–278.

Shields, F. D., R. C. Copeland, P. C. Klingeman, M. W. Doyle, and A. Simon. 2003. "Design for Stream Restoration." *Journal of Hydraulic Engineering* 129 (8): 575–584.;

Sholtes, J. S., and M. W. Doyle. 2011. "Effect of Channel Restoration on Flood Wave Attenuation." *Journal of Hydraulic Engineering* 137 (2): 196–208.

Short, Cathleen. 1988. *Mitigation Banking*, ed. U.S. Fish & Wildlife Service. Washington, DC: U.S. Fish & Wildlife Service.

Smith, Sean M., and Karen L. Prestegaard. 2005. "Hydraulic Performance of a Morphology-Based Stream Channel Design." *Water Resources Research* 41 (11). https://doi.org/10.1029/2004WR003926.

Spence, L., B. Copp, X. Kent, D. Vermeer, and M. W. Doyle. 2017. *Environmental Impact Investing in Real Assets: What Environmental Measures Do Fund Managers Consider?* Nicholas Institute Report 17-01.

Sudduth, Elizabeth, Brooke A. Hassett, Peter Cada, and Emily Bernhardt. 2011. "Testing the Field of Dreams Hypothesis: Functional Responses to Urbanization and Restoration in Stream Ecosystems." *Ecological Applications* 21 (6): 1972–1988.

Swanson, Gustav A. 1979. *The Mitigation Symposium: A National Workshop on Mitigating Losses of Fish and Wildlife Habitats*. Fort Collins, CO: Rocky Mountain Forest and Range Experiment Station, Forest Service, U.S. Department of Agriculture.

Tarzwell, C. M. 1937. "Experimental Evidence on the Value of Trout Stream Improvement in Michigan." *Transactions of the American Fisheries Society* 66 (1): 177–187.

ten Kate, K., J. Bishop, and R. Bayon. 2004. *Biodiversity Offsets: Views, Experience, and the Business Case*. The World Conservation Union. Cambridge: IUCN.

Thompson, Douglas M. 2005. "The History of the Use and Effectiveness of Instream Structures in the United States." In *Humans as Geologic Agents*, ed. J. Ehlen, W. C.

Haneberg, and R. A. Larson, 35–50. Boulder, CO: The Geological Society of America Reviews in Engineering Geology.

Thompson, Douglas M. 2006. "Did the Pre-1980 Use of In-stream Structures Improve Streams? A Reanalysis of Historical Data." *Ecological Applications* 16:784–796.

Thompson, Douglas M. 2013. *The Quest for the Golden Trout: Environmental Loss and America's Iconic Fish*. Lebanon, NH: University Press of New England.

Thompson, Douglas M., and Gregory N. Stull. 2002. "The Development and Historic Use of Habitat Structures in Channel Restoration in the United States: The Grand Experiment in Fisheries Management." *Geographie physique et Quaternaire* 56 (1): 45–60.

Tullos, D. D., D. L. Penrose, G. D. Jennings, and W. G. Cope. 2009. "Analysis of Functional Traits in Reconfigured Channels: Implications for the Bioassessment and Disturbance of River Restoration." *Journal of the North American Benthological Society* 28:80–92.

U.S. Army Corps of Engineers—Wilmington District. 2018. Wilmington District Mitigation Bank Processing Procedures. Updated October 15, 2018. U.S. Army Corps of Engineers, Wilmington District Office, Wilmington, NC.

U.S. Congress. 1958. "Fish and Wildlife Coordination Act." In *16 U.S.C. 661–666*. Washington, DC: Government Printing Office.

U.S. Regulatory Council. 1980. *Innovative Techniques in Theory and Practice: Proceedings of a Regulatory Council Conference*. Washington, DC.

Van Cleef, J. S., 1885. "How to Restore Our Trout Streams." *Transactions of the American Fisheries Society* 14:50–55.

Violin, Christy R., Peter Cada, Elizabeth Sudduth, Brooke A. Hassett, David L. Penrose, and Emily Bernhardt. 2011. "Effects of Urbanization and Urban Stream Restoration on the Physical and Biological Structure of Stream Ecosystems." *Ecological Applications* 21 (6): 1932–1949.

Walker, Susan, Ann Brower, R. T. Theo Stephens, and William G. Lee. 2009. "Why Bartering Biodiversity Fails." *Conservation Letters* 2 (4): 149–157.

Walsh, Riley, and Adam S. Ward. 2019. "Redefining Clean Water Regulations Reduces Protections for Wetlands and Jurisdictional Uncertainty." *Frontiers in Water*, April 18, 2019. https://doi.org/10.3389/frwa.2019.00001.

Walter, R. C., and D. Merritts. 2008. "Natural Streams and the Legacy of Water-Powered Mills." *Science* 319 (5861): 299–304.

Weidenbaum, Murray. 1997. "Regulatory Process Reform: From Ford to Clinton." *Regulation: The Cato Review of Business and Government* 20:20–26.

White, C., C. Costello, B. E. Kendall, and C. J. Brown. 2012. "The Value of Coordinated Management of Interacting Ecosystem Services." *Ecology Letters* 15:509–519.

Wilen, B. O., and M. K. Bates. 1995. "The US Fish and Wildlife Service's National Wetlands Inventory Project." *Vegetatio* 118 (1–2): 153–169.

Wohl, Ellen, Stuart Lane, and Andrew C. Wilcox. 2015. "The Science and Practice of River Restoration." *Water Resources Research* 51 (8): 5974–5997.

Wohl, Ellen, Katherine Lininger, and Jill Baron. 2017. "Land before Water: The Relative Temporal Sequence of Human Alteration of Freshwater Ecosystems in the Conterminous United States." *Anthropocene* 18:27–46.

Womble, P., and M. Doyle. 2012. "The Geography of Trading Ecosystem Services: A Case Study of Wetland and Stream Compensatory Mitigation Markets." *Harvard Environmental Law Review* 36:229–296.

Yergin, Daniel. 2011. *The Quest: Energy, Security, and the Remaking of the Modern World*. New York: Penguin Press.

Zeedyk, Bill. 2006. *An Introduction to Induced Meandering: A Method for Restoring Stability to Incised Stream Channels*. 3rd ed. A Joint Publication from Earth Works Institute, The Quivira Coalition, and Zeedyk Ecological Consulting. http://altarvalleyconservation.org/wp-content/uploads/pdf/75-Induced_Meandering_Field_Guide.pdf.

Index

Page numbers followed by f refer to figures.

2008 Mitigation Rule, 68–69, 78, 79

Balancing environment and development, vii–viii, 141, 147–148. *See also* Compensatory mitigation, trade-offs between ecological complexity and economic stability; Markets for ecosystem services, rationale for
Best professional judgment, 27, 98–99
"Build it and they will come," 31, 43, 124. *See also* Channel morphology; Channel stability
Bush, George H. W., 52, 56, 58. *See also* No Net Loss

Capitalism, vii, 4–5, 55–56. *See also* Markets for ecosystem services; Neoliberalism
Carbon credits
  afforestation, 3, 24–25, 150–151
  and coal, 16
Carter, James, 51–52
Channel morphology. *See also* "Build it and they will come"; Channel stability; Hydraulic geometry equations; Sinuosity
  and channel reconfiguration, 34, 35–39

as proxy for ecological function, 41, 46, 70–71, 74, 83–84, 140
Channel reconfiguration, 34, 35–42, 123
  environmental outcomes, 70–71, 140–141, 149
  privileged form of stream mitigation, 70, 123, 139–140, 149
  and uncertainty, 139, 154
Channel stability, 41–46. *See also* "Build it and they will come"; Channel morphology; Natural Channel Design
  letting go of stability to imagine other options, 140–143, 153
  in mitigation banking, 68, 70, 84, 93–96, 124–125, 136–138, 148–149
Chicago District, U.S. Army Corps of Engineers, 109, 168n16
Chicago School, 50, 51. *See also* Neoliberalism
Civilian Conservation Corps (CCC), 33–34
Clean Air Act Amendments, 52, 53
Clean Water Act (CWA), 6–7. *See also* Waters of the United States
  and mitigation, 57–64, 69, 70–71, 76–78, 98, 141, 149–150
  Section 404, 57, 98

Clinton, William, 52–53
Command-and-control, vii, 51, 53, 141
Compensatory mitigation, 56–69, 74, 76–77, 94. *See also* Fish and Wildlife Coordination Act; Clean Water Act, and mitigation
 in-kind vs. out-of-kind, 59, 68, 98
 in lieu fee (ILF), 64, 66, 164–165n34, 169n17
 mitigation banking in relation to ILF and PRM, 61–64
 permittee responsible (PRM), 61–64
 trade-offs between ecological complexity and economic stability, 9, 19–21, 28, 100–101, 110, 141–145, 147–151
Conservation banking, 25–28, 150–151, 155. *See also* Endangered Species Act
 red-cockaded woodpecker, 27, 150
 vernal pools, 27
Conservation easements, 20–21, 87, 112, 158nn4,11
 and Hawthorne Stream Bank, 115–118
 and trading ratios, 23
Costanza, Robert, 55
Credit chasing, 83
 via restoring tributaries, 131–133
 via sinuosity, 125, 130–131
Credit release schedule, 80, 92, 108–110, 112–113
Credits, 5–6, 11, 13, 19. *See also* Debits; Stream credits
 abstract and simple, 16–18
 by area, 27, 59
 durable, 14, 17, 25
 easy to measure, 18
 and equivalence, 15, 16–18
 producers (*see* Mitigation bankers)
 privileging channel reconfiguration, 70, 123, 139–140, 149
 purchasers (*see* Permittees)

 stable and predictable, 17–18
 and trading ratios, 21–22
 and uncertainty, 19–20

Dales, John, 50–51, 52
Daly, Herman, 55
Dam removal, 81, 85, 99, 140, 154–155, 174n10
Debits, 5–6, 11, 13, 16–17, 21–22, 59, 64, 65. *See also* Credits
Designer ecosystems and streams, 152–153
Designers, 81–83
 and channel reconfiguration and stream restoration, 35–41, 84
 and liability, 165n14
 and Natural Channel Design, 75, 121, 130–131
 and regulators, 168n15
 and scientists, 45, 84–85
 and short courses, 39–41, 83
 and site selection, 102
 and stream mitigation, 81–83, 102–103, 105–108, 117–118, 130–131, 137–138
 and uncertainty, 93, 94, 124
Draft Mitigation Banking Instrument. *See* Mitigation Banking Instrument
Drainage basin size, 35, 36f, 126–128. *See also* Hydraulic geometry equations; Stream order
Dynamism vs. instability, 43–45, 94–95, 153–155

Ecological economics, 55. *See also* Dales, John; Environmental economics
Ecologists
 development of ecosystem services concept, 53–56
 involvement in stream restoration and mitigation, 46, 85–86
Ecosystem Investment Partners, 90. *See also* Investors

Ecosystem service markets. *See* Markets for ecosystem services
Ecosystem services, 5, 53–56, 69–70, 147
 and equity, 14
 and equivalence, 15, 123–24, 152–153
 measurement of, 18
 and time lags, 14
 and uncertainty, 124–125
Endangered Species Act (ESA), 4, 25–28, 159n21. *See also* Conservation banking
Environmental economics, 53. *See also* Dales, John; Ecological economics
Equivalence, 14–18, 22
 in carbon markets, 24–25
 in conservation banking, 27–28
 for designers, 82
 imagining other options for mitigation, 151–153, 155
 for regulators, 76–77, 80, 95, 101–104, 109–110

Field of Dreams. *See* "Build it and they will come"
Fish and Wildlife Coordination Act (FWCA), 56
Friedman, Milton. *See* Chicago School
Function-specific ecosystems. *See* Designer ecosystems and streams

Gore, Albert, 53
Gore, James, 39
Grant-funded stream restoration, 82–83, 122, 127–128
Guidance documents, 67–68. *See also* Mitigation sequence
 balancing market and regulatory needs, 100
 and carbon credits, 25
 case-by-case flexibility, 98–99

 and conservation banking, 26
 influence of the Southeastern Division of the Corps, 121, 142
 lack of scientific influence, 85–86
 and preference for channel reconfiguration, 70
 and stream restoration, 37

Habitat banking. *See* Conservation banking
Harman, William, 83, 161n20
Hawthorne Stream Bank, 113–119
Headwater streams, 60, 92–93, 127, 131–133, 139–140. *See also* Drainage basin size; Stream order; Waters of the United States
Hydraulic geometry equations, 35–37, 43, 45. *See also* Drainage basin size; Regional curves
Hyporheic exchange, 152, 158n5

Impact site, 14–15, 22, 74–75
In lieu fee (ILF) mitigation. *See* Compensatory mitigation
Interagency Review Team (IRT), 63, 65, 76, 77, 106–107, 168n14
Inter-Fluve, Inc., 37–40, 83. *See also* Koonce, Gregory
Investors, 74, 80, 88–90, 92, 110–111

Jurisdictional waters. *See* Waters of the United States

Kelly, George, 165n1
KKR, 169n19
Kondolf, G. Matthias, 39
Koonce, Greg, 37–39. *See also* Inter-Fluve, Inc.

Land acquisition, 79, 100–101, 115, 124, 131. *See also* Conservation easements; Site selection

Land owners, 74, 86–88
and permittee responsible mitigation (PRM), 63
Hawthorne Stream Bank, 114–115, 118
public, 166n29
Leopold, Luna, 40

MacBroom, James, 37
Markets for ecosystem services (MES), 5–6, 11–23. *See also* Carbon credits; Conservation banking; Wetlands mitigation
equivalence, 14–18
history of, 50–56
importance and inertia of MES metrics, 141–145
physical impacts of, 140–141, 148–151
possibilities for improvement, 147–155
rationale for, 5, 11, 147
uncertainty, 15, 19–23
Martin Dairy Creek, 1–3
Metrics, 16–18, 21–23, 27–28, 141–145, 150–151
Michigan School, 32–34
Mitigation bankers, 74, 78–81, 88–90, 99–113, 142, 144–145, 149
Enhancement Bank, The (TEB), 113–119
in North Carolina, 124–125, 128–133, 138–139
Mitigation Banking Instrument (MBI), 77, 103–110, 111–112. *See also* Credit release schedule; Monitoring; Service areas; Success criteria; Uncertainty, regulatory
incentives to use standard approaches that meet regulators' expectations, 79–80, 81, 94–95, 104–105
Mitigation sequence, 7, 57, 60–62
Mitigation site. *See* Site selection

Monitoring, 20–21, 107–108, 111–112
lack of, 27

Nature Conservancy, The (TNC), 4
Navigable waters. *See* Waters of the United States
Neoliberalism, 50–53, 56, 69. *See also* Chicago School; Markets for ecosystem services, rationale for; Regulators, regulatory reform
Nitrogen retention, 152–153
No Net Loss (NNL), 58, 63. *See also* Wetlands mitigation
North Carolina. *See also* Wilmington Corps District
impacts of mitigation banking, 121–145, 148–149
in-kind mitigation for streams, 59
Martin Dairy Creek, 1–3
role of scientists in mitigation policy, 83, 85

Offsetting. *See* Compensatory mitigation

Palmiter, George, 164n43, 173–174n9
Performance standards. *See* Success criteria
Permittees, 60–64, 73–75, 76, 90–91, 93, 113. *See also* Compensatory mitigation, permittee responsible
Permittee responsible mitigation (PRM). *See* Compensatory mitigation

Quayle, Daniel, 52

Radius of curvature, 1–3, 133–137
Rapanos v. United States, 59–60, 68. *See also* Waters of the United States
Reagan, Ronald, 52–53, 56
Reference reaches, 43
and radius of curvature, 171n14
Regional curves 43, 45. *See also* Hydraulic geometry equations

Index

Regulated public. *See* Permittees
Regulators, 74, 76–78, 79–80, 98–100.
See also Regulatory markets; U.S. Army Corps of Engineers; U.S. Environmental Protection Agency; U.S. Fish and Wildlife Service
and channel stability, 70, 137–138
credit release schedules, 109–110
equivalence, 17–18
Mitigation Banking Instruments, 104–107
monitoring, 107–108
in North Carolina, 121–124, 130, 142, 143
regulatory markets, 11–13, 83, 93, 148 (*see also* Carbon credits; Clean Air Act Amendments; Conservation banking; Mitigation banking)
regulatory overreach, 91
regulatory reform, 139–145, 151–155
and restoration short courses, 83, 122–123
and scientists, 84–85
service areas, 101–102
uncertainty, 20–23, 90–96, 101–102, 109–110, 124
Restoration Systems, 81
Riley, Ann, 41, 43
Riparian vegetation, 16, 18, 109, 111–112, 144, 164–165n44
Rosgen, David, 39–41, 45. *See also* Natural Channel Design
channel stability, 45
short courses, 39, 43, 83, 122–123
use of Rosgen's work in mitigation banking, 70, 123–125, 130

Scientists. *See also* Ecologists; Michigan School
equivalence and uncertainty, 21, 23, 94–95, 124–125
influence on policy (or lack thereof), 84–86, 141–145

role in mitigation banking, 74, 83–86, 141–145
Self-forming channels, 154
Service areas, 101–102, 109–110
Shields, F. Douglas, 39
Short courses, 39–41, 43, 83, 122–123
Sine wave curves. *See* Radius of curvature
Sinuosity. *See also* Channel morphology
and mitigation, 95, 125, 127f, 128–129, 130–131
and radius of curvature, 134–139
in stream restoration, 32
and urbanization, 44
Site selection, 101–103, 128, 133
agricultural or dairy sites, 102
public land, 166n29
Site visits, 74, 118
Soil and Water Conservation Districts, 122. *See also* U.S. Natural Resources Conservation Service
Sotir, Robbin, 37
Standard Operating Procedures. *See* Guidance documents
Standards of practice
vs. flexibility, 98–100
in mitigation banking, 76–77, 80, 82–83, 90–91, 101, 123–124
in regulatory markets, 12, 19
varying across Corps districts, 67–68
Stream credits, 7, 69–71, 75, 139–145, 149–150, 155. *See also* Credit chasing
and Rosgen's classification system, 69–71, 122–126, 130
as defined in North Carolina, 122–126, 129–131
emphasis on channel stability, 94–95, 136–138
producing credits, 78–80
and sinuosity, 129–131
Stream order, 126, 128, 130–132. *See also* Waters of the United States

Stream temperature, 16, 140, 145, 152–153
Success criteria, 77, 105, 107–108. *See also* Mitigation Banking Instrument
  adding biological and/or chemical criteria, 83–84, 91–92, 143–145
  channel form/physical, 83, 94–95 (*see also* Channel stability)
  dynamism vs. stability, 94–95, 112, 136–138, 143–145, 151–155
  and monitoring, 107–108, 137

Trading ratios, 21–23, 70, 119

Uncertainty, 15–16, 19–23, 90–96, 145, 153–155
  ecological, 20–21, 84, 94–95, 102, 139
  financial, 19–20, 78–80, 88, 92, 139
  implementation, 92–93, 139
  leading to standardization, 80, 81, 94–95
  random, 95, 139
  regulatory, 17, 60, 75–77, 90–92, 138
  reputational, 93–94, 139
  trade-offs between different types, 19–21, 96, 110, 119–120, 123–125, 138–139
U.S. Army Corps of Engineers (Corps of Engineers), 67–68. *See also* Regulators
  channel straightening, 29–30
  Clean Water Act, 6–7, 57, 59–60
  dam removal, 85, 155
  guidance documents and regulatory flexibility, 98–100, 111
  mitigation, 56–57, 59–61, 68–69
  mitigation banking, 59, 65, 74, 76–78, 121
  role in Mitigation Banking Instruments, 105–107, 109–110
  and scientists, 85
U.S. Bureau of Reclamation, 29–30, 56
U.S. Department of Agriculture
  Agricultural Research Service (ARS), 39

U.S. Environmental Protection Agency (EPA), 6–7, 57–58, 60–61, 68, 76, 122. *See also* Regulators
U.S. Fish and Wildlife Service (USFWS), 58, 64–66, 76. *See also* Regulators
U.S. Forest Service (USFS), 41
U.S. Geological Survey Hydrologic Unit Codes (HUCs), 101. *See also* Service areas
U.S. National Environmental Protection Act (NEPA), 51
U.S. Natural Resources Conservation Service (NRCS). *See* U.S. Soil Conservation Service
U.S. Soil Conservation Service, 56. *See also* Soil and Water Conservation Districts

Valuation, 55–56. *See also* Ecological economics; Markets for ecosystem services
Van Cleef, John Spencer, 31–32, 43
Vyverberg, Kris, 45

Waters of the United States, 57–58, 60. *See also* Rapanos v. United States; Stream order
  ephemeral vs. intermittent vs. perennial, 74, 171n12
  navigable waters, 57, 60
Wetlands. *See also* No Net Loss
  ecosystem services provided, 54–55
  National Wetlands Inventory Project (NWI), 58
Wetlands mitigation, 5–6, 58–60, 66, 122
Wilmington Corps District, 59, 85, 106–107, 121, 165n45. *See also* North Carolina

Zeedyk, William, 154